Remembering Mattie:

A Pioneer Woman's Legacy of Grit, Gumption, and Grace

Remembering Mattie

A Pioneer Woman's Legacy of Grit, Gumption, and Grace

Barbara Russell Chesser, Ph.D.
A *New York Times* Bestselling Author

with

Phillip ("Russ") and Rita Russell

Lewis ("Bo") and Marilyn Chumbley

Charlene Johnson Hutson

Copyright © 2007, 2008 by Barbara Russell Chesser
Printed and bound in the United States

All rights reserved. No part of this publication may be reproduced or transmitted in any form or by any means, electronic or mechanical, including photocopy, recording or any information storage and retrieval system (except for brief quotes used in reviews), without permission in writing from the author. However, copyright protects only the verbatim expression of information in this book, not the facts. Therefore, information in this book may be used freely for further family history research. Permission is required to reproduce any of the pictures.

Please send any queries or corrections to the holder of the copyright:

    Dr. Barbara Russell Chesser
    2617 Regency
    Waco, Texas 76710
    barbarachesser@sbcglobal.net

Library of Congress Cataloging-in-Publication Data

    Chesser, Barbara.
  Remembering Mattie : a pioneer woman's legacy of grit, gumption, and grace / by Barbara Russell Chesser.
    p. cm.
  ISBN 978-0-86534-687-1 (softcover : alk. paper)
 1. Kinney, Mattie, 1896-1988. 2. Chesser, Barbara--Family. 3. Women pioneers--New Mexico--Biography. 4. Pioneers--New Mexico--Biography. 5. Frontier and pioneer life--New Mexico. 6. New Mexico--Social life and customs--20th century. 7. New Mexico--History--20th century. 8. Portales (N.M.)--Biography. 9. Alvord (Tex.)--Biography. 10. Role models--United States--Biography. I. Title.
  F801.K54C47 2008
  978.9'05092--dc22
  [B]
                                            2008027018

WWW.SUNSTONEPRESS.COM
SUNSTONE PRESS / POST OFFICE BOX 2321 / SANTA FE, NM 87504-2321 /USA
(505) 988-4418 / ORDERS ONLY (800) 243-5644 / FAX (505) 988-1025

Table of Contents

Acknowledgments ix

Introduction...xi

> *This remarkable woman overcame great difficulties throughout her life, and all the while she helped others to also survive and surmount calamities. She provided a tremendous role model and left a golden legacy to us all.*

PART I: GRIT

Chapter One: BEGINNINGS (1896 - 1905) 1

> *How will our children know who they are*
> *If they don't know where they came from?*
> — Ma in *Grapes of Wrath*

Chapter Two: "…DOWN TO THE BONE" (1906 - 1913) 9

> *Keep your face to the sunshine and you will not see the shadows.*
> — Helen Keller

Chapter Three: DANCING ALL NIGHT (1913 - Oct. 11, 1918) 29

> *In the long run all love is paid by love…give thy love freely, do not count the cost, so beautiful a thing was never lost in the long run.*
> — Ella Wheeler Wilcox, *In the Long Run*

Chapter Four: "I WILL KEEP MY GIRLS!" (Oct. 11, 1918 - Sept. 27, 1920) 49

> *To have courage for whatever comes in life – everything lies in that.*
> — Mother Teresa

PART II: GUMPTION

Chapter Five: MOVING ON (Sept. 28, 1920 - May 1, 1933)............................67

> *Home is where the heart is.* — Old American saying

Chapter Six: A BEND IN THE ROAD (May 1, 1933 - Dec. 18, 1935).........................101

> *It's a long road that doesn't have a bend in it somewhere.*
> — Old American Saying

Chapter Seven: GRANDDAD AND A NICKEL FOR A SPOOL OF THREAD
(Dec. 18, 1935 - Feb. 8, 1972)..117

> *A woman's work is never done, and happy is she whose strength holds out to the end.*
> — Martha Ballard, eighteenth-century writer

Chapter Eight: MATTIE'S CAFÉ (1939 - 1967)..........139
*Where I was born and where...I lived is unimportant. It is what I
have done with where I have been that should be of interest.*
— Georgia O'Keeffe, famous New Mexico artist

PART III: GRACE

Chapter Nine: HOW ABOUT A CUP OF COFFEE? (1940 - 1980s)..........161
*Family stories reveal our family values, character, and personality.
They connect our past to the present, and they can shape the kind
of person we become.*
— Helen Armstrong, successful businesswoman, political activist,
daughter of first mayor of Portales, New Mexico, and first governor
of New Mexico – and Mattie's friend

Chapter Ten: ROOM FOR ONE MORE (1950s - Early 1970s)..........189
*Let there be kindness in your face, in your eyes, in your smile....
Don't only give your care, but give your heart as well.*
— Mother Teresa

Chapter Eleven: RED SILK PAJAMAS (Early 1900s - 1980s)..........211
*The best and most beautiful things in life cannot be seen or even
touched...they must be felt with the heart.*
— Helen Keller

Chapter Twelve: A GOOD CAR (1913 - 1970s)..........231
A good car can get you to where you want to go.
— Mattie Kinney

Epilogue: A REMARKABLE LEGACY: LUCKY US!..........253
A good person will be remembered as a blessing.
— Proverbs 10:7

Appendices:
    Assorted Photos..........257
    Family Histories..........267
        The McPeak Family..........267
        The Smith Family..........273
        The Deatherage Family..........277
        The Creek Family..........289
    Mattie's Genealogy..........295
        The Smith Family – First Generation..........295
        Mattie's Family – First Generation..........297
    Martha/Mattie Timeline..........299

Acknowledgments

As I embarked on this project, several of my most experienced writing colleagues warned me that writing a biography, especially of a deceased person, a relative, and an awesome one at that, would be a difficult and daunting undertaking. They were right! Only with the help of others committed to this project have I been able to bring it to this point. Grateful acknowledgment is made to the following:

Phillip and Rita Russell for their diligence in reviewing and selecting pictures from the E.N.M.U. Special collections, gathering pictures from relatives, and making available other pictures and legal documents – including homesteading papers from the early 1900s. In addition, they researched important historical and genealogical information and reviewed numerous versions of the manuscript.

Lewis and Marilyn Chumbley for making various pictures available and for the tedious task of getting pictures ready for publication, for providing a draft of the McPeak family history and for providing a draft of Martha/Mattie's Timeline.

Charlene Johnson Hutson for having the courage to get the project started and to offer help along the way, including extensive genealogical information, and for providing a draft of the Smith family history and the Deatherage family history. Charlene also contributed significantly to the author's cost of developing this book.

Aunt Lillie, a precious lady, who provided an amazing gold mine of memories, facts, and pictures from her 90+ years of living life generously and fully.

Uncle Leroy and Aunt Weesie, who also helped financially with the development of the book and critiqued and corrected the manuscript.

Dennis Hill, my friend, for the original drawings throughout the manuscript.

Alan Hunt, another friend, for pictures and information about cars.

Various other friends, such as Jim Moore and Karon Freeman, who offered input and encouragement along the way.

Griffin Photography, Ltd., for photos of Mattie's Heritage china.

Mollie Cook for patience beyond compare and excellent expertise in formatting the manuscript and masterfully getting the photos "just right" and inserting them into the manuscript, plus the ongoing edits and changes to the manuscript to keep everything "just right."

Various other relatives (especially daughter, Christi, and cousin Carolyn) and friends who provided pictures, information, and advice and encouragement along the way.

And last, but certainly not least, Del Chesser, my husband, who has given information, dates, and editorial input on countless drafts. But most of all, he has provided support and encouragement and has made room in his own life for this all-absorbing, demanding book and accepted an unpredictable schedule in every aspect of our lives as this book has taken on a life of its own and has been our constant companion for the last several years.

Introduction

This remarkable woman overcame great difficulties throughout her life, and all the while she helped others to also survive and surmount calamities. She provided a tremendous role model and left a golden legacy to us all.

The most influential lives are not always the best-known lives. I know a person whose life profoundly affected countless others. Yet her name never appeared in any Who's Who listings, bestselling books, or major newspapers. This extraordinary person's life story needs to be written so it can be shared with others, for her life was a wellspring of enduring character, courage, and devotion to helping others triumph over tragedy just as she had done.

Calamities of every sort shaped her life – a rattlesnake bite nearly killed her as a young child, and only a week after she celebrated her eleventh birthday her mother died unexpectedly. Along with other pioneers, she fought an ongoing and exhausting battle with the sometimes cruel forces of nature. Her young husband died in the Spanish Flu epidemic of 1918. She struggled as a 22-year-old widow to rear her three young daughters. She faced other challenges throughout her life, including the death of her first son the day before his first birthday and the death of her second husband, leaving two young boys fatherless. Through it all, this woman survived; she was a trailblazer for others suffering relentless difficulties.

This unique lady was known by different names – Martha Jane. Martha. Mrs. Deatherage. Mrs. Creek. Mother. Mrs. Kinney. Mumsie. Grandmother. Mattie. These different names reflect how she was special to many different people. Over the last 50 years of her life, most people came to call her Mattie. Even though I usually called her Grandmother, I often thought of her as Mattie because most others called her Mattie. Whatever the name, people expressed it with genuine affection and respect.

Because this unique lady had such a far-reaching impact on so many people and her influence is still felt strongly by many, a book should be written about her. Knowing about this person would inspire and encourage others. Several people, including myself, made a commitment several years ago to capture and record the essence of Mattie the best we could. Charlene (Johnson) Hutson agreed to spearhead the gathering of family anecdotes and genealogy that would perhaps provide insight into all that went into her life and all that had gone before. Phillip and Rita Russell immediately began the time-consuming search for pictures, various documents like homestead papers and marriage records, and other historical information that would help portray Mattie's incredible life. Rita tracked down genealogical information about Mattie's ancestors and compiled a treasure trove of invaluable material. Lewis ("Bo") and Marilyn Chumbley assumed the daunting task of preparing pictures and other items for publication. Because of my professional writing background, I agreed to attempt to weave all the true-life stories, historical information, and pictures into a meaningful book. Mattie's five children — Lillie, Juanita, Winnie, Paul, and Leroy – offered invaluable information and insight. In her nineties, Lillie especially shared a goldmine of memories and a never-ending fountain of encouragement. While I could not have put together this book without the information, documents, and pictures all these people provided, I assume full responsiblity for any errors in reporting and interpreting.

Another major reason others thought I was the logical choice for writing this book – I spent the first 25 years of my life with this generous and noble lady. I was eight months old when my father was killed; Mattie sheltered my 24-year-old widowed mother, my two young brothers, and me under her compassionate wings just as her in-laws had taken her and her three fatherless daughters into their home. This quarter of a century living with Mattie gives me a unique vantage point for sharing firsthand stories about a woman who loved her children, grandchildren, her other family members, and friends and helped them overcome countless hardships just as she had survived them. I also had the privilege of working closely with her in business – not only was she a marvelous matriarch, she was an astute, outstanding business woman.

The power of memory is strong. Thoughts of this unique lady still dance through my mind and echo in my heart. Hardly a day goes by that something does not remind me of her. Others should also have the opportunity to know about Mattie. They could hold the heartwarming stories of her life close to their own hearts when they need them most. It is people like Mattie who have strength of character, strength of conviction, strength of faith, strength of grace and dignity that have shaped our generations. The stories of ordinary people doing extraordinary things to overcome hardships and encouraging others to do the same still have a special place in the hearts of all people.

Like any valuable tapestry, age only adds to the value; the stories woven into this book become more precious as the years go by. They let us know the rich legacy Mattie left was one of grit, gumption, and grace. Our gift to others is to celebrate this great legacy and to pass it on.

Chapter One:
BEGINNINGS
(1896 - 1905)

*How will our children know who they are
If they don't know where they came from?*
— Ma in Grapes of Wrath

Life at Grandmother Mattie's house was good. I loved being in the midst of the heartfelt fun and laughter and even the shared tears of family members. There we exchanged stories and lived out life together. The sound of long-ago laughter echoes most loudly in my earliest memories. But other warm memories also flood my mind – the smell of fresh brewed coffee, open face apple pies with tiny cinnamon candy bits, and the best enchiladas in the entire world. Bouquets of brightly colored dahlias and roses on tables throughout the house. The fresh smell of clothes and bed linens dried in the dry, hot New Mexico sunshine. The lingering aroma of Granddad's Roitan cigar. The set of dishes with tiny pink roses displayed on the shelves of the china cabinet in the kitchen.

I am now much older than Mattie was when I was a young girl enjoying the relatives drawn to her house. One of my favorite pastimes is reminiscing as I sip coffee out of a cup from that set of china dishes. The memories I recall of life with Mattie are even more beautiful than the small pink roses and the delicate gold leafing. Reminiscing renews the heartwarming love felt in those family gatherings, and the friendly laughter rings across the years.

The china dishes were special to Mattie because employees, family members, and friends had given them to her. My grandmother was a compassionate person and an astute businesswoman who treated everyone like a valued member of her family. Someone she had given special encouragement – or maybe some much-needed cash – would give her a piece of china. Wanting to also show their respect and appreciation, others joined in this outpouring of thankfulness, including the mayor of the town, bankers, storeowners, and various other individuals. These dishes were a tangible tribute to a remarkable lady whose lending a helping hand had touched the lives of many people. "Including me," I say to myself as I drink the last sip of coffee.

As I turn the cup over in my hand and look on the bottom of the cup, the pattern of this set of dishes is indicated – Heritage. The pattern is coincidentally appropriate, for this beloved matriarch had indeed left a far-reaching heritage. Her various possessions were parceled out to relatives when age and deteriorating health left her no longer able to remain in her home. Inheriting these dishes means more to me than I can find words to express, for they evoke a rainbow of emotions – love and gratitude – and a treasure chest of heartfelt memories. But they represent a far greater heritage. This grand lady's legacy is beyond measure; it is one of grit, gumption, and grace, and it extends to a vast array of fortunate heirs.

In stark contrast, the heritage Mattie had received was dramatically different. Looking back to the late 1800s, so the story goes, the McPeak family of Tunica, Mississippi, owned a plantation and enjoyed prestigious social standing in the community. The wealthy family disinherited Lillie Camilla McPeak and her sister, Mary Olivia, when they married Joseph Smith and Joseph's brother, both from Tennessee and day laborers on the McPeak plantation. Perhaps because of the disdain of the McPeak family, Joseph and Lillie Camilla moved to Alvord, Texas, after the birth of their first two sons. On U.S. Highway 287/81 and not far from Dallas, this town is 10 miles northeast of Decatur in northeast Wise County. Settlement began there in the early 1880s. It was originally called Nina but later adopted the name of Alvord in honor of the president of the Fort Worth and Denver Railway Company. By 1890 Alvord had become a retail center for area farmers.

It was near Alvord that Joseph and Lillie Camilla lived on a farm and raised cotton – and kids, including sons Alonzo, Shelby (Sheb), John, Jim, and "the baby," Charlie Roy (not born when family photo was taken), and daughters May, Mary, and Martha Jane (Mattie). Even though Lillie Camilla's parents had disowned her, she named at least two sons after the McPeaks, including the first son, Shelby Clark, named after both of his grandfathers – Clark Smith and Isaac Shelby McPeak. In addition, Grandmother Mattie was named Martha Jane after Lillie Camilla's mother, Mary Jane, and her grandmother, Jane, whose own grandmother was also named Jane.

Smith Family, Alvord, Texas, about 1899. Photo courtesy of Louise Smith.

Mattie was born on March 5, 1896. She and others born that year had a life expectancy of less than 50 years of age. Many died of various infections, for antibiotics such as penicillin had not yet been developed. Chlorine was not used to make water safe to drink until 1908, so many died of infectious diseases, such as cholera and dysentery, carried by bad water. Beating the odds, Mattie and her brothers and sisters all lived into adulthood and past the 50-year mark.

In spite of grandparents disinheriting her parents, Mattie wore her middle name proudly; she was especially pleased when her eldest daughter, Lillie Levi, named her second daughter Charlene Jane. Being born into a disowned family did not keep the family from using the family name of Jane; it was used for six generations. And neither did being born in a disowned family keep Martha Jane Smith from growing into a remarkable woman – affectionately called Mattie – who lived out her life with grit, gumption, and grace!

Working in the cotton fields was etched indelibly in Mattie's memory. Even in her later years, Mattie would recall picking cotton near her birthplace, Alvord, Texas, and how the members of her family would get to the field before sunup and wait at the end of the row until it was light enough to pick. Adults traditionally pulled six-foot canvas bags along behind them, filling a bag with up to 80 pounds of cotton before "weighing out." "I was so little," Mattie was heard to say many times, "that I had to use a flour sack to pick cotton."

Even as a youngster, Mattie was tenacious and courageous. Throughout her entire lifetime, she remembered vividly how she had taken little Charlie out behind the shed – indoor bathrooms were just about non-existent except for the well-to-do families. The Smith family definitely did not fit into that category. After Martha sat Charlie down and stepped back, she immediately saw the rattlesnake between them. Putting Charlie's safety above her own, she darted toward him to pick him up. At the same time, the coiled snake made its vicious strike, sinking its fangs firmly into her ankle.

Decades later, as Mattie looked at the fang marks, her eyes sparkled like flint. "I remember it like it was yesterday," she said of the life-threatening ordeal. She recalled how she became hysterical in spite of everyone telling her that the snake had not bitten her. When a lamp was lighted, the fang marks became obvious, verifying that Mattie knew what she was talking about. She emphasized, "I knew the snake had bitten me."

When the family realized that the rattlesnake had indeed bitten Mattie, they immersed her leg in kerosene. One of her older brothers was sent for a doctor. When the doctor finally arrived, he was not overly encouraging. Back then rattlesnake bites often resulted in death, and the prognosis for a small girl was especially grim. Years later Mattie described her leg, "It puffed up so much that reaching around it required the hands of three men."

The doctor later said that soaking her leg in kerosene had saved the brave little girl's life. With her determination and unremitting will to live, healing began. Recovery, however, was slow and arduous. Nearly 60 years after the rattlesnake bite, Mattie said, "After the swelling went down, the flesh began to rot and fall away." A crutch was required while the flesh and muscle grew back on Mattie's small, withered leg. She hobbled around the house on the crude, homemade crutch. While learning to manage the crutch, she had a few mishaps, including falling off the porch. But with her innate optimism, she remembered thinking, "One good thing about it, I don't have to pick cotton anymore this year." Mattie's optimism and wry sense of humor began early in life!

Surviving the rattlesnake bite was a defining milestone in Mattie's life. Although she had almost added to the high death rates for those precarious years of the early 1900s, she had looked death in the face and defied it. After she endured the painful recuperation from the rattlesnake bite, she believed that she could overcome anything. Little did she know that attitude would serve her well as she faced the tumultuous challenges in the years ahead.

Eking out a living on a small Texas cotton farm evidently was a challenge, or at least not fully satisfying. Of course, life anywhere in the early 1900s was not "living on easy street," as Mattie was heard to say during her adulthood. More than 95 percent of the births took place in homes; Mattie's two oldest brothers were undoubtedly born at home in Arkansas, and all the other Smith children were probably born in their home in Alvord, Texas. Back then only 14 percent of the homes in the United States had a bathtub, and only eight percent had a telephone. Rare anywhere but more likely in urban areas, these luxuries were simply not available to the Smith family on their farm, far from a city of any size.

The allure of free land and a better life made Joseph Smith eager to join the Westward Movement. Signed into law in 1862 by Abraham Lincoln, the Homestead Act provided that any person over 21 and a U.S. citizen could obtain 160 acres of land if he or she lived on it five years and improved it. Later legislation provided 320 acres could be homesteaded. This Act turned over vast areas of the public domain to private citizens from all walks of life – newly arrived immigrants, farmers without land of their own, single women, and freed slaves took on the challenge of "proving up" and keeping this "free land." More than 270 millions acres or 10 per cent of the land in the United States was claimed and settled under the Homestead Act. Successful Homestead claims dropped sharply after the Taylor Grazing Act of 1934 substantially decreased the amount of land available to homesteaders in the West. But some land was available for homesteading until the Homestead Act was repealed in 1976, with provisions for homesteading in Alaska until 1986 – one of the last places in the country where homesteading remained a viable option into the latter part of the 1900s. Under the Homestead Act, by 1900 about 600,000 individuals in 30 states had received clear title to 80 million acres of farm and ranch land.

The Homestead Act was just one of several laws enacted in 1862 that totally transformed the American West. Among other laws, thirteen new territories, including New Mexico Territory, were admitted to the union, and grants were given to the four transcontinental railroads to extend rail transportation from the Atlantic to the Pacific. The Smith family may not have felt personally affected by some of the laws, but having rail service available in remote Eastern New Mexico did wield a personal impact on them. For in 1906, Joseph and Lillie Camilla joined thousands of others to pursue better opportunities for their families. No more picking cotton for the Smith family!

Cotton farming, early 1900s. *Texas Almanac*, 1998-99

"Pioneer family by covered wagon." Courtesy Palace of the Governors (The New Mexico History Museum), Negative no: 015069

Like many others, Joseph and the older boys loaded their farm tools on wagons and herded their livestock to New Mexico.

Lillie Camilla and the younger children later rode the train to join them in search of their dream for a better life.

Westward ho to New Mexico!

Early 1900s train engine, E.N.M.U. Special Collections.

Chapter Two:
"...DOWN TO THE BONE"
(1906 – 1913)

Keep your face to the sunshine and you will not see the shadows.
— Helen Keller

Homesteaders by the hundreds were drawn to New Mexico before it became the 47th state in 1912. They came because it promised to be the Land of Enchantment long before it was given that name officially. Beckoning sunshine and blue sky stretched from horizon to horizon in the wide-open vastness of this eastern part of the New Mexico Territory. Crystal clear air offered the promise of healing to many hopeful homesteaders. Majestic sunsets painted a panorama of rich colors. Bright stars sparkled like jewels scattered across the night sky. To top it all off, coyotes could be counted on to provide an evening serenade.

The Joseph Smith family members found themselves in this intriguing setting in 1906 when they arrived on the wind-swept High Plains of Eastern New Mexico. Many homesteaders, just like Lillie Camilla and the younger children – including ten-year-old Mattie – were met at the train depot by other family members who had arrived earlier to stake out their claims.

The train depot and Light Hotel in Elida, New Mexico, 1905, E.N.M.U. Special Collections

The few other buildings in Elida clustered near the train depot were dwarfed by the endless sky and faraway horizon. The buildings struck dramatic silhouettes against the starkness of the treeless terrain. The exuberant band of reunited families told a compelling story of people determined to make a new start despite past unfulfilled ambitions, the vicissitudes of nature, and the sheer magnitude of the seamless, never-ending landscape surrounding them.

Before the homesteaders arrived, the spacious area was occupied by the Apache, Comanche, and Kiowa tribes and large herds of buffalo. When Texas became a state in 1845, hunters came into West Texas and Eastern New Mexico and killed most of the buffalo while the U.S. Government drove out the Indians. These actions – and the Homestead Act of 1862 – made way in the area for new settlers, eager to claim "free land."

Going back even further in time, in 1540 this expansive area of "free land" was named Llano Estacado, Spanish for "staked plain," by the Spanish explorer Francisco Vasquez de Coronado. Most authorities believe that the term originated from the stockade-like appearance of the formations on its boundaries while some think that Coronado and his men drove wooden stakes into the ground so that they could find their way out of the tall prairie grass. Later explorers, however, did not find wooden stakes. Rather, they found markers of rocks, buffalo bones, and dung. Another version of the origin of the name claims that the "stakes" were the stalks of the yucca plants growing all over the vast tableland. Regardless of the origin of the name of the flat land, Coronado's expedition mapped a trail used by colonists over the next three hundred years.

Later known to early explorers and settlers as the Great American Desert, this large, semi-arid mesa has elevations rising from 2500 feet in the east to more than 5000 feet in the west. The Llano Estacado covers approximately 32,000 square miles; it is larger than all of New England and comprises all or part of thirty-three Texas counties and four New Mexico ones, including Roosevelt County, where Elida is located.

The land and the sky seem to reach further than time in the open prairie of Eastern New Mexico. Photo by Phill Russell

The first ranch on this area of the Llano Estacado was established in 1879 – the T-41. In 1898 the Pecos Valley and Northeastern Railroad reached Portales, then only a box-tent settlement located near some springs several miles from the current location. The name Portales, Spanish for "porches," refers to the cliffs of the springs – these overhanging formations resembling porches of traditional adobe houses. Railroad service to this remote part of New Mexico would do more than any other factor to transform the wide open grazing ranchlands to a fenced-in agricultural area. Longstanding resident of Portales, wife of a former New Mexico governor, and New Mexico historian, Jean Burroughs offered this description: "Rutted wagon trails soon became grassed over and unused when shining steel rails and cross ties, like a broad zipper, connected Pecos, Texas, with southeastern New Mexico and the Portales Valley."

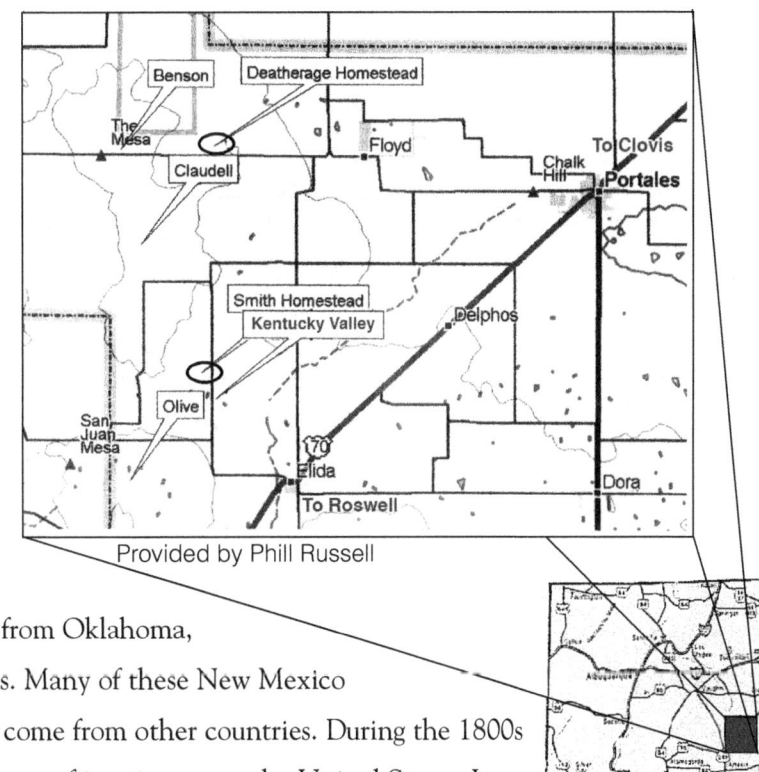
Provided by Phill Russell

The Elida train depot was a happy place on that milestone day in 1906 when the Smith family members were reunited and began their dusty, 12-mile wagon trek from Elida to Kentucky Valley, the location of the Smith homestead. The first homesteaders arriving in that area were from Kentucky and so named the area. Other homesteaders came from Texas, like the Smiths, while some came from Oklahoma, Tennessee, and various other states. Many of these New Mexico homesteaders or their parents had come from other countries. During the 1800s Germans were the largest single group of immigrants to the United States. In the 1840s nearly a million Irish immigrated to the U.S.; they made up about 45 percent of all immigrants in that decade. Other immigrants came from England and Scotland. Regardless of their country or state of origin, those choosing New Mexico as their destination came mostly by train or covered wagon, and they came from all walks of life, eager to meet the challenge of "proving up" and keeping their "free land."

Affidavit claiming specified land issued to Joseph A. Smith by the Dept. of Interior (United States Land Office) and signed/dated Aug. 11, 1906. Provided by Phill Russell

Affidavit identifying Joseph A. Smith from the Dept. of Interior (United States Land Office), and signed/dated Aug. 11, 1906. Provided by Phill Russell

Homesteaders had to be at least twenty-one, live on the land, build a home, make improvements, and farm the land for five years. Four legal documents record Joseph Smith's steps required to acquire his homestead. The first two are signed on August 11, 1906, while the third and fourth ones are dated August 13, 1906. The fourth one is a receipt for the fee of $16.00 paid by Joseph Smith. The last two forms indicate they were issued by the United States Land Office in Roswell, New Mexico, the seat of Chaves County; the first two probably were also issued by that Land Office. By 1906 the area encompassing Elida had been aligned with Roosevelt County, but evidently there was no Land Office in Portales, the county seat. Roswell was older than Portales; it was founded in 1869 when a professional gambler established a lone store on the cattle trail whereas Portales was established much later.

Homestead application issued by Roswell, N.M. Land Office, dated August 13, 1906. Provided by Phill Russell

Receipt from the Roswell, N.M. Land Office, Dept. of the Interior, for $16.00, received from Joseph A. Smith on August 13, 1906. Provided by Phill Russell

Roosevelt County was carved from Chaves and Guadalupe Counties in 1903 and named to honor Theodore Roosevelt, then a hero not only to the Rough Riders but also prominent for his rise in politics. At that time only 800 people claimed Roosevelt County as their home. The Census report of 1900 showed only 383. But a great influx of people began moving into Roosevelt County, and by 1904 the population had jumped to 3,000.

By 1906 the population had reached 6,000, and by 1910 more than 12,000 people had settled in Roosevelt County. Clovis, the county seat of neighboring Curry County, was incorporated in 1909, and by 1910 its population was 3,225. Because Roosevelt County covered such a large area and the people were scattered all over it with no easy way to communicate, the Smiths were probably unaware that they had joined 3,311 other homesteaders filing in Roosevelt County just from January until mid-August of 1906.

Portales in 1903, E.N.M.U. Special Collections

Many homesteaders had also settled in Curry County, including Francis Jackson ("Jack") Smith, Joseph's brother. Mattie never saw her Uncle Jack and his family after 1906 when both families left Wise County, Texas, to homestead in New Mexico. There is no evidence that the two brothers even knew the whereabouts of each other. The Smiths, other Texans, and homesteaders from a variety of states helped the population of the entire Territory of New Mexico grow; in 1900 it was only 141,282. By 1910 the population had more than doubled to 327,296.

Joseph and Lillie Smith, Martha's father and mother. Photo courtesy of Louise Smith

Like other pioneers, the Joseph Smith family had joined the historic Westward Movement across the American frontier. Also like many other homesteaders, this bold and resolute couple and their family undoubtedly had no idea they were playing a significant role in this important expansion of the United States. Some called them nesters or squatters, but whatever the label, these homesteaders were part of the epic story of people who were shaped by the land and who also shaped the land – one sod dugout at a time, one small farm at a time, and eventually one town at a time. Before the Homestead Act was repealed in 1976, under this law private citizens had claimed more than 270 million acres in the United States. To put it another way, private citizens just like Mattie's father (and later, Mattie's husband Lewis) had homesteaded and settled more than 10 percent of the land in the United States.

Exterior of one of the more "luxurious" half-dugouts – "home" to many homesteaders in the early 1900s. Photo taken by Phill Russell at the Pappy Thornton Museum, Clovis City Park (Curry County, New Mexico)

Upon arriving at their claim in Kentucky Valley, the Smiths' first task was to make some sort of shelter. Because there were no trees within more than a hundred miles from their homestead and no easy way to transport them anyway, lumber to build their new home was out of the question. So the Smiths did what most all the other homesteaders were doing. They dug a hole in the ground so that the majority of their new one-room home was underground with the top part above ground. The top might have been covered temporarily with canvas wagon sheet, dirt, or whatever else was at hand. Later the roof was probably covered with wood shingles or maybe with wood planks and sod. Whatever the roof, fine dust generally sifted through to settle on the people and furniture within. To add further insult to injury, the roof almost always leaked whenever it rained.

In late years Mattie told about one family that was roused in the middle of the night by loud noise on the roof of their dugout. By the time they got outside to investigate all they could find were wagon tracks in the sod. It turned out that a doctor was returning to town after seeing a patient too ill to travel the bumpy road to the doctor's office. Navigating by the stars, the doctor ran over the sod roof. Mattie commented, "It couldn't have been a very heavy wagon."

Half-dugouts were the accepted "blueprint" for New Mexico homesteaders' bungalows, and pioneers like the Smith family worked as a team to make theirs as comfortable as possible. With the floor and walls swept as clean as dirt floors and walls could be swept from excess dirt, the Smiths made themselves at home. Bugs, snakes, and other "critters" also made themselves at home; they pervasively and persistently resisted the pioneers' invasion. As

Interior of half-dugout in the early 1900s. Photo taken by Phill Russell at the Pappy Thornton Museum, Clovis City Park (Curry County, New Mexico)

an adult Mattie recalled in those early years how she could tolerate co-existence with bugs, mice, and dust – but not snakes. She knew all too well the long-lasting damage a striking snake could cause.

The construction of the Smiths' dugout was simple and easy to understand. In contrast, a staircase built nearly four decades prior to the Smith's dugout and several hundred miles away was much more complicated and is still shrouded in two mysteries – the identity of its builder and how the staircase was constructed. The location of this mysterious construction was Santa Fe, the capital city of New Mexico, founded in 1610 and the oldest continually used seat of government in North America. When the Loretto Chapel in Santa Fe was finished in the 1870s, there was no way to get to the choir loft. Carpenters insisted that a ladder would be the only solution because a staircase would take up valuable seating space in the small Chapel. The Sisters of Loretto began to pray, and on the ninth day of prayer, as the story goes, a man with a toolbox showed up looking for work. After several months the carpenter completed the staircase and disappeared without pay or thanks. The staircase was built with wooden pegs – no nails, and it has two 360 degree turns with no visible means of support. Whoever designed the magnificent structure and built it still perplexes experts today.

Faraway from the miracle wooden staircase in New Mexico Territory's capital, the Smiths grappled with more mundane matters such as gathering dried cow manure to make a fire for cooking meals. Because wood was almost non-existent in the remote, treeless, wind-scrubbed prairie, dried cow dung – frequently called cow chips – was commonly used to provide fuel for preparing meals. Cooking was considered a female responsibility; Mattie and her two sisters gathered cow chips and helped their mother cook in the dugout during cold weather and outside during warmer weather. This practical solution was just another one of the many pragmatic ways pioneers responded to the harshness of the land with creative resourcefulness. Mattie's ability to learn quickly coupled with childhood experiences such as selecting and gathering the best cow chips for fuel served her well as she faced new challenges. She easily earned the reputation of "making things happen" and "getting things done."

Like other homesteaders, the Smiths raised peas, corn, squash, and beans. They ate some of the fresh vegetables and dried the rest for winter eating and the next year's seed. Food consisted of whatever could be grown in the family garden and dried or stored in the coolness of the dugout. Watermelons were raised since the climate in Eastern New Mexico was wetter in the early 1900s than it is now. Because uninvited coyotes helped themselves to the watermelons, the homesteaders tried to raise enough to feed their family as well as their canine neighbors. Coyotes also enjoyed feasting on the homesteaders' chickens; the homesteaders depended on chickens for meat as well as eggs. So the newcomers fought a constant battle with relentless coyotes.

The homesteaders also depended on livestock such as a cow or two for milk and some pigs for meat. Stories of early homesteaders also mention eating a lot of jackrabbits and some pronghorn antelope. Considering that jackrabbits can run up to 40 mph, and pronghorn antelopes, the fastest animal in the western hemisphere, run in 20-foot bounds at up to 60 miles per hour, having one of them for a meal required a sharp shooter in the truest sense of this challenge. In his memoirs of his maternal grandmother, Sadie Greathouse – another New Mexico pioneer woman – my brother Bob offered this commentary:

> *She told us once that she raised her family with a .22 rifle and flour gravy. She routinely shot running jackrabbits, but cottontails were easier and tenderer. As for the antelope, they would take a four to six foot stick and tie a handkerchief to it. They would crawl into a small depression within three or four hundred yards of the antelope herd, then set the stick into the ground and wait. The antelope would see the new thing in the landscape, and eventually get curious and approach until they were within easy shooting range of the .30-30 or .25-35 rifle with open sights. It might take a couple of hours, but it worked most of the time.*

The gutsy pioneers were simply carrying on a food-gathering tradition begun thousands of years ago in this area. Only seven miles north of Portales on the way to nearby Clovis is Blackwater Draw, where the earliest occupants of the New World lived thousands of years ago, trying to "live off the land" just like the homesteaders. Stone and bone weapons, tools, and processing implements have been found at this important archaeological site. Back then the area was populated with extinct forms of the giant mammoth, elephant, wolf, bison, and horse, as well as deer, wolves, wild hogs, and the four-pronged antelope hunted by the Smiths, the Greathouses, and other early 1900s homesteaders.

The Smith women and other pioneer women were very inventive in food preparation. One reported making sausage with jackrabbit, hog lard, and spices – another pioneer experience that gave Mattie courage to experiment when she became the "head cook." When someone asked Mattie if her family ate prairie chickens, she quickly replied, "Not unless we had to." She explained, "They are not very appetizing. The meat is bloody and smells 'gamey.'"

Crops the homesteaders planted included corn, kaffir, maize, broom corn, and haigari (higear) grown for the grain. The grain was "headed" with a knife whereas the stalks were cut and stacked for fodder. Although farmers never planted bear grass, they sometimes harvested it. Also called yucca, this plant was made the state flower in 1927. Put into bales, this native plant was shipped to places where it was used to make rope. Some old-timers remembered that during WWI many train car loads of baled bear grass were shipped from Eastern New Mexico.

Life was demanding and precarious on the prairie. There was no reliable or accessible source of water. Some years it rained a lot, and some years hardly at all. There was neither river nor lake to provide easy access to water. Portales Springs served only a very limited area. Although a plentiful supply of water existed beneath the ground, this source was not recognized or utilized until the late 1800s and early 1900s when technology made drilling possible. This source was one of the world's largest aquifers – the Ogallala Aquifer. Also known as the High Plains Aquifer, it is a vast yet shallow underground water table aquifer located beneath portions of eight states – Nebraska, South Dakota, Wyoming, Colorado, Kansas, Oklahoma, Texas, and New Mexico.

Until a well could be dug near the home site, water had to be hauled long distances on a horse-drawn wagon. On some homesteads, drilling for water was never successful, or settlers ran out of money before "striking water." So the weary pioneers deserted their claims and returned to their former homes or resumed their search for greener pastures.

Just as "no water" was one of the main reasons homesteaders gave up and moved on, "no water" was also probably the reason the earliest inhabitants as well as others over the centuries moved on. But before moving on early inhabitants tried to get water from the ground. Even in the historic period, Comanche Indians camped here and dug shallow wells. These ancient wells are considered the oldest wells in North America. Failure to get reliable sources of water as well has other reasons may have also discouraged staying in this area – constant wind (the wind velocity is greater on the High Plains than on any other area in the United States), blinding sand storms, searing heat, relentless insects, devastating prairie fires, empty horizons, isolation from more populated areas, and pure loneliness.

But life elsewhere was not always free from struggles either. An earthquake and fire in San Francisco in 1906, for instance, killed as many as 3,000 people and destroyed nearly 25,000 buildings. In that same year, famine in Chile left 20 million dead. A coal dust explosion killed 1,060 in France. Many new settlers in New Mexico suffered ill health – asthma, tuberculosis, or other lung ailments; they had responded to the advertisements of New Mexico as a haven where they could recover their good health. New Mexico itself suffered an ongoing struggle; in Santa Fe, America's oldest capital city, the big issue in 1906 was that of statehood – many people in the Territories of New Mexico and Arizona voted on joint statehood, New Mexico voting in favor and Arizona against – Arizona won. In 1906 a fire called The Great Prairie Fire destroyed many homesteads from Fort Sumner, New Mexico, to Hereford, Texas, and from the Caprock north of Clovis to within 10 miles of Melrose. In 1908 and 1909 fires destroyed 25 businesses in Portales, and about that same time fires destroyed numerous businesses in Clovis, including three saloons.

Far from the concerns of California, Chile, France, the capital of New Mexico – or even of neighboring counties or the towns of Portales and Clovis, the Smiths had worries of their own.

The basic necessities of life – like getting water for drinking and cooking – were an ongoing challenge. "Mother worked hard," Mattie was heard to say many times later in her life. Like the days of other pioneer women, Lillie Camilla's days began early and ended late as she cared for her husband and children. Life as a pioneer in New Mexico was in stark contrast to the life Lillie led on her family's Mississippi plantation. When she left that life at sixteen to marry one of the plantation's day laborers, she could not have possibly imagined how her life would change and how dramatically different the lives of her children would be from her childhood on a Mississippi plantation.

Life on the Eastern New Mexico frontier in the early 1900s was demanding and difficult in part because there was no electricity, which meant no lights, no refrigerators, no freezers, no air conditioning, no heating systems, and, of course, no television, no computers, and no e-mails. Only homes in more metropolitan areas in the United States had electricity; the first electric lights were turned on in Albuquerque during the 1890s. Faraway New Mexico farms and ranches did not get electricity until the early 1950s.

New Mexico was a land apart from the rest of the United States, and remote Eastern New Mexico was a land apart from the rest of New Mexico. Isolated with virtually no communication with the "outside world," homesteaders in remote Eastern New Mexico relied on neighbors and word-of-mouth. Families spread sparsely over the far-reaching plains enjoyed getting together for community dances, and they also depended on an area church for social interaction as well as for

Church group in Kentucky Valley, early 1900s. E.N.M.U. Special Collections

spiritual strength. Telephones were also almost non-existent in that distant part of New Mexico. Santa Fe had a few telephones in 1881, but the few telephones in Eastern New Mexico came years later and were in Clovis and Portales. Elida had the nearest Post Office; it was established in 1902. Mail was sporadic and trips in a horse-drawn wagon were long and grueling. Kentucky Valley never got a Post Office although Claudell did get one in 1907. Because mail was virtually the only means of communicating with faraway places, the homesteaders were willing to do what was required to get it.

With neither modern conveniences nor machinery, the hardy homesteaders had to rely on themselves – their energy was devoted to tilling the land and caring for their farm animals. The terms "manpower" and "horsepower" might well have been coined by hard-working homesteaders! Women are the unsung heroes of "taming the West," for they carried out all the traditional "women's work" – caring for the babies and children, raising the gardens, preparing meals, washing clothes, and keeping the dugouts as clean as possible – as well as helping the men folk with the "man's work." Livelihood of the homestead families was mainly farming and ranching – both were at the mercy of the weather, and it could be temperamental and unpredictable.

Death was also unpredictable on the windy plains of Eastern New Mexico. In March of 1907, tragedy struck the Smith family – Lillie Camilla died unexpectedly. She was 43 years old. Even though the average life expectancy in the United States in the early 1900s was only 48, Lillie Camilla's life was snuffed out even before reaching that age. One account of her sudden death is that in the afternoon she had gone to the home of her oldest daughter, May. Her husband, Dennis Lamb, and she had staked their claim about one mile from the Smiths' homestead. While there, Lillie Camilla drank some water that she said "seemed to stick in my throat."

Suffering from chest pains the remainder of the afternoon, Lillie Camilla "took it easy." In the evening when she and Joseph went to bed, she asked Joseph to get her some camphor. When Joseph gave her the container and she took off the stopper, it fell to the floor. By the time Joseph lit the kerosene lamp, his wife and the mother of their seven children was dead. Cardiac disease and cancer, the current top killers, were relatively uncommon at that time – people didn't live long enough to get them. Perhaps Lillie was an exception and died of heart problems.

Or maybe Lillie's chest pain was caused by an upper respiratory infection, for prior to the mid 1930s – before the introduction of antibiotics – infectious diseases were the top killers in the United States. Poorly insulated housing, inadequate sewage treatment, and "bad" water may also have contributed to Lillie's death, just as they adversely affected countless other early pioneers.

Mattie had celebrated her eleventh birthday only a week before her mother died. All her life, according to Winnie (Mattie's youngest daughter), she "remembered vividly the dreadful night her mother died." Years later when I was about 10 or 11, Grandmother Mattie told me that the coyotes howled "louder than ever" that night. My grandmother also said that she would lie awake during the nights after her mother's death and listen to the coyotes wailing. "The sound of coyotes in the dark nights," she recalled, "was the saddest sound I ever heard." The coyote's serenade in the Land of Enchantment had turned into a funeral dirge.

More than 55 years have gone by since Mattie first told me about the impact of her mother's death – I still cannot hear a coyote howl without feeling the sadness a little girl must have felt at the death of her mother. Mattie described to me the inconsolable suffering at losing her mother and compared it to the pain of the earlier threat to her own life – the rattlesnake bite. "The pain of the bite itself," she explained, "was not the worst. It was when the flesh on my leg rotted away." She emphasized, "That hurt down to the bone!"

Then my grandmother's eyes faded into a faraway, forlorn expression as she added sorrowfully, "But Mother's death hurt worse – and longer…it still hurts." She emphasized, "Mother's death truly hurt down to the bone."

Lillie Camilla McPeak Smith was buried in the cemetery at Kentucky Valley, New Mexico. By this time, this community consisted of a church, a schoolhouse, and a community center. Winnie recalled, "Years later when the cemetery had deteriorated into a cow pasture, my grandmother's body was moved to the cemetery in Elida." Changing grave sites was very

Rubbing of the quotation on Lillie Camilla's tombstone.
Provided by Phill Russell

emotional for Mattie; it dredged up all the grief-stricken memories of the long-ago heartbreak of a young 11-year-old losing her mother.

Joseph never remarried. Rather, he devoted himself to keeping the children together until they were married. Years later, Winnie said that at the time of Lillie Camilla's death, "Aunt May was the oldest girl and she had just gotten married…she took charge of the younger ones…including 'Baby Charlie' as he was called long after he was a baby." Winnie continued, "Mattie, being next in line, soon took charge."

Deserted homestead – windmill, wagon, and half-dugout.
Source unknown

Many stories of the early settlers speak loudly of their courage and determination in the face of perils and uncertainty. Treasured dreams and hopes for the future staked their claim on the Land of Enchantment, but much of this changed. The Promised Land lost some of its allure. The large thunderhead clouds sometimes failed to deliver life-giving rain needed for thirsty crops. The glorious sunsets were sometimes hidden by blinding sandstorms. The stars were sometimes masked by driven snow and bitter cold. Those difficult times shaped the lives of the New Mexico homesteaders in countless ways, large and small. Character was put to the test – a strong work ethic, treating others with respect, willingness to work together, honesty, fairness, perseverance, and determination. Those who failed the test fled the land, deserting their homesteads and searching for an easier life. Those who survived became even stronger.

Other traits and rigorous habits also had their historical roots in those early homesteading days. Grandmother's insistence on clean clothes, for example, stemmed from her past pioneer days. Winnie recounted that "Keeping clean was not so easy as it is today – water was scarce and precious. It usually meant a weekly bath in the wash tub and clean underwear – longhandles in the winter."

Winnie continued her story, "Charlie broke his arm. Only broken bones or near death situations called for a doctor in those days. They took Charlie to a doctor in Elida. When the doctor asked Charlie to take off his overalls, you could see his underwear – and they were not clean." Winnie emphasized, "Even as a young girl, Mother was so embarrassed! Among other childhood experiences, this particular one taught Mattie a lesson that stayed with her all her life." All Grandmother's children and many of her grandchildren remember her routinely checking, "Are your undies clean?"

Work on the homestead sometimes required trips to Portales, the largest town in the area, to get materials and supplies not available in Elida. Portales was 25 miles from Elida so trips there were rare, and the long grueling trip by wagon was reserved for grownups. In 1898 the Pecos Valley and Northeastern Railroad had begun its run to Portales, bringing the supplies homesteaders required for developing the land and building communities.

A Pecos Valley and Northeastern Railroad – Pea Vine, for short – in the early 1900s, E.N.M.U. Special Collections

Two most significant events affecting the history of New Mexico occurred less than fifty years apart. First, three centuries of Hispanic authority was concluded when the Treaty of Guadalupe

Hidalgo was ratified in 1848; the United States gained not only Texas but New Mexico and Upper California and the rights of U. S. citizenship were guaranteed to all New Mexicans. The second important event or force was the coming of the railroad in 1879, bringing in a variety of machines and tools for the farmers and ranchers. The train traveling through Portales was popularly called the Pea Vine. In addition to its delivering important supplies to the area, many settlers rode it, bringing with them to the Portales area their children and their hopes, dreams, and belongings.

Among the numerous people bringing their hopes, dreams, and belongings to New Mexico from other states was the first governor of New Mexico when it achieved statehood in 1912 after sixty-two years as a territory. Born in New York, William C. McDonald taught school and studied law before moving to Kansas in 1880 and then on to New Mexico in 1881. After working nearly ten years as a U.S. deputy mineral surveyor, he entered the cattle business. A very strong Democrat, he was elected as the first governor of New Mexico, working until 1917 to serve his adopted state.

Work of a different nature fell to Mattie and her younger sister, Mary, after their mother died. The youthful girls had to assume responsibilities such as housekeeping, cooking, and washing clothes. But they also attended school. According to Winnie, her mother reminisced about how all the school-age Smith children sometimes walked to the school at Kentucky Valley and how they sometimes rode burros or were taken in a horse and buggy. Early in the 1900s, one-room schools dotted the sprawling stretches of prairie because poor roads and inadequate transportation made it impossible for children to attend centrally-located schools. I remember my grandmother's saying numerous times how she felt bad that she completed only the eighth grade of school. She did not complain about all the other work she had to do; she was simply expressing her disappointment that she "didn't have much schooling."

Mattie was not alone; many children during that period of time completed no more than the eighth year of school. In 1906 – the year the "hot dog" was introduced – only six percent of all Americans graduated from high school. New Mexico only became a part of the United States in 1850 when it was organized as a territory. As late as 1888 there was not a single public college

Portales street scene, 1910, E.N.M.U. Special Collections

or high school in the entire territory; a system of public education was not established until 1890. Even by 1906, the total enrollment in New Mexico was merely a little more than 39,000. The 1900 census indicated a population of 141,282, of which 33 percent was illiterate. This problem was compounded by the fact that English was not the first language of a majority of New Mexicans but was officially the language required to read everything from newspapers to school books. This situation was a legacy of the territory's former position as an isolated frontier province of Spain and Mexico.

This legacy did not affect Roosevelt County, for there simply were not any Spanish-speaking people there. Most of the people had moved to this barren, uninhabited area from Texas and other English-speaking states. Nevertheless, there were some educational obstacles. For instance, the average length of the school year was only a few days over five months. Especially on the homesteads and other rural areas, children like Mattie and her sisters and brothers were needed to help with the work, leaving little time for formal education. Those children living in town were much more likely to be able to attend school and possibly graduate.

As Joseph's children grew, they "made their own entertainment," and a favorite was dances. Neighbors for miles around took turns having them, and the entire family attended, bringing loads of home cooked food to share with the others. They would dance all night and get home by daylight in time to start their day's work. They were doing their best to reclaim some of the enchantment that had drawn them to this new land.

Joseph Smith's homestead deed, July 29, 1913. Provided by Phill Russell

Joseph Smith's homestead deed, Aug. 16, 1913. Provided by Phill Russell

Days of special celebration would come when all the hard work of Joseph and his family paid off and they received the deeds to the Smith homestead. These deeds to their "free land" bore the signature of the twenty-eighth President of the United States, Woodrow Wilson.

As I consider the lives and values of my grandmother and her family and measure my life and values against this remarkable legacy, I am filled with awe. There are so many lessons to be learned from even the briefest recollections of these ancestors. Their moving to a faraway land to improve their life was a monumental act of faith. The outrageous demands of this new land truly tested this faith. Many times the Smith family – our family of only a few generations ago – was afflicted with disappointments, their possessions were meager, and tragedies occurred that hurt "down to the bone." Yet this motherless pioneer family survived.

Mattie not only "survived," she emerged as a stronger person. Her experiences – her interaction with people and the land – would shape her personality and weave the fabric of her character. She was learning at an early age that life is fragile; she was learning to overcome an awful loss and to go on living despite heart-breaking grief. She was learning a work ethic that would serve her well the remainder of her life. She was growing rich in resourcefulness – she was learning to "make do or do without." She was developing self-reliance and learning to help and encourage others to also become independent. She was learning to treat others with respect and dignity; she was learning to regard relationships as precious and to handle them carefully and with compassion.

In each of us is a tiny part of this remarkable woman who began early living out her life with grit, gumption, and grace. As her descendants, we carry within us some of her genetic makeup, and descendants and non-relatives alike can adopt the values and attitudes forging a foundation – a bedrock of values and character – that enabled her to build a solid life. Revisiting the enormous mosaic of this resolute pioneer woman's life story will hopefully give added meaning and resolve to each person reading it. The story of the indomitable Mattie can be essentially our story – one of grit, gumption, and grace.

Chapter Three:
DANCING ALL NIGHT
(1913 - Oct. 11, 1918)

In the long run all love is paid by love…give thy love freely; do not count the cost;
so beautiful a thing was never lost in the long run.
— Ella Wheeler Wilcox, *In the Long Run*

"Love at first sight!"

That is what happened when Martha Jane Smith and Lewis Campbell Deatherage met. Lewis was from Benson, and she was from Kentucky Valley – both areas a grueling day's wagon trip to Portales, the nearest town and the seat of Roosevelt County. Lewis played the fiddle for all the dances in both areas, and it was at one of these dances that the two met.

A couple of other men also played their fiddles for the dances, including Mattie's father, later called "Grandpa Smith" by many relatives. One of these men would occasionally play the fiddle in Lewis' place so that he could dance with the love of his life. She never missed a set, dancing all night – she square danced, two-stepped, and spun to "Cotton-Eye Joe" and the polka. Lewis enjoyed a reputation as "the best fiddler ever heard," carrying on a rich family tradition. The Deatherage family history tells of others who played the violin and some who also made them. Martha's family history describes congenial people who wholeheartedly followed their dreams. Even as a teenager, Martha was no exception. She loved life passionately, and whatever she did, she did with great gusto – including dancing.

Decades later when Mattie was a great grandmother, she could still remember the fun of those dances. I recall visiting her at Aunt Lillie's after she could no longer live by herself. It was a beautiful summer evening, and we were listening to some Floyd Cramer music. When "Last Date" filled the air, Grandmother's feet went into motion and her body captured the rhythm of the song. With obvious happiness of years gone by written all over her face, she said softly but with deep feeling, "I loved dancing all night."

As the music played on, she continued, "About sunup, we'd all load into the wagon and get on home…just in time to eat breakfast, change clothes, and get back to work."

Photo by Ben Wittick, Courtesy Palace of the Governors (New Mexico Museum of History/DCA) Negative no: 003083

Someone asked the same question that many before had asked, "Weren't you too tired to work after dancing all night?" She knew the answer without thinking, and she always replied the same, "Yes, we were tired. But we had to work…and the dancing was worth it." Starting early in life, Mattie worked hard, but she also enjoyed some occasional good clean fun as counterpoint to the long periods of work.

Like Mattie's mother and father, Lewis Campbell Deatherage's mother and father had also come from Texas to homestead in New Mexico. The Deatherage family had been a large one – eleven children according to older family members although public records account for only six children. Margaret lived to be sixteen while others died as babies or before reaching their teenage years. Will and Lewis were the only ones to survive as adults.

An unusual name, Deatherage was quite a contrast to Smith, Mattie's maiden name. Some historians contend Deatherage is of French origin. As the story goes, a man from Flanders named D'Aeth married a French woman named Etherage in the late 1000s. Upon marriage, their names were combined to form Deatherage. Some of their descendants traveled to Germany and settled there while others went to England. Deatherages from both Germany and England immigrated to the United States.

Cousin Maggie and Lewis

Lewis as a young boy in Texas who probably never knew he had famous ancestors

Deatherage grandparents and other relatives

Deatherages from Germany tended to say Deatherage was a German name; some "Americanized" it by changing it to Richardson when they arrived in their new homeland. Immigrants from England, including the ancestors of Lewis Deatherage, contended the name was English and did not change it. Lewis Deatherage never spoke to Mattie of his early ancestors, probably because he was unaware of his long-ago family history. But his family ties can be traced through his mother back to Pocahontas, an Indian princess who was vital to the goodwill between the Indians and the early colonists in Virginia, and John

Roelfe, an early English colonist and successful tobacco planter. After the two married, they had one son before Pocahontas's untimely death.

Although Lewis did not know about his renowned ancestors, he did know that there were various small communities of immigrant Deatherages in Texas. In addition, Lewis knew that several of these families accepted the railroads' free passage to homestead in Eastern New Mexico just as did many families named Smith.

Early 1900s train bringing prospective homesteaders and other passengers to Eastern New Mexico. E.N.M.U. Special Collections

The origin of the Smith name is much simpler. Derived from the Anglo-Saxon "to smite or strike," the Smith name and its derivations are an occupational name for a person who worked with metal, one of the earliest jobs for which specialist skills were required. People were frequently named after what they did to make a living, hence Locksmith, Blacksmith, Goldsmith, etc. Later the part of the name designating the specific job was dropped, and the person's surname simply became Smith. No wonder that name is the most common last name in the United States as well as Canada, Australia, New Zealand, and the United Kingdom. Smith is the last name of one out of 100 persons in each of these countries. The widespread use of this name accounts at least in part for the difficulty tracing Mattie's lineage, resulting in little information about her father's ancestors. It seems fitting that her maiden name was work-related, for Mattie was known from her earliest days to be a very diligent worker.

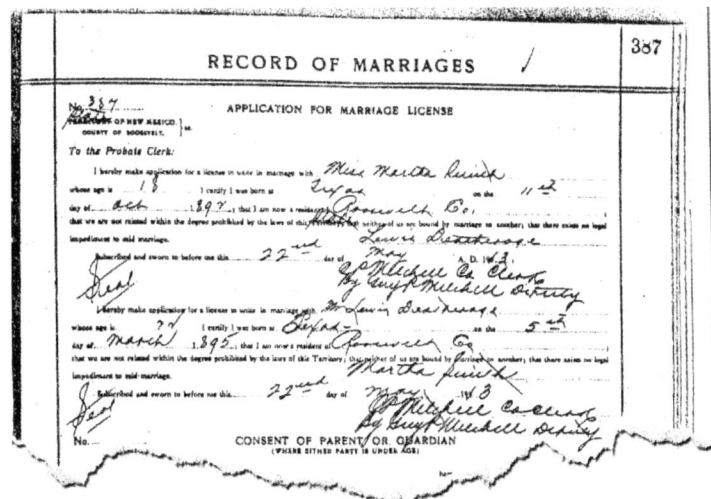

Mattie was also known to care deeply for Lewis, the good-looking, popular fiddler, and he was known to be equally smitten with Mattie. So on May 22, 1913, Martha Jane Smith became Martha Jane Deatherage, or Mrs. Lewis Deatherage. Mattie indicated on the application for a marriage license that she was 18 and her birthday was March 5, 1895.

As it turned out, Mattie's birthday was actually March 5, 1896. In Wise County, Texas, where she was born, only ten percent of the births were reported in the late 1800s. With the family not having a copy of her birth certificate, there being several children in the family, her mother dying at an early age, and there being more pressing concerns than "keeping records," Mattie probably truly believed that she was born in 1895. That is, until several years passed. More about that later. But for that May day in 1913, a wedding was uppermost on the minds of Lewis and Martha, and young love prevailed.

John Smith, Mattie's brother, and Sarah Emelia Eminger, from a large group of German homesteaders, were also planning to get married. The two couples finally decided to have a double wedding. A friend drove the foursome into town with his "old car with no top," as Emelia put it. Neither Emelia nor anyone else knew the kind of car it was, but it probably was a Ford Model T because that car accounted for three-fourths of all cars on America's roads at that time. Emelia said they were all "just excited to have a ride in a car," for it was the first time either she or Mattie had ever ridden in one.

Uncle Will, Lewis' brother, worked in a bar in town. He thought it would be a funny prank to go to the court house and tell the officials that they should not give Lewis a marriage license because he was not old enough to get married. But one of Lewis' friends found out what Will had done. So he waited for the foursome and told them about the proposed prank.

Lewis and John gave their fiancés some money so they could go shopping while Lewis went to confront Uncle Will and insist that he undo his mischief. As for the shopping, Mattie and Emelia each bought a sailor hat – a flat top with a brim and a long ribbon down the back – and a pair of long white gloves. With all the confusion – and the shopping – the wedding was detained but finally carried out "without a hitch," as Mattie put it years later.

About 4:00 the four newlyweds got back to Mattie's new in-laws, Lewis Jordon and Mattie Deatherage. The new mother-in-law warmed over the food, and the newlyweds and everyone else ate the wedding dinner. The foursome planned to go back to Grandpa Smith's for their wedding night, for Grandpa Smith and his family had recently moved to a bigger, nicer house with three bedrooms and a dining room. Like many other disillusioned homesteaders, the previous owners had returned to their former home.

Late when they arrived, the newlyweds were told by Mattie's brother, John, not to undress and go to bed because a crowd was forming at their brother Jim's house to chivaree them – that is, play tricks on them like short-sheeting their bed, tying bells underneath the bed, or hiding in their house until they arrived and bursting out in song when they entered the room. Not married long themselves, Jim and Ola lived in the house that Joseph Smith and his family vacated when they moved to the larger house. Jim and Ola likely wanted to play some of the pranks on the newlyweds that had been played on them. John said he knew there were some people at Jim's because he could hear the dogs barking. Aunt Emelia lived to be over 100; about 80 years after the festivities of this double wedding, she recalled the details fairly clearly. She concluded, "The chivaree, or 'wedding tricks,' didn't amount to much."

Although Lewis and Mattie kept in close contact to Mattie's father, they lived in Claudell with Lewis' parents after they got married. Probably the main reasons they lived with the Deatherages is that they did not own a home – not even a half-dugout, and jobs and money were scarce. Of course, prices of everything were also lower in 1913 than they are now – for example, the average cost of a new house in 1913 was $3,395. The average family income was $1,296, a new car cost $490, a loaf of bread cost six cents, a gallon of milk was 36 cents, and a gallon of gas cost 27 cents.

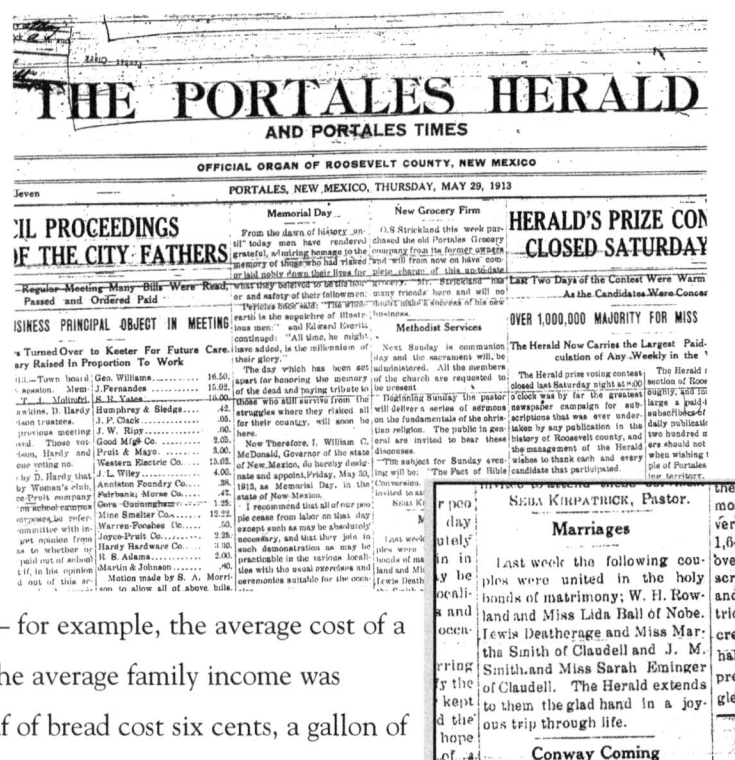

Typical New Mexico homestead of that era – quite an improvement over the half dugout! Near Elida. E.N.M.U. Special Collections

The newlyweds moved to Clovis sometime during the first year of marriage so that Lewis could work in the roundhouse for the Santa Fe Railroad. Lillie was born in Clovis on March 18, 1914. Only days later – March 31, 1914 – Lewis filed an application for a homestead of 320 acres.

When Lillie was only six weeks old, the family of three traveled on the train from Clovis to Elida, where Grandpa Deatherage met them at the train station. They lived on a farm near Floyd to be closer to the Deatherages but soon moved to their own homestead. Mattie recalled in later years how she was always eager to "make things better" and to "improve the situation."

Lewis and Mattie's homestead had some buildings on it. While they certainly were not fancy, they were an improvement over the half-dugout that was her first New Mexico home. The young couple's homestead papers gave this description:

Provided by Phill Russell

Finally living on the land they hoped to someday own and in their own house was "very good fortune," as Mattie put it.

On March 9, 1916, the people of Columbus, New Mexico, were not so fortunate. Pancho Villa and his force of about 485 men raided the small village, causing massive destruction and countless deaths. This deadly attack would go down as one of the most infamous entries in New Mexico history and was reported in large headlines across America. Only three miles from the Mexico border, Columbus was 300 miles from Portales. In those days over news traveled slowly into the remote areas of New Mexico's large land area of 121,593 square miles (it was the fourth largest state at that time). Furthermore, Roosevelt County covered 2000 square miles. This vast expanse of land in Eastern New Mexico was far from the larger towns, it was a less populated area, and the people were spread out over the land – with neither radio nor television. From time to time historians and other writers have called the High Plains the forgotten frontier or the last frontier. Like other significant happenings in New Mexico, the Columbus massacre may have captured the attention of only the residents of the towns in remote Roosevelt County.

Another exciting – but happy – event also occurred in March of 1916. Although it did not make the newspaper headlines in the towns of Roosevelt County, Lewis and Mattie rejoiced over it. Their second daughter, Juanita, was born on March 26, 1916. Grandpa Smith and the Deatherage grandparents celebrated with the young parents and helped them care for both the new arrival and her toddler sister. All three grandparents also gave their support and encouragement to the young couple in their efforts to qualify to own their homestead.

In the original Homestead Act, a person was required to live on the land, build a home, make improvements, and farm for five years before they were eligible to "prove up." However, on a document signed on October 9, 1917, by J. C. Compton, the Probate Judge in Portales, and sent to the U.S. Land Office in Fort Sumner, New Mexico, indicates a "final three year proof." This provision had changed in 1912.

The Portales newspaper undoubtedly did report the horrible Columbus massacre; but no record of the Deatherage births could be found although births – and deaths – were routinely recorded in local

```
                              Portales, New Mexico.
                              Oct. 9, 1917.
          OFFICE OF J.C.COMPTON PROBATE JUDGE.

Register and Receiver,
      U.S.Land Office, Fort Sumner, N.M.

Gentlemen:
        I HEREBY CERTIFY that final three year proof
on homestead entry No. 011212    Entryman, Lewis C.
Deatherage, for the N.1/2 Sec. 13, T. 1 S. R. 30 E.
N.M.P.M.; was made before me on the 9th day of Oct.
1917, between 1:00 P.M. and 3:00.P.M.; that the names
of the witnesses to the said proof were John M. Price,
of Benson, New Mexico and Arthur S. Davidson of Floyd,
New Mexico; that there were no protests or objections
of any kind offered against the said proof.
        Given under my hand and official seal at Portales,
Roosevelt County, New Mexico, this the 9th day of Oct. 1917.
                              J. C. Compton
                              Probate Judge.
```

Provided by Phill Russell

Provided by Phill Russell

newspapers. The first newspaper in the county was the *Progress*, printed weekly in Portales. It was followed by the *Portales Herald*, beginning in 1902 and lasting until 1907. Then there was the *Portales Times*, printing papers from 1903 to 1913. The two papers merged in 1913 to become the *Portales Herald-Times*, which published newspapers until 1916. There were also other newspapers in the county, including the *Kenna Record*, publishing the news from 1907 until 1924.

Besides printing news – such as the account of the tragedy in Columbus – newspapers printed notices about homesteaders' intentions to "make proof" of their homesteads; the Homestead Act required that a notice be published five consecutive weeks in a newspaper near the particular homestead. The *Portales Valley News* was the name of the Portales newspaper publishing Lewis and Martha's notice; this information is recorded near the bottom (left side) of the document on this page.

Martha and Lewis worked as partners in the struggle to survive the drought. To reply to the letter from Washington, they had to complete another document – about twenty questions. At the right is an excerpt summarizing the conditions in the three "prove up" years.

The young homesteaders' third daughter, Winnie, was born on November 6, 1917. The next day, November 7, 1917, the Homestead Certificate was signed and issued from the United States Land Office in Fort Sumner, New Mexico. This document confirmed that Lewis had "paid in full" all the required fees and was entitled to receive a Patent for the homestead. As further approvals were given, additional dates were stamped on this Certificate.

While the young couple was happy to be making progress on completing the requirements to own their homestead, caring for their family was a challenge for them. But because of so little rain and virtually no crops for several years, an even bigger challenge loomed over them. Lewis had to leave the

Provided by Phill Russell

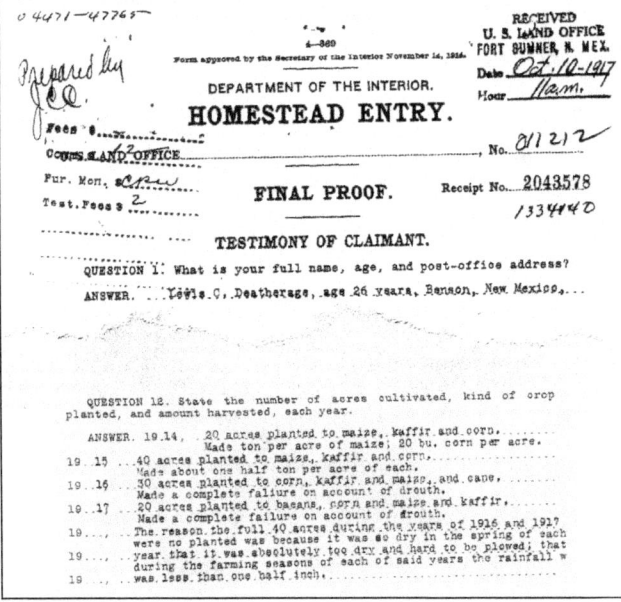

homestead to find work in early 1918; Mattie was left to fend for herself and their three daughters, all under the age of four.

"Leaving the land" was not unusual. The dream for "a good living" held by many of the homesteading families had simply not come true, and husbands were frequently forced to travel to other places to find work. The song, "O, Fair New Mexico," was adopted as the state anthem only a year or so before. Elizabeth Garrett, the New Mexico woman who wrote it, was blind and from a rather tumultuous and controversial family. She was the daughter of Pat Garrett, best known for killing in 1881 the infamous Billy the Kid, leader of a gang of the most feared outlaws in the Southwest and involved in the Lincoln County War. As an accomplished musician, Elizabeth Garrett was one among many prominent women leaving their mark on New Mexico in spite of personal or circumstantial adversity. Moreover, the wives left to tend to the homesteads and care for the children while their husbands searched for other work also made an indelible imprint on the land and history of New Mexico.

Lewis traveled to Hurley, near Silver City, New Mexico, in his search and lived with his brother, Will, and his wife, Venus. According to Will's WWI draft card, Will worked in the Chino Copper Mine where Lewis hoped to also get a job. In later years Mattie recalled those early hardscrabble years when Lewis was gone weeks on end and she did all the chores on the homestead and cared for three young children. Obviously a self-reliant young wife and devoted mother, she expressed no self-pity but simply commented, "I just had to tough it out."

While in Hurley looking for a job, Lewis wrote letters to Mattie dated January 13, 17, and 20, 1918. Although telephones were available in larger cities and there was telephone service between Berlin and New York City, most people in remote Eastern New Mexico did not have access to telephones. New Mexico was a land apart from the rest of the United States, and Eastern New Mexico was a land apart from the rest of New Mexico. There were some advantages of being "apart" or isolated – for instance, all the violence – murders, gunfights, and cattle rustlings – associated with the Lincoln County War posed no threat to the people living in Roosevelt County. When the feud erupted in 1877 among rival cattle barons, John Chisum, namesake of the Chisum Trail, Lincoln County covered one-fifth of the entire New Mexico

Territory; it was the largest county in the United States. A large expanse of land also cushioned Roosevelt County from Fort Sumner, where Pat Garrett killed Billy the Kid after he killed two guards to escape jail.

Fortunately, Lewis did not fear for Mattie's safety from battling factions. But means of communication had not improved much since the Lincoln War. So Lewis wrote letters to Mattie. In one of them he told her that even if he found a job in Hurley he would not be able to work because of his difficulty breathing in the higher mountainous altitude. There was speculation that Lewis had some type of heart problem that caused his breathing problem.

Writing to his father, Lewis asked if he would send him $25 so he could come home. He obviously was concerned about his health because he told his father that he "was really scared." When "Pa," as Lewis' father was often called, sent him the money, he came home on the train. The wife and two daughters of Charlie Greathouse were on the train; their destination was also Portales. They would join Charlie, who had homesteaded in the vicinity and would become a well-known early rancher in Eastern New Mexico. His family reported that Lewis was sick when he boarded the train in Belen.

In one of his later letters, Lewis told Mattie he had rented a house and for her to "have Grandpa Deatherage move you and the girls." Lewis also explained that it was a little yellow house where "old man McPhearson" lived when Lewis was younger and went to school in Portales. Lillie's first memory of "Papa" was during the move to this house. She recalled throwing a spoon down into the cellar and his spanking her for doing it.

When the anxious young couple had not received word about their homestead, Lewis wrote this note dated May 7, 1918, to the U.S. Land Office in Washington D.C.:

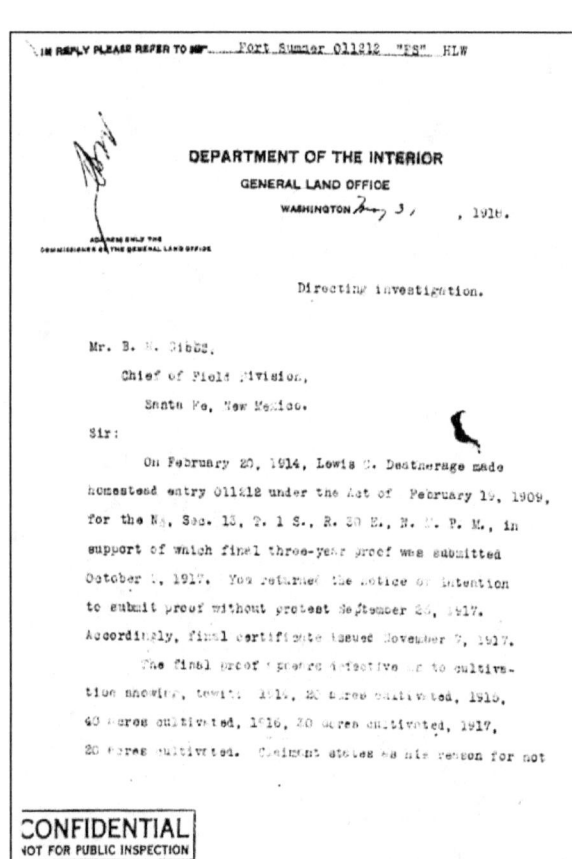

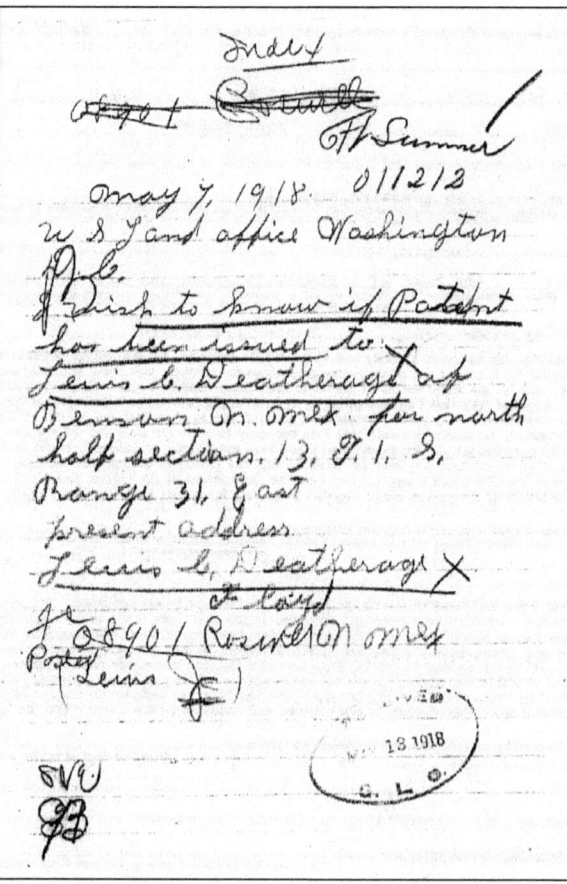

Provided by Phill Russell

Later that month the Department of the Interior, Washington D.C., sent a letter to the Chief of Field Division in Santa Fe summarizing Lewis' claim that "his reason for not cultivating the required land…it was so dry and the soil so hard that it was absolutely impossible to do plowing." Because of the drought, Lewis and Mattie had cultivated only 30 acres in 1916 and only 20 acres in 1917. A local newspaper reported only one inch of rain one of those "prove up" years. The federal office asked the state office to advise it regarding this cultivation requirement.

A letter received nearly a month later from the Chief, Santa Fe Field Office, confirmed that "the facts justify relieving the claimant from cultivating the required area." In other words, the reality of the severe drought in Eastern New Mexico was finally being recognized and acknowledged.

Lewis recovered enough to work when he returned to Portales, and by July, 1918, he was living in Portales with a job loading livestock. The cattle business had grown significantly in Portales but was never as large as it was in Roswell, 90 miles away. Names of the great cattle barons like Chism, Goodnight, and Loving are associated with Roswell, for in the 1870s and 1880s it was the watering place for the Pecos Valley cattle drives. Kenna, even closer to Portales than Roswell, had also enjoyed a thriving cattle business; in 1909 it was one of the largest cattle shipping operations in New Mexico. But the cattle industry in the entire area had suffered greatly because of ongoing extremely dry weather from 1916 through 1918.

The government agencies handling all the paperwork for carrying out the provisions of the Homestead Act of 1862 finally began taking appropriate action regarding the drought in Eastern

Provided by Phill Russell

Early Portales scene — Farmers Wagon Yard and Camp House, E.N.M.U. Special Collections

New Mexico. A two-page letter from the General Land Office in Washington D.C. to Fort Sumner summarizes the situation and concludes that the area of cultivation be reduced and finally that the "Patent will be issued in due course." Good news to Lewis and Mattie!

Although Lewis and Mattie both worked hard, they still occasionally attended community dances after they had their three daughters. Mattie told years later how she and Lewis, like many other couples, would take their young children to the dances and "put them to bed in a room or put them to bed in the wagons." Mattie also recollected that "It was a prank for someone to change babies, and the parents wouldn't know it until they got home." Times have certainly changed; this would not be considered "funny" nowadays!

Most of all, Mattie emphasized how much fun the dances were and that along with church they were the most important social gatherings in the entire area. She said that Lewis was always a favorite fiddle player; people liked for him to play because he did it so well and obviously enjoyed doing it. As a youngster, he had been given a fiddle by someone who told him he could keep the fiddle "until I come back after it." This individual apparently never returned, so Lewis kept the fiddle and became very

Provided by Phill Russell

Roswell Evening News, Sat., Oct. 5, 1918. Provided by Phill Russell

Roswell Evening News, Oct. 12, 1918. Provided by Phill Russell

skillful at playing all the popular music of that time. He was well known as "the left-handed fiddler." Decades later when Lewis and Mattie's three little girls had grown up and had children of their own, they could all remember Mattie's referring to obviously treasured memories:

"We loved dancing all night."

But the infamous Spanish Flu epidemic of 1918 changed all that, just as it changed lives for millions of other families. This deadly epidemic created a state of panic in communities around the globe, and many people believed the world was coming to an end. The epidemic struck at the end of World War I, killing more people in six months than the war had killed in four years. To put it another way, the deadly Spanish Flu snuffed out ten times as many lives in America as did World War I. Worldwide, this dreadful infectious disease proved fatal for more than 50 million people – including 675,000 Americans.

New Mexico was among the last states to be invaded by the cruel killer, but neither its sparse population, its normally ideal climate, nor its relative isolation could halt the spread of the disease once it had crossed into the Southwest. Only six years old as a state, New Mexico was the only state without a Department of Health. This lack proved to be a serious deficiency when the Spanish Flu struck. To make matters even worse, New Mexico experienced its coldest autumn and winter in more than 25 years as temperatures dropped to as low as 30 below in many places.

Nearly everyone in the Smith and Deatherage families suffered from the deadly illness. This strain of flu struck with amazing speed, often killing its victims within just hours of the first signs of infection. Not only was the Spanish Flu virulent, but it had an unusual preference in its choice of victims – it tended to target young healthy adults over those with weak immune systems, the very old, and the very young. This was true in the area where Lewis and Mattie lived. Lewis' parents were among the few who escaped it, and it was said that "Grandpa and Grandma Deatherage came to help take care of the sick." Only 26, Lewis was one of the young stricken with this dreaded illness.

The 1918 strain of flu overwhelmed the body's natural defenses so fast that the usual cause of death in flu patients – a secondary infection of fatal pneumonia – oftentimes never had a chance to establish itself. In the month

HEALTH PROCLAMATION

Whereas, at a special meeting of the Board of Trustees of the Town of Portales, New Mexico, held on the 7th day of October, 1918, a number of cases of Spanish Influenza were reported, and

Whereas, after due investigation and consultation, the Board of Trustees have definitely ascertained that Spanish Influenza exists in the Town of Portales, and that same is rapidly spreading, and

Whereas, the health of the citizens of the Town of Portales and of the public in general is seriously jeopardized by the continued operation of amusement places, and places where crowds gather, by reason of the possibility of the great spread of Spanish Influenza, and

Whereas, the co-operation of all cities and towns in stopping the further spread of the disease has been asked by the surgeon general of the United States, and

Whereas, the Board of Trustees of the Town of Portales has fully considered all means of properly safeguarding the public health during the epidemic of Spanish Influenza, and has by a unanimous vote reached the conclusion that an emergency now exists in regard to the public health, now, therefore, be it

"RESOLVED by the Board of Trustees of the Town of Portales, New Mexico, that all places of amusement, motion picture show houses, theaters, churches, dance halls, and all schools shall be indefinitely closed immediately on the passage of this resolution, and that all public indoor gatherings of any kind or character be and the same are hereby indefinitely prohibited; that the school children, and all other persons, not engaged and in the pursuit of some useful business are hereby prohibited from loitering upon the streets, plazas, buildings, or any other place in town except their own homes and premises. And be it further

"RESOLVED, that the inhabitants of the Town of Portales are urged to take all possible precaution to prevent the further spread of the Spanish Influenza, by remaining as much as possible in their own homes, by not attending gatherings of people in houses or buildings, by keeping the windows of their homes open day and night, by isolating as much as possible any member of the family afflicted with the disease, by calling in attendance a physician as quickly as any possible symptoms of the disease appear, and by strictly adhering to the sanitary instructions and preventative measures advised by such physician. And be it further

"Resolved, that it is the unanimous sense of this board that all meetings incident to the sale of Liberty Bonds during the present campaign, and all other patriotic gatherings, be held in the open air and not in enclosed public places.

Passed and approved this the 7th day of October, 1918, and ordered that publicity be given by means of circulars being printed and publicly distributed.

E. B. HAWKINS, Mayor.

Attest:—W. H. BRALEY, Clerk.

Portales Valley News, Oct. 12, 1918. Provided by Phill Russell

of October alone, the Spanish Flu claimed the lives of 200,000 individuals in America. Lewis did survive the flu long enough to develop pneumonia. But unfortunately, the young father of three small girls could not fight off the ravages of pneumonia. The exuberant left-handed fiddle player with enough stamina to play the fiddle and enjoy dancing all night, Lewis Deatherage was one of these victims. He succumbed to the infamous virus on October 11, 1918, his 27th birthday.

The undertaker came to the house and in the front room prepared Lewis' body for burial. The other family members stayed in the kitchen with the door shut. Although Lillie was only five years old, that dreadful time remained indelibly etched in her memory her entire lifetime: "I remember how Mother cried and beat on that door." She also remembered that her father's coffin was opened before burial at the Floyd cemetery and that "they tried to get me to look at him."

For Lewis Deatherage and Martha Jane Smith, it had been "Love at first sight." But now their love story was over. Lewis was laid to rest in the Floyd, New Mexico, cemetery with a piece of petrified wood as his monument – a monument his father had planned to use on his own grave. The heartbroken widow later placed a more traditional monument beside that petrified wood.

Maybe for many people today the Spanish Flu epidemic of 1918 has merely the substance of a tenuous memory, but for Mattie and her three young daughters – Lillie was five, Juanita was two, and Winnie

Provided by Phill Russell

was 11 months old – it turned their lives upside down. Mattie and Lewis had dreamed of carving out a great life with each other in the Land of Enchantment. But this dreadful illness destroyed their dream and replaced it with dramatic life-long consequences, reaching across generation after generation.

For the 22-year-old widow, there would be no more dancing all night. The beautiful music had ended.

Provided by Marilyn Chumbley

Chapter Four:
"I WILL KEEP MY GIRLS!"
(Oct. 11, 1918 - Sept. 27, 1920)

*To have courage for whatever comes in life –
everything lies in that.*
— Mother Teresa

Lewis' death left Mattie with a broken heart and no money. Well-meaning people told the grief-stricken 22-year-old widow she couldn't possibly keep her children …she should give them to someone who could care for them adequately. Her reply was quick and resolute: "No…I will keep my girls!" Like most women of that era, the young widow had no special skills for making a living. Neither were there any government programs to help out; Social Security was not launched until 1935. New Mexico had been a state only six years; it had no programs or resources to help Mattie and her children. Although the first life insurance company in the United States was founded in 1732 and many companies were started in the late 1700s and early 1800s – including at least one in New Mexico – very few survived. Furthermore, most homesteaders were not known to have much money; they probably

considered life insurance an unattainable luxury. As a young woman, Mattie might not have even known about life insurance. But one thing Mattie did know for sure, and she made it very clear: "I will keep my girls!"

From the age of eleven, Mattie had felt the awful emptiness of not having a mother. The sadness caused by her mother's death perhaps added to her resolve to keep her children. Because her father knew firsthand the challenge of rearing children as only one parent, he came to live with Mattie soon after Lewis' death to help her with the three little girls.

As for Lewis' parents, they loved Mattie "like a daughter," she recalled in later years. Perhaps Mattie was like the daughter they no longer had. All their eleven children had died except Lewis and Will. Lewis' death undoubtedly opened old wounds of grief and left a new gaping gash in their hearts. Grandma Deatherage's father had died when she was about a year old; she had experienced the sadness of growing up without a father. So without hesitation, the young widow's in-laws supported Mattie's vow to keep her young girls.

Only a few months had passed after Lewis' death when Mattie received the deed to their homestead; it was dated December 27, 1918, and signed by Woodrow Wilson, the twenty-eighth President of the United States. Only about one month after Lewis died, the Germans signed the Armistice –

November 11 – and on the eleventh hour of the eleventh day in the eleventh month of 1918, the world rejoiced and celebrated. The "war to end all wars" was over. Wilson presented to the Senate the Versailles Treaty, containing the Covenant of the League of the Nations, and asked, "Dare we reject it and break the heart of the world?" While Mattie was concerned about the war and grateful that progress toward peace was being made, she lacked the emotional energy to "rejoice and celebrate." Her heart was already broken, and she was facing the most grievous battle of her life – coping with the tragic death of her young husband and considering how she would take care of their three little girls.

Ownership of the homestead would help immeasurably. As a couple, Mattie and Lewis had worked hard to reach this goal, and the money from its sale would literally help put food on the table. Because Lewis died with no will, Mattie had to go through probate court to establish her sole guardianship of their children before she could sell their portion of the 320-acre homestead. Legal guardianship was finalized on May 5, 1919, whereas proceedings to settle the estate lasted from March 19, 1919, until August 2, 1920.

```
IN THE PROBATE COURT,
ROOSEVELT COUNTY, NEW MEXICO.

Honorable Cleveland Compton, Judge of said Court.

In the Matter of the Estates of
Lillie Levi Deatherage,
Flora Juanita Deatherage, and
Winnie Mary Deatherage, Minors.

    NOTICE OF APPLICATION FOR LETTERS OF GUARDIANSHIP.

    Notice is hereby given, That Martha J. Deatherage has filed
with the clerk of this court a petition, praying for letters of gua-
rdianship of the persons and estates of Lillie Levi Deatherage, Flora
Juanita Deatherage and Winnie Mary Deatherage, minors, and that Monday
the 5th, day of May, 1919, at ten O'clock in the forenoon of said day
at the court room of said Court, in the Court House in Roosevelt Cou-
nty, New Mexico, has been fixed by said court for hearing said peti-
tion, when and where any person interested may appear and show cause why
said petition should not be granted.

Dated 3-19  1919.                    _____, Clerk
                              By _____, Deputy
                                 Clerk.
```

The young widow sold the property to Isaac Greathouse for $1,600. Two claims made against the estate said that Lewis owed them money before his death. One said he had loaned Lewis $20.00 whereas the other claimed that Lewis owed him $38.60 for "goods sold and delivered…at his request." Mattie paid the two men from the money she received from the sale of the homestead.

As required by law, a notice about settling Lewis's estate had to be published weekly for four consecutive weeks. The first notice appeared in the June 17, 1920, *Portales Valley News*, and the fourth one in the July 8, 1920 issue.

A legal document called the FINAL ACCOUNT, REPORT AND PETITION FOR DISCHARGE provides a summary of this sale as well as other issues.

Finally, the long, laborious proceedings came to an end on August 2, 1920. Mattie was relieved and happy when she received the DECREE OF FINAL DISCHARGE.

IN THE PROBATE COURT OF ROOSEVELT COUNTY, STATE OF NEW MEXICO

IN THE MATTER OF THE ESTATE OF)
LEWIS C. DEATHERAGE, DECEASED.)
) No. 171.

FINAL ACCOUNT, REPORT AND PETITION FOR DISCHARGE.

Martha J. Deatherage, administratrix of the estate of Lewis C. Deatherage, deceased, renders to the Court her final account, report and presents herewith her petition for discharge as such administratrix:

1st. That letters of administration were duly issued upon the said estate to the undersigned on the 5th day of May, 1919.

2d. That notice to creditors has been duly posted as required by law, proof thereof being on file in this cause.

3d. That all the property in the said estate consisted of a half section of land located in Roosevelt County, New Mexico, described as follows:— The North half of Section Thirteen in Township One South of Range Thirty East, New Mexico Meridian, New Mexico, of a value of approximately $1600.00 (sixteen hundred dollars)

4th. That all the claims that have been presented and allowed against the estate of said deceased have been paid and settled in full.

5th. That more than one year has passed since the issuance of letters of administration upon said estate to the undersigned and the posting of the notice thereof.

6th. That in strict pursuance of the orders of this Court in case No. 172 thereof, the undersigned administratrix sold the land herein above described to Isaac R. Gratehouse for a consideration of $1600.00; that the report of such sale has been duly approved by the Court and a deed conveying the same to the said purchaser has been duly executed and delivered.

7th. That all the costs of this proceeding have been duly paid to the clerk of this Court.

8th. That no money or personal property in any ... belonging to the estate of the said ... or knowledge of this administratrix.

... Deatherage, administratrix of ... deceased, prays that this her final ... ed and settled; that she be ... said estate and that she, as well as ..., acquitted and relieved from all ... all and every other necessary and

Martha J. Deatherage
Administratrix.

... Deatherage, being first duly sworn,
... has read the foregoing statement

IN THE PROBATE COURT OF ROOSEVELT COUNTY, STATE OF NEW MEXICO.

In the matter of the estate of Lewis C. Deatherage,)
deceased.)
Martha J. Deatherage, administratrix.) No. 171.
)

DECREE OF FINAL DISCHARGE.

Martha J. Deatherage, administratrix of the estate of Lewis C. Deatherage, deceased, having this day shown to this court by the production of satisfactory vouchers that she has paid all sums of money due from her, and has delivered up all the property of said estate to the parties entitled thereto, that she has performed all the acts lawfully required of her and that nothing further remains to be performed by her as such administratrix,—

IT IS THEREFORE ORDERED, ADJUDGED AND DECREED that said Martha J. Deatherage, administratrix of the estate of Lewis C. Deatherage, deceased, be and she is hereby discharged from all liability to be hereinafter incurred as such administratrix and her sureties are likewise released from further liability.

Dated and entered at Portales, New Mexico, this 2d day of August, 1920.

J. C. Campbell
Judge of the Probate Court

Mattie refused to give in to feelings of futility, despair, and sheer exhaustion during the nearly eighteen months of working her way through the maze of legal proceedings and about thirty pages of legal documents. During this tedious time she was also working day and night – literally – to generate some income, and, of course, caring for her three daughters. This grueling legal experience coupled with day-to-day home and work responsibilities and heartrending grief could easily have destroyed a young widow, forcing her to relinquish her children to others and to even become dependent on others herself. But Mattie pressed on with unflappable resolve.

Qualities that enabled the pioneers to move to this New Mexico frontier and to survive the harsh land and unanticipated obstacles were the very qualities Mattie drew upon as she faced a frightening and unfamiliar frontier of shattered dreams. Though she had no roadmap to guide her in this personal journey, she never considered quitting, turning back, or giving up her girls. The fire of fierce determination had been ignited early in Mattie's life; this dire situation fanned it to even greater intensity. Her human spirit responded with uncanny courage, resourcefulness, and self-reliance.

With her portion from the sale of the homestead, Mattie bought a small four-room house on an acre of land at the edge of Portales. Located on the Clovis highway, her purchase included a windmill, a cow barn, a red coal shed, and a smokehouse where she dried apples. To complete her new home place, Martha bought a cow named Spot and a few chickens. No zoning ordinances regarding farms animals were yet established. The economy of Roosevelt County was becoming increasingly agricultural, and the spirit of independence that had brought people to Eastern New Mexico was evident even in the small New Mexico towns and villages.

In addition, Portales was relatively small at that time, so people could do whatever they wanted as long no one protested. The population of Roosevelt County peaked at about 12,000 by 1910 but had shrunk to about 6,000 by 1918 because many disheartened homesteaders had abandoned their dreams. On the wind-scoured plains there was nothing to break the sameness of the endless sky and vast horizon – no scenic mountains, no misty valleys, no lush forests, no deep green grass carpets. In O. E. Rolvaag's novel about life on the Plains, *Giants in the Earth*, a young woman thinks, "Here there was nothing to even hide behind." Many homesteaders returned to their former homes or went elsewhere. Even after New Mexico became a state in 1912, it continued to be somewhat apart from the rest of the United States, and Eastern New Mexico especially continued to experience some aspects of frontier life such as isolation and the lack of amenities enjoyed in more developed parts of the country. There truly was "nothing to even hide behind." Only the toughest stayed.

Going elsewhere never occurred to Mattie. For one reason – she had nowhere else to go. And she was tough! To complete her new "setup," the industrious young widow planted a small garden at the back of her house. This may well be symbolic of her "putting down roots," but even more so, it was a matter of economics. Store bought food was expensive! A loaf of bread cost 10 cents, a gallon of milk cost 55 cents, and fresh vegetables cost a lot at the store. While the average national salary was $1,144.00, Mattie's income was undoubtedly even less; at first she had no job or income at all. When she did work "outside the home," she worked in the fields by day and did laundry for others by night. There was no federal law setting a minimum wage, but had there been, the kind of work Mattie had to do would have brought the minimum. Furthermore, the difference in what men and women were paid for the same work was even more startling in the early 1900s than it currently is.

Mattie poured herself into her new "setup," for she and her three young fatherless girls needed a house and a home. No time for wallowing in self-pity! Mattie later said that she thought "that little four-room house was the grandest house I ever saw." Lillie described the house:

> *We called it the "Little White House." It had a red roof and a fence around the yard with a board on the top that we used to walk around on. A big salt cedar tree was in the corner of the yard…*

Each daughter received $200 from the sale of their parents' homestead. Mattie immediately deposited her young daughters' inheritance in the bank for safekeeping. Shortly afterwards, this bank "went broke" according to one account. Grandmother Mattie elaborated to me years later that an unscrupulous banker took the bank's money and fled, never to be apprehended.

Unfortunately, the girls lost their meager inheritance because at that time there was no agency or program for protecting the depositors in a bank. The FDIC (Federal Deposit Insurance Commission) was not founded until 1933. Nevertheless, the undaunted widow steadfastly continued to honor her commitment to keep her girls.

Adding to the young widow's sorrow was the fact that she and Lewis had not had the son they had wanted to carry on the Deatherage name. One way Mattie believed she could at least partially fulfill that lost dream and pay tribute to her dead husband was changing the middle name of her youngest daughter to Lewis. She carried out this legal transaction soon after Lewis' death. It would be decades later before it was fashionable to give boys' names to girls. With little concern about what was "fashionable," Mattie preferred to do her own thinking. Furthermore, she had her own compelling reason for changing her baby daughter's middle name. She said "handing down Lewis' name" was a desperate attempt and a tangible way to "keep the memory of my dear husband alive."

When Winnie was born, she was named Winnie Mary. The "Mary" was probably after Martha's sister, Mary Rebecca. It is not known why Martha chose Winnie to change her middle name to "Lewis." Winnie quipped that it was probably because she was supposed to have been the baby boy the two young parents had hoped for after having two girls. But she was happy that "Winnie" was not changed because she liked that name. As she put it, "An English war bride told me that Winnie was a popular English name." In Winnie's memoirs where she tells about this name change, she jotted down the Scripture, "Thou shalt be called by a new name, which the mouth of the Lord shall name" Isaiah 62:2. As an adult, Winnie commented that she was proud to have her father's name.

As soon as Mattie's father came to live with her to help with the girls, she sought work outside the home to generate some income. The young widow found a job working on Bill Kenyon's farm, one of the first irrigated farms in the Portales valley. Her long days were spent setting out onions and sweet potatoes and then later hoeing them and finally harvesting them. Her work, however, did not end when the day's grueling farm work ended. Mattie would return home and do the cooking and housework. In the evenings she also did washing on the rub board and ironing for other people. The tireless mother had no time for "what ifs." Just as she never complained about the backbreaking work on the New Mexico homestead, neither did Mattie complain about her increased workload after Lewis died. Mattie never wasted time or energy forlornly "looking back."

No photographs are available of Mattie as she labored tirelessly to keep her girls. But if there had been any pictures, they would show a woman in her early 20s wearing a dark, long dress for work, including her work out in the hot, muddy fields. Like most women of that time, Martha's selection of clothes was limited. Regardless of the work, custom required women in those days to wear a long dress. Even though Mattie had to work like a man, she could not dress like one. Pictures would portray her with her long hair swept away from her face and secured on the back of her head with multiple hair pins. On her face there would be no makeup – no "base" or powder, no blush – or rouge, as it was called back them – no eye shadow, no lip liner or lipstick. Her face had on it only perspiration from the long hours of exhausting work and her eyes reflected steel-strong determination. What a stark contrast to the earlier times when Mattie and Lewis held love in their hearts for each other and wore smiles on their faces as they enjoyed dancing the night away together!

A recent picture of the age-old tin box and treasures Mattie kept and protected the rest of her life. The treasures include love letters from Lewis, locks of hair from Lewis and her three daughters, and an intricate pecan basket meticulously carved by Grandpa Smith.

At least Mattie had someone to care for her children while she worked. Child-care centers were not even heard of till decades later. "Grandpa Smith," as the girls called Mattie's father, lived with her and her daughters and watched after the girls. Of course, he needed a home – he did not want to live on his homestead by himself. In addition, he was not able to work the long hours as he had when much younger. This may well be the first of many situations in which Mattie gave someone an opportunity to meet a need or fill a position she had available.

Grandpa was definitely a positive in Mattie's modest little home. He took watch care over his three young charges very seriously. He would sit in front of the smokehouse whittling and overseeing their play. The doting grandfather made toys such as puzzles, balls inside a box with bars, and a wooden man with jointed hands and legs attached to a string so he could hold it over a hand saw to make it "dance," much to the delight of the three little girls.

The most poignant items in the treasured tin box were the letters from Lewis. Here are two typical excerpts from them:

So precious were all the letters that Mattie saved even the envelopes, including ones Lewis had saved and brought home with him when he returned home.

Mattie's father was a gentle, patient man. Lillie said she and the other two girls loved him very much and were happy for him to live with them in their "grand house." Lillie and Winnie both said they could never remember their grandfather saying a harsh word to them. Perhaps this was because Mattie was known to discipline her daughters, and so they probably knew better than do anything that would require Grandpa Smith to raise his voice.

Lillie remembered well that salt cedar tree in their yard and commented on her mother's method of discipline:

> *That tree made dandy switches and Mother would make us go get our own.*
> *If we picked one too small, we could have to go back and get another one.*

Aunt Lillie's description brings back my own memories. Two generations later when Mattie was "Grandmother" to me, she used the same simple discipline method only the switches came from the two willow trees in the back yard of her house in Portales on South Dallas Avenue. When either one of my brothers, Phillip or Butch, or I misbehaved, we were sent for willow switches. Sometimes Grandmother did not trust our judgment; she would select the switches herself. The sting of those switches on the back of the legs of us three mischievous children always worked, just as the salt cedar switches on the bare legs of Lillie, Juanita, and Winnie were effective child psychology.

In addition to Grandpa Smith's help with Mattie's three young girls, Lewis' parents also assisted in the care of them. "Grandpa" and "Grandma," as the Deatherages were called, lived about a quarter of a mile from Mattie's house.

Lillie shared this memory:

> *I always loved to go to Grandma's house. She let us do about anything we wanted to, but we minded her and never talked back to her. Uncle Will had two girls and a boy who came, and they sassed her. But Mother made us understand that if we did, the cedar limb would be a big one.*

Winnie provided this description of Grandpa and Grandma Deatherage's house:

When one went in the front door, a big bedroom opened to the left. To the right was the "front room." In the front room was a coal stove, their bed, a stand table that held the coal oil lamp, and the two rocking chairs – a big one for Grandpa and a little sewing chair that was Grandma's.

The little sewing chair had been her mother's. To the back of the room was the kitchen. It had a big black [cooking] range with a warming closet on top; a reservoir at the side for heating water; a table, with a long bench at one side; and an old-fashioned "safe" for the dishes. On both sides of this room were porches. Later Grandpa built a little room – a shed – on the back of this room with a coal oil stove to use in the summer and a place for Grandma to keep her milk and do the churning.

Grandpa always had a big garden, and Grandma had a yard full of flowers. I always tried to have a few cosmos flowers because they remind me of her. Her front porch was covered with little pale pink roses. There was also a chicken house.... Grandma and Grandpa always went to bed before sundown in the summer and were always up at 4 a.m., sitting in their chairs waiting for sunup.

Lillie also remembered the schedule kept by their grandparents:

They went to bed before dark, and I couldn't get to sleep. The clock would strike every hour and every half hour. I'd finally get to sleep, but at 4:00 they would get up and wake us all up so we could get up and eat breakfast. Mother said that was the only thing that she and Grandma ever had any difference over. Before Papa died, Mother and he had lived with Grandma and Grandpa off and on a lot. Grandma wanted everyone up, even the little babies. Of course, Mother wanted the little kids to sleep.

Grandpa and Grandma Deatherage milked cows, including one named Pet. Using a big churn called a "daisy churn," Grandma churned the milk from those cows every morning. Mattie's daughters said that Grandma would "sit in the door and churn and talk to anyone who happened by."

Daisy churn

The Deatherage grandparents also had some chickens; they sold the eggs and the butter Grandma had churned as well as buttermilk to two hotels in town. Mattie's three daughters could remember riding to town with Grandma in a buggy pulled by a horse named Peaches. The little girls loved riding in the back of the buggy with their legs hanging down.

Other memories include the traditional menu for the evening meal. Lillie put it simply, "We always had milk and mush for supper." She said the girls always wanted sugar on their mush, but Grandma did not think it was good with sugar on it. Grandpa would always say, "Oh, Ma, let them have sugar if they like it that way." Winnie said she was always grateful that Grandpa won that argument.

As for what the three young girls cooked, it was mud pies. This childhood make-believe was one of their favorite pastimes. They frequently spent the night at their grandparents' home; that's where they did their "cooking." Grandma Deatherage never let anyone touch their mud pies until the girls came back to see about them. I have often wondered if those early fun-filled "cooking" experiences accounted at least in part for how all three of these little girls grew up to enjoy cooking and were very good at it.

In 1920, the famous Babe Ruth was sold to the New York Yankees for $125,000. The first Agathie Christie mystery was published. Woodrow Wilson was not a candidate for re-election in 1920, and his proposal that the U.S. enter League of Nations was rejected when Warren Harding was elected President of the United States. Octaviano Ambrosio Larrazolo followed Portales resident, Washington Ellsworth Lindsey, as governor of New Mexico. Larrazolo would enjoy the distinction of being the only native of Mexico elected governor of the state of New

Mexico, and he would be the first U.S. Senator of Hispanic heritage. In 1920, women in New Mexico were finally given the right to right to vote. The population of the United States had reached 106,521,537 whereas the population of New Mexico had reached 360,350, and the population of Roosevelt County was 6,548. Life expectancy for males wsas 53.6 and for females it was 54.6. Average annual earnings was $1,236. Teachers' annual salary was $970. There were 387 miles of paved roads in the United States; it took 13 days to drive to California from New York. But all these paled in significance compared to the milestone in the life of Mattie's oldest little girl. Lillie started to school!

Adjusting to school was easy in comparison to another major occurrence in Lillie's small, young world. When there was an outbreak of measles, Lillie and Eva Shaw, Lillie's best friend, both had them. Sadly, Eva died. When Mattie broke the bad news to Lillie, she was inconsolable at the death of her best friend. But she was also terrified! Perhaps she had heard of other children dying from measles, for it was not that unusual – measles and death from that childhood disease was at an all time high from 1915 into the 1920s. Although the measles vaccine was not introduced until 1963, death rates went down in the later 1920s probably because of changes in sanitation, including cleaner roads, improved water supplies, and more effective sewage control. Lillie knew nothing about these improvements in sanitation – she just knew she would be the next to die, and she kept thinking every day would be her last.

Abandoned School and Church in Eastern New Mexico, E.N.M.U. Special Collections

Lillie survived, and at age 90 she chuckled at her childhood fear, but emphasized that it made her realize throughout her life how very real children's fears are.

While Lillie was recovering from the measles, Juanita and Winnie came down with them. Just as Grandma Deatherage had come to help take care of their father when he had the flu, she came to help care for her three young granddaughters while they were sick. Fortunately, all three little girls recovered from the measles.

When I was just a little older than these young girls were when they had the measles, I became aware of what an orphanage was because of the one located

Mattie's three little girls, the two older ones holding their hats while Winnie refused to even hold hers – Winnie never liked a hat!

in Portales, New Mexico. This orphanage was founded in 1919 – just months after the deadliest month of the Spanish Flu epidemic – October, 1918. Countless children were orphaned and families devastated. The pastor of the First Baptist Church in Portales was aware of nine children in Portales who had been orphaned and simply did not have anyone to care for them. So he began an orphanage in a home; pictured here is a drawing of this home, the beginning of the longest continuously operating residential child-care facility in the state of New Mexico.

Photo of very old drawing of the first building of the New Mexico Baptist Children's Home, about 1920. Provided by administrator, Geraldine Dooley.

As I attended school with several of the children who lived there and played games with them during recess, I learned that many of them had lost a parent through death. I was reminded of Winnie, just eleven months old when her father died, Juanita only three years old, and Lillie only five years old. I harbored heartsick thoughts of kids not having their mother close to them, especially when they were sick. How fortunate the girls were that their mother had not had to put them in an orphanage but could be by their bedside when they had the measles and other illnesses throughout growing up. For Mattie kept her promise, "I will raise my girls some way."

Mattie was building a legacy that would profoundly affect her children and her children's children in years to come. She had no foreshadowing, for example, that a tragedy similar to her own would strike one of her precious girls. Winnie's husband was killed in a horrible accident just days before Winnie's 24th birthday, leaving her with three young children to rear. But Mattie's invincible role model helped Winnie survive and find meaning and joy in life just as she had. And that legacy was passed on to Winnie's three young children.

I know this legacy well, for I was an eight-month-old when Winnie's husband – and my father – was killed. My brothers and I were too young when we lost our father to have any memories of him. But as three fatherless children we soon became acutely aware of the painful and far-reaching vacuum his death left in our lives. We also soon became aware of our grandmother's life-long "helping hand."

We were just a few of many other family members – and friends – whose destiny was determined by Mattie and her promise to keep her girls.

Thoughts of Lewis comforted Mattie and encouraged her as she carried out her promise. She later admitted she constantly and desperately needed that comfort and encouragement. "Thinking about Lewis," she said, "kept me going." One effort to keep her memory of Lewis alive was a having a family picture made. About eighteen months after Lewis died, she had a picture taken of herself and her three daughters; then she had a picture of Lewis put into that picture – the picture of Lewis was taken from their wedding picture.

This picture enjoyed a prominent place in Mattie's house – and in her heart.

Chapter Five:
MOVING ON
(Sept. 28, 1920 - May 1, 1933)

Home is where the heart is.
— Early American Saying

After a couple of years working in the fields by day and washing and ironing other people's clothes in the evenings, the young widow with three young daughters saw a way to improve her situation. She met Harve Creek, a landowner whose marriage partner had also died in the flu epidemic of 1918. Mattie enjoyed the affectionate attention Harve gave her. The love letters she received from him calling her "My Dear Little Girl" reflected his protective, fatherly attitude toward her. She was 25; he was 50.

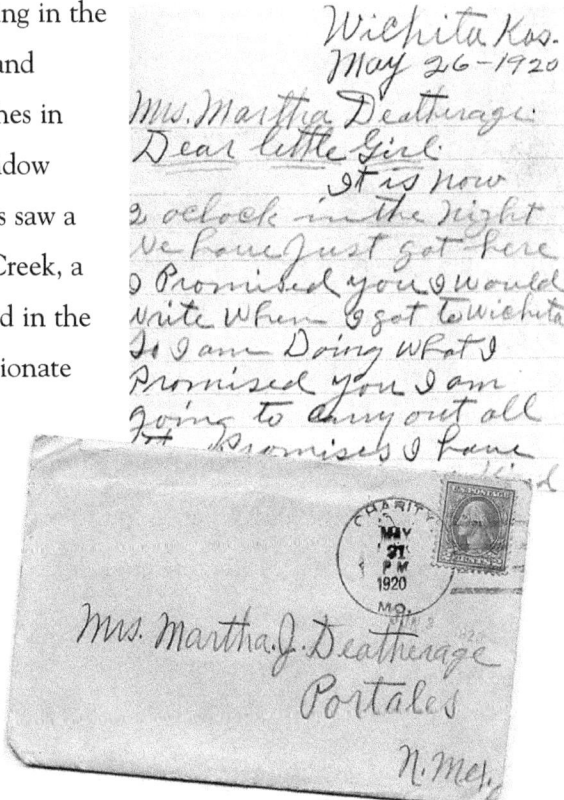

Mattie cherished Harve's letters. Although a first class letter in 1920 required only a 2-cent stamp, Harve's letters were invaluable to the young widow. She vowed to "keep them forever." And she did.

After a short courtship Mattie and Harve married, and their marriage provided many treasured memories, to name just a few:

> *Following several relocations, Harve moved the blended family to Graham, Texas, in hopes of better opportunities. They stopped in Seymour, Texas, spending the nights in a tent and the days in fields picking cotton to make enough money to go on to Graham, where the kids enrolled in school. It was mid-term, and Lillie was behind the other kids. To add insult to injury, she had to wear some "sharp-pointed old lady shoes" bought on sale. The other kids made fun of Lillie's shoes, and she got in a fight with a little girl whose ridicule was especially painful. When Lillie got home, she said she was not going back to school. Harve took his last dollar and bought her a pair of children's shoes so she could go to school without other children making fun of her.*

> *At about four years old, Winnie had the responsibility each morning of emptying the chamber pot down by the water storage tank. Many years later she recalled that to her delight she quite often found a penny near the tank placed where she could easily find it. She said, "I am sure my step-dad put it there for me."*

Alice said in the book, *Alice in Wonderland*, "The best place to begin is at the beginning." So let's go back to the beginning of Mattie and Harve's life together. Reminiscing about their meeting, Mattie said, "We seemed to really 'hit it off.'" Harve also "hit it off" with Winnie and Juanita; he brought them candy – including a flat coconut bar with a strip of white, pink, and chocolate. Not so with Lillie; she did not want Harve coming to see her mother, and she would not eat his candy – she was old enough to remember her father, Lewis, and perhaps did not want anyone taking his place. Maybe she considered Harve an "intruder" in the pleasant life that her mother had developed with her, her two sisters, Grandpa Smith, and Grandpa and Grandma Deatherage.

The "intruder" readily gained Grandpa and Grandma Deatherage's acceptance. One night when all three little girls went to their house to spend the night, Grandma told them that their mother was going to marry Harve and that they would have to call him Daddy. Lillie stated flatly, "He isn't my daddy, and I will never call him Daddy."

In spite of a little opposition most people approved of Mattie and Harve's getting married.

After they married, Mattie and her new husband lived on one of Harve's two farms at Rogers, a small farming community near Dora, New Mexico. Lillie stayed with Grandpa and Grandma Deatherage to finish first grade but joined her mother and new stepfather as soon as the school year was finished. Living with the newlyweds were two of Harve's five children – Ruby, 18, and Webster, 16. Grown and married, Harve's other children included Roscoe (one year older than Mattie), John, and Obannon.

Harve's children and grandchildren from his first marriage showered attention and affection on the three little girls. Lillie recalled, for one example, how Obannon, who worked in the oil fields, came to visit them in his new car. She said, "He took us riding…we thought he was rich!" Harve's married children frequently returned to visit their dad and his new family. They all liked Mattie and her little girls; as Lillie put it, "They were very good to us and treated us like little sisters." Their friendliness and Harve's kindness and congeniality finally influenced the six-year-old Lillie to relent and called him Daddy.

Mattie and Harve's wedding picture, September 28, 1920

Mattie said she felt like "a happy woman" to be marrying Harve. In 1920 all women in New Mexico had reason to be happy – the adoption of the 19th Amendment gave women the right to vote! As early as 1869 women in Wyoming had earned this right and Colorado in 1893; by 1912 nine other Western states had granted this right. But the Land of Enchantment did not achieve statehood until 1912, and opposition was firmly entrenched. Except for local school elections women in New Mexico could not vote until 1920. Not that they didn't try! Nina Otero-Warren and Julia Brown Asplund were two New Mexico women trailblazers. In 1915 Asplund lead a parade of women to the Santa Fe home of Senator Thomas B. Catron to urge him to support the woman suffrage. He resisted, contending that he "did not want to demean the fine women of New Mexico by subjecting them to the responsibility of voting." He had failed to recognize that many of New Mexico's women – just like Mattie – were already successfully assuming some very challenging responsibilities.

Moreover, some men in New Mexico undoubtedly were not discerning voters, and some simply did not honor all their responsibilities. Case in point: In 1921, Juanita started first grade in Dora and Lillie went to second grade there. Because they lived on a farm, they rode the bus to school – the bus was an old Model T touring car. One cold, wintry morning Juanita and Lillie had almost arrived at the bus stop. The driver saw them approaching the bus stop, but he drove on without stopping for them. Had Mattie had her way, this irresponsible bus driver would've lost his job – as well as the right to vote!

Lillie shared another memory – painful at the time, but one to chuckle at years later. Several of the children were picking up cow chips to burn for fuel. Lillie explained how she crawled under the wagon to "get some nice black ones – for they burned better and made a hot fire. The horse was startled and ran over my leg." Fortunately the wagon was light and Lillie's leg was not seriously injured, and there was one advantage of the mishap. Lillie explained, "I got to stay home for several days."

There were other memories of life on this farm. Winnie recalled going to a Mt. Zion church about two miles from where the family lived. Winnie said that she enjoyed going to church because, "We got a pretty Sunday School card every Sunday with the lesson on it." She added that she remembered most of all "the penny they gave me to put in the offering plate."

One of the happiest memories was the birth of Harvey Joe Creek on October 17, 1921. The three little girls were overjoyed at having a baby in the house! Since Harve was twice the age of Mattie, it had been quite some time since he had been a new father. So he and his older children also loved the new arrival.

"Little Harve," as the newcomer was often called, took a special liking to Lillie, seven years old by then. But the delight Lillie and everyone else took in their newest family member was short-lived, for when little Harve was nearly a year old, he became gravely ill. To the heartbreak of everyone, the precious little baby died. Although Winnie was only five years old at that time, she had a vivid memory of Little Harve and their mother's grief over the death of her baby:

Little Harve in his casket

> *I remember well the first time I saw Mother cry. Harvey was a very special little boy – very smart and much loved.... A few days before his first birthday he took sick. The doctor came out a few times but couldn't diagnose his illness. One night he died in Mother's arms.*

People generally did not have cameras back then and did not routinely take pictures. If no picture had been taken before a person died, special effort was made to find someone to lend a camera so a picture could be made of the deceased loved one – as in the case of Little Harve. This is the only picture ever taken of Little Harve.

 Little Harve died one day before what would have been his first birthday. Later the doctor said that he might have had polio. After little Harve's death, Winnie said she had a different feeling about the church at Mt. Zion:

> *When my baby brother died, his funeral was there, and he was buried there.... I remember sitting in the pew and looking out the side door...I could see Little Harvey's grave. That always gave me a sad lump in my heart.*

MT. ZION ITEMS

Sunday school is progressing nicely. You are invited to come out and take a part. Rev. Parker Fortner will fill the pulpit next Saturday at 2:00 and Sunday at 11:00. Come out and hear him.

Miss Iona Edwards has been real sick the past few days.

Among those that were Roswell visitors last week were: Vane Victor, Ben Bennett and wife, H. L. Capps and daughter, Marorie Harve Creek and family.

Raymond Lott purchased himself a car a few days ago.

The Spranger family and Dug Bowen left Wednesday for Arkansas, where they expect to make their home. They will make the trip in their Fords.

Little Harve Creek, age 1 year, was buried at Mt. Zion Sunday. The cause of his death is unknown.

An account of another incident that could have easily turned into another tragedy was given by Winnie:

> *I remember one time when Grandpa Smith was with us when the windmill fell on him. I don't know if they were building a new tower, but the tower was down on the ground and they had wires tied to it and were pulling it up with some kind of vehicle. My step-dad and step-brothers were doing this...it was at the little white house that Mama had bought when she moved to town.*
>
> *My step-sister, Ruby, was going to town, and I was going with her. She had stood me up in a chair and was washing my feet with a washcloth...I had a good view of the whole works. Grandpa was down on his hands and knees with the hammer, working on the ladder. They had the windmill about halfway up when one of the wires broke, and the mill started swinging around. They all yelled at Grandpa, and he started crawling real fast. The mill swung around and when it got right above him, it just dropped right on top of him. They all ran to him...Daddy, Roscoe, and Webster. They lifted it off him.*

God was with Grandpa! The big fan had hit the ground first, with such force it bent the iron blade but held it off Grandpa. He crawled out with only a skinned ear and nose. That afternoon I remember looking at him sitting in a straight-back kitchen chair. It was miraculous; the only evidence of this near calamity was a bandage on Grandpa's ear and "monkey blood" on his nose (a red medicine, probably mercurochrome, used in those days).

From all accounts, Grandpa Smith and Harve enjoyed each other's company, and Grandpa's visits were pleasant ones. One relative said the fact that the two had such different personalities probably accounted for their getting along well together. Winnie offered this comment:

My step-dad was from Missouri, and Grandpa had lived in Tennessee, Mississippi, Arkansas, and Texas. I can remember their exchanging "panther stories" and other tales of "the old days."

As in all families, some conversations were not so pleasant. Juanita and Lillie both remember when Harve had fallen off a horse and broken his shoulder. As he was recuperating in bed one afternoon, he watched Mattie churn. Grandpa Smith was sitting by the fire in the same room. Mattie's "churn" was actually a syrup bucket that she shook up and down until the cream became butter. Something provoked Mattie – Lillie and Juanita never knew what – but she lost her temper and threw the bucket down as hard as she could and stalked out of the room. The lid came off and cream went all over the room and on the ceiling. No one, including Harve, said a word; Grandpa Smith just quietly cleaned it up.

Happy times far outnumbered the tense times like this "churn incident." For example, Harve's teenaged daughter Ruby loved Grandmother's three daughters and enjoyed helping take care of them. She spent a lot of time caring for Winnie simply because Winnie was the youngest and required more care. Winnie recalled one of the special times with Ruby:

When I was about four years old, I sang a song at a church program. My step-sister Ruby coached me. I don't remember what the song was, but I remember standing in the middle of the bed singing it for Ruby. Then I remember being on the stage and looking out over all the people, but I wasn't scared. When they all clapped, I wondered why they did that. I also remember going to church in the wagon, and going home in that wagon after the program – and wetting my pants.

Other memories Winnie recalled include these comments about the man she learned to call "Daddy":

He was an old man with a young family and young ideas. He loved to go, and, to him, the grass was always greener on the other side. So we went a lot – we went through the Carlsbad Caverns when it was very new, made two trips to Missouri – which I loved, and took a trip to Arkansas. And we always visited various relatives on the weekend. In later years Mother said she did not realize it at the time, but she was learning to enjoy going places, seeing things, and meeting new people. We were all learning to "feel at home" with all kinds of different people wherever we visited.

In addition to the visits or sightseeing trips, Harve frequently moved his new family from one "home place" to another. No one could remember anyone ever questioning his desire to relocate. One relative said that he was often domineering, and it was just easier to go along with whatever he decided. Even Mattie, who had demonstrated fierce independence after Lewis died, did not at first offer resistance to Harve's frequent decisions to "move on." After all, the relocation was in search of "greener pastures."

Decades later as family members discussed why Mattie tolerated the constant moves, they concluded that she was actually operating from a point of strength. She had resolved to keep her three daughters after Lewis died; cooperating with Harve and moving from place to place actually required an inner strength that helped her accomplish that goal. In other words, she was doing whatever it took to provide a home for her three girls. At least, she was not working in the fields by day and taking in laundry by night. In addition, Harve and his extended family provided a wellspring of companionship and camaraderie and fostered a spirit of hopefulness and positive expectations.

After living on Harve's farm near Dora, the new family moved to the Walker house near Rogers. The 1920-1921 depression and widespread drought "hit" farmers very hard, and Harve's farming operation was no exception. Lillie was old enough to remember in later years that money was very scarce. Another one of Lillie's vivid memories while living at this house was her stealing a few of Ruby's pennies to buy some candy. Like most thieves, she got caught! Lillie's mother made her pay Ruby back and apologize to her. Harve supported Mattie, for he was also a very moral person who valued honesty and "obeying the law." The lesson evidently stuck, for that ended a life of crime for eight-year-old Lillie.

Just as Mattie was diligent in instilling important lessons and values in her children, other New Mexico women were "taking a stand" and compiling to their credit a number of "firsts" nationwide. Secretary of State Soledad Chacon and Superintendent of Public Instruction Isabel Eckles were the first women in New Mexico to hold statewide office. Bertha Paxton from Doña Ana County was the first woman elected to the state legislature, serving in the House from 1923 to 1925. In 1924 Chacon served as acting Governor in the absence of Governor Hinkle since Lieutenant Governor Baca had died earlier that year. This was especially notable in that New Mexico was the first state to acknowledge a woman as its chief executive.

That same year the Deatherage-Creek family moved back to Mattie's "Little White House" in Portales. Some thought this move was probably Mattie's "executive decision." While the top-ranking New Mexico female officials had been reared in relatively privileged families, Mattie's background included a day laborer father, a disinherited mother, early childhood poverty, a near-death rattlesnake bite, her mother's untimely death, loss of her young husband in the Spanish Flu epidemic, and working in the fields by day and taking in laundry by night to keep her three young daughters. Mattie's "executive decision" to move might well have required as much grit and gumption as many of the state-level decisions made by the female public servants.

Mattie also was learning to use another strategy – one undoubtedly used by Chacon, Eckles, and Paxton in their positions. Mattie was learning to "choose her battles." There was no income-producing job near the Walker house. Realizing the futility of the situation, Mattie insisted on moving to a location nearer prospective jobs. When her daughters and granddaughters asked her for marriage advice, she nearly always emphasized, "Choose your battles," a strategy historically used by successful women in positions at every level the world over.

Harve worked nights at a café in Clovis and in the ice plant there in the daytime. Going to Clovis on Sunday and returning to Portales the next Saturday night, Harve had only a brief weekend to spend with his family. Led by Mattie, everyone cooperated to make this situation "work." During this time, Paul Norris was born December 17, 1924. The entire family greeted this new baby with open arms! And virtually all arms were needed, for the newborn suffered from colic the first six months of his life; he cried from early evening until midnight. Mattie held him and carried him around until she was exhausted, and then 10-year-old Lillie sat on the edge of the bed, bouncing him until finally he went to sleep. Mattie decided he was crying at least partly because he was hungry. So she started feeding him on a bottle, and he did indeed get better. Breastfeeding was considered the "best" way to feed a baby, so Mattie had to muster a great deal of courage to go against peer pressure and public opinion. But as the relieved mother put it, "Thank goodness, Paul turned the corner." Winnie commented:

> *After a shaky beginning, we quit worrying that Paul was going to die just as little Harve did. We really enjoyed him…Mother would let us help take care of him and play with him. While Mattie was happy at the birth of Paul, she was saddened by the death of her oldest sister, May, from lockjaw, now usually referred to as tetanus. May had surgery in Lubbock and seemed to be improving when she developed tetanus. It is not known if May's worsening condition was misdiagnosed, not diagnosed soon enough for the vaccine to be effective, or if the vaccine wasn't available. The vaccine for tetanus was discovered in 1884 and became widely used in World War I. It seems that the vaccine should have been available. However, it wasn't until the early 1940s, after other scientists had refined the potent antibiotic, that drug companies began mass-producing it.*

Because May's death occurred so soon after the birth of Mattie's baby, Mattie could not travel to Lubbock to attend the funeral. May's death left several young children motherless. Mattie remembered all too well the sadness when her own mother – and May's mother – died. The heartbreaking loss of a mother was when life "turned a corner" for many of the Smiths.

Around the time Paul was born and May died, some Americans had "turned the corner" in a different sense. In 1923-24 oil was discovered on the Navajo Reservation, which dramatically increased the income of countless American Indians in New Mexico. In 1925, 207 Americans enjoyed incomes of one million dollars, and seven had incomes of above five million dollars. In contrast, most families made considerably less than that, and the average annual family income was $1,300. Prices, of course, were also lower. The First Class stamp Harve used in May of 1920 to send his letter to Mattie cost only 2 cents. A loaf of bread was about 10 cents. The basic Model T Ford sold for $290 – a nice car was indeed a luxury afforded by only a few.

The ten families who owned cars in early Portales days posed in front of the Roosevelt County Courthouse. Jim Stone (grandfather of Dave Stone, as of 2007 a third-generation Portales bank president) drove the Cadillac at right front. Doug Stone, a one-year-old, was held by his mother while his sister Roma sat beside Lula Stone. Gladys and older brother James Toliver were in the front seat with their dad. Credit: E.N.M.U. Special Collections

From all that was known of Mattie's family, there were times that it did not enjoy even the average income. Failure to become millionaires or even to earn the average American family's income was not because the family didn't work – Mattie made sure everyone helped with the work that had to be done around the house. Lillie's job was to bring in a couple of buckets of water for cooking, drinking, and washing hands and faces. Juanita's job was to bring in

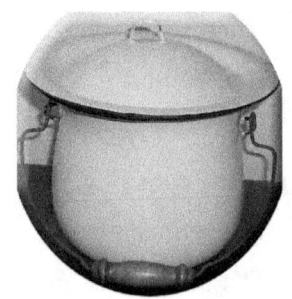 kindling three times a day to help start a fire in the coal-burning cook stove.

Winnie's biggest responsibility was to bring "the pot" in before dark. The pot was a bucket with a lid; it was usually stored under a bed and offered welcomed relief from going to the outhouse in the dark and in bad weather. She forgot it one night; her mother warned her that the next time she forgot it, she would wake her up to go get it. Well, Winnie eventually forgot it again one night! When Mattie went in to wake her up, older sister Lillie offered, "I'll go get it!" But Mattie would not let Lillie get it for her four-year-old sister; she said, "It is Winnie's job, and she will have to do it." Winnie was sound asleep, but Mattie pulled the cover back, gave her a spat, and told her to go get the "slop jar." Winnie said she was "scared to death," but she went out to the tank in the dark by herself and got it. She never forgot that pot again! Kindhearted Harve probably would have liked to go get it for Winnie, but he never dared interfere when Mattie was teaching one of her children – even "little Winnie" – to "do their work."

A lot was happening in the world in 1925. Wyoming had elected the first woman governor in the United States. Arthur T. Hannett followed James F. Hinkle as New Mexico governor. Chiang Kai-shek became the leader of China. Hitler published his book, *Mein Kampf*. The "Charleston" was the latest dance craze. The production of bread was automatized in all stages. Al Capone was running organized crime in Chicago, and George Herman "Babe" Ruth was patrolling the outfield of Yankee Stadium.

Meanwhile Mattie and Harve were preoccupied with plans for their combined families – Mattie and her three girls; Harve and his two sons, Obannon and Webster; and Harve and Mattie's baby, Paul. They were organizing a trip to Buffalo, Missouri, to visit Harve's father, Norris Creek. Two cars were required for the large family; Harve and Mattie provided one car while Obannon provided the other one. When crossing a river one day, the two cars got separated. Mattie's carload spent the night by a small creek where the mosquitoes were so bad that Lillie got sick from countless bites. Fortunately she recuperated in a few days. But many youngsters did not survive some of the various maladies and illnesses that befell them. A New Mexico state health bulletin in 1925 reported that 13 percent of New Mexico babies died before their first birthday. Mattie was frantic about the entire situation, but on the second day the two carloads of relatives found each other and happily resumed their caravan to Missouri.

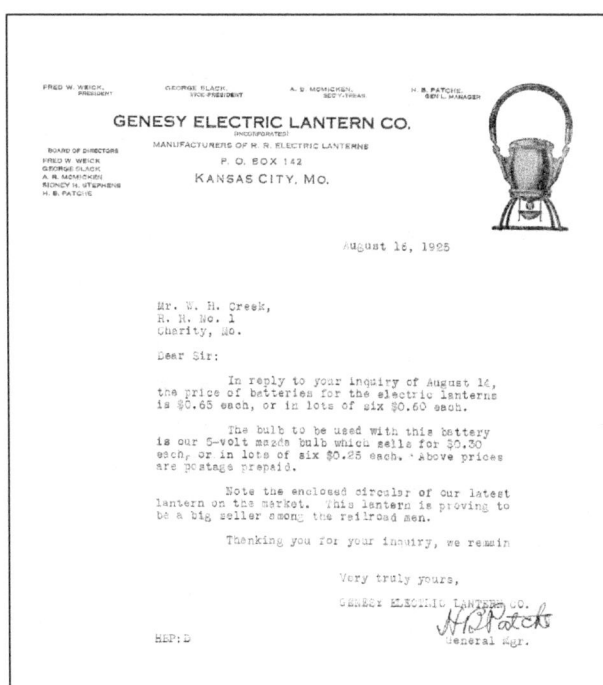

Courtesy Carolyn Creek Holder

When they reached their destination, Harve took a job as night watchman. A pipeline was being built across Missouri, and Harve's job was to watch over the tools so no one would steal them. A letter to Harve from a lantern company indicates he had inquired about the cost of batteries for electric lanterns. Harve probably used this lantern in his work as a night watchman.

In addition to Harve's working as a night watchman, the entire family pitched in to work in one of the numerous stands selling hamburgers and lemonade to the picnickers in Buffalo and the surrounding communities. They worked to make enough money to return to New Mexico. It was literally "Pay as You Go" – no credit cards to pay for vacations in those days! Furthermore, Mattie was honing her skills as the "team leader" of all the family members as they worked together to get the job done.

Winnie was too young to be worried about finances and other practical concerns. But she was not too young to enjoy the long trip to Missouri. Years later here is what she said about it:

> *I was five years old. It was the first time I had been out of the vicinity of Portales. I loved the ride in the model T Ford – a three-day-trip at 25 mph. It was the first time I had ever seen trees, water, and waterfalls. I was so excited....*

Soon after returning to Portales, Harve traded the little white house for a house in Graham, Texas. This is where Harve spent the last dollar of his pension to buy Lillie some children's shoes to spare her from the ridicule of the other school children. Another memory from Graham, Texas, involved a lady with two children who lived next door to them, and how she had been married to one of the infamous Dalton gang. These neighbors had a vacant lot where the kids in the neighborhood gathered and played. Harve never allowed Lillie, Juanita, and Winnie to play with the other kids. "I never knew the reason," Lillie said in later years, but she doubted that it had anything to do with the connection to the Dalton gang. Mattie did not try to dissuade Harve. Rather, she emphasized the family members doing things with one another, the three girls getting their homework done, and "getting the work done" around the house. Mattie was still learning to "choose her battles," and the early roots of her work ethic were growing deeper and deeper.

In 1926 the large family moved back to Portales. Harve had traded the house in Graham for a section of land between Elida and Roswell. They never lived on that land, and no one remembered what ever happened to it. They stayed for awhile in Aunt Alice's rental house about two blocks from the high school in Portales and the children continued to find interesting things to do to entertain themselves.

Portales, about 1926. Someone probably used this wagon and sheep to make a few dollars – the owner would go from neighborhood to neighborhood and from town to town and offer to have children's pictures made for a fee.

Next the family moved to a farm at Floyd called "the Slim Snell place." Mattie's three daughters could remember that they milked cows and made a crop of some kind – and they also had a white pony. Even though they had no saddle, the girls enjoyed riding the pony to bring the cows in from the pasture to milk them. To attend school, they rode a bus about 10 or 12 miles – which was not quite as much fun as riding the white pony. Mattie, however, was resolved that her girls would get an education!

First Floyd school bus. In the mid 1920s. E.N.M.U. Special Collections

But the three daughters and even young Paul were more excited about something else. Even though Paul probably did not fully comprehend, he joined in the enthusiastic anticipation – their mother was "expecting," and the three sisters and the "big brother" were eager for a new baby in the family!

Before the baby was born, the Creeks moved back to Portales into what they called the "shack" on 20 acres about five or six miles out of Portales. It was well named! The structure originally was one long room, but then another room built on the side of it. When the time came for the baby to be born, Uncle Will took the other children home with him so full attention could be given to the home birth of Leroy – most babies were born at home, not in a hospital, during those days. On February 24, 1928, Leroy made his appearance on the same day as Shirley Temple. But Shirley Temple's birth – had the four children even known about it and her later fame – paled in significance to the birth of their new little brother.

Another significant event occurred in 1928. At the age of sixty-nine, Octaviano Ambrosio Larrazolio was elected by the state of New Mexico as the first native of Mexico, the first Latin American, to serve in the United States Senate. Larrazolio already enjoyed the distinction of being the only native of Mexico serving as governor of New Mexico when on November 5, 1918, he was elected as the first Republican governor of New Mexico. Like Mattie, his marriage partner died at an early age, leaving him the sole responsibility of rearing his family. Also like this remarkable pioneer woman, he remarried within the second year after the death of his partner. Back in those days there were no day care facilities, no child development centers, no "latch-key" programs, no after-school or extended school programs, and no professional nannies. Remarriage was simply the most pragmatic solution for a man or a woman left with children to rear.

Only three years older than Mattie, Carlsbad-born Georgia Lee Lusk was another "first" female in New Mexico. Upon the untimely death of her husband, as a young woman she was thrust into the role of manager of the family ranch. In addition to mastering this job, she assumed numerous civic responsibilities included serving as Lea County Superintendent of Schools from 1924 to 1928. Next she became State Superintendent of Public Instruction in 1930. Various positions prepared her well for her election as a Democrat to the Eightieth Congress during the 1940s, making her New Mexico's first congresswoman.

With the same fervor and work ethic as Georgia Lusk, Mattie was honing skills and abilities that would later serve her well in her business ventures. Mattie was baking pies for Harve's son, Roscoe, who owned a restaurant. Mattie quickly earned a Marie Callender reputation for baking delicious "homemade" pies! But the growing family needed more income, so Mattie and Harve purchased a small short order café. The building was long and narrow with six stools, a small kitchen with a stove, a cook table, and a tub for washing dishes. Harve was the public relations person – he "worked" the counter, for he was really good at making the customers feel welcome and want to come back to eat with them again. As usual, Mattie planned and purchased the food and did the cooking. She was increasing her cooking expertise, pie by pie, as well as broadening the menu, which by then consisted of hamburgers, chili, and Irish stew. Mattie also supervised the "employees" – Lillie, about 14, would leave school at the lunch hour and work behind the counter; she would barely get back to school before the bell rang. Winnie – about 11 – was the dishwasher; she had to stand on a box to reach into the large washing tub. Twelve-year-old Juanita had the job of watching over Paul and Leroy.

Lillie recounted how she had trouble making change at the café, so she used only dimes. No one could ever understand why the cash register kept running out of dimes. Lillie did not say whether or not she ever told "the rest of the story," as Paul Harvey would say.

Mattie's days began early and ended late. While some women in New Mexico – like Soledad Chacon, Isabel Eckles, Bertha Paxton, and Georgia Lusk – strengthened the fabric of the state by managing their families and serving in public office, Mattie's contribution was being the linch-pen at the family's small café in Portales, incorporating her family members into the café's work, and rearing her children. Few women worked outside the home at that time; Mattie was an exception. Many women simply did not consider becoming active in government, especially those living in Eastern New Mexico, a land quite apart – geographically and psychologically – from Santa Fe, the hub of government for New Mexico. Only a few men from this remote part of the state became involved in state government. Washington Lindsey, the first mayor of Portales, was probably the most notable one; he served as Governor from 1917 to 1919. Coincidentally, Mattie later became a good friend of Lindsey's daughter when both of them had established themselves as outstanding businesswomen in Portales.

Although not many individuals from Eastern New Mexico served in Santa Fe, decisions were being made in the state capital regarding the interests of this part of the state. For example, on February 12, 1929, New Mexico, Texas, and Colorado signed the first Rio Grande Compact in Santa Fe. This agreement placed a five-year moratorium on water projects until water could be measured for apportionment. This measure would be just one among much legislation authorizing the use of New Mexico's scarce – and diminishing – water supply. The decreasing level of the Ogallala Aquifer has continued to pose a problem to the farmers and ranchers of Roosevelt County.

In spite of the challenges of a decreasing water supply, many homesteaders had "stuck it out" and stayed in Eastern New Mexico, including Lewis's parents. They said all along they wanted to grow old being with their children and grandchildren, and that is what they did. During this busy time with day-to-day living, Grandma Deatherage died after a lengthy illness. Lillie said she always felt guilty because she had not been able to spend much time with her grandmother – the grandmother who had been so good to the three little girls left fatherless when her youngest son, Lewis, died. Mattie's strongest emotion was heart wrenching grief, an emotion all too familiar to Mattie.

In contrast, joy was brought to some lucky children who received the Marx "Joy Rider" tin wind-up toy car and the Buddy L ratchet dump trunk, popular toys across the United States that year. But these two toys were not found under the Creek's Christmas tree. In fact, there was not even a tree at the Creeks. But the archway between the living room and kitchen had ornaments and cards for everyone to enjoy, and for the two young boys two stockings filled with small toys like those in boxes of cracker jacks along with an apple, orange, nuts, and hard candy. Although in 1929 the FM radio was introduced, this family did not own one or sense the need for one. Their Christmas music was "live," provided by a hired hand, Ray Widner, quite good with his guitar and singing.

Although the three girls and two little boys did not have a tree or many toys, they enjoyed the few they had. Besides, most other families they knew did not have any more than they did. Following their mother's example, they found special pleasure in small things – including a little bantam hen that chose the dirty clothes basket as its favorite egg-laying place. The little hen would also perch on Mattie's shoulder and rub her head against Mattie's neck and cackle and sing – much to the delight of everyone!

Laughter was also found in other everyday events. Lillie, for instance, had assumed the role as head housekeeper, and her way of making things "look nice" was to put everything out of sight. Once Harve's hat was missing for a long time before it was finally discovered crumpled up at the bottom of the dirty clothes basket. Everyone thought this was funny, and even Harve joined the laughter about it.

That year the fun and laughter came to a halt when word came that Joseph Smith – Grandpa Smith – had died. The sad news came by word of mouth. Mattie's father had meant a lot to her; he had been mother and father to all his children after Lillie Camilla died when Mattie was still a young girl. Grandpa Smith had been living with Charlie, his youngest son, and Charlie's wife, Amy. When the family gathered at Charlie's ranch between Floyd and Elida, New Mexico, Amy lifted young Paul up to view Grandpa Smith in the casket. This apparently was frequently done with small children. Lillie recalled that Paul was "really scared." She also remembered how it was almost dark when the funeral procession reached the Elida cemetery; the headlights of cars were all shined toward the grave so people could see as Grandpa Smith was laid to rest next to Lillie Camilla, the mother of their eight children. Just as Mattie courageously "carried on" after her mother died, she "carried on" after her father died. After all she had a family to encourage and to care for.

Mattie's family moved to Portales, about one block from the Clovis highway, where Harve and Mattie opened another short order café, calling it the Little Brick Front Café. Each family member had a job, assuming the usual "assignments." Harve was the PR person, Mattie planned the purchase of food, cooked, and supervised all the others – Lillie worked the counter, Winnie washed dishes, and Juanita took care of Paul and Leroy.

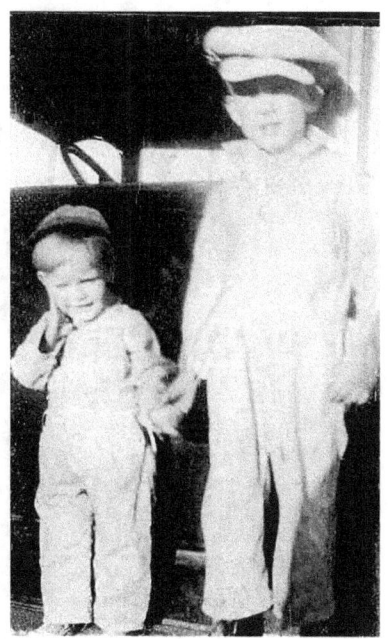

New Mexico's state motto, adopted in 1913, is Cresit Eundo, "It Grows As It Goes." This motto could well have described Mattie. As she and Harve moved from place to place, Mattie was growing – in confidence and in skills and abilities that helped ensure current success and also would serve her well in the future.

Mattie and Harve decorated their new café by painting it dark green. The one bucket of paint left was taken to their house. One day while Mattie and Harve were working at the cafe, the children decided to use that bucket of green paint on the furniture. They painted two iron beds, a wooden box Grandpa Smith had made for Leroy to store his clothes, a dresser, the kitchen table and chairs, and a cabinet. They worked hard all day and felt extremely proud of their accomplishment. When Mattie came home, she looked silently at the furniture in the first room. Still without a word, she went into the other rooms and surveyed all the other green furniture. She sat down deliberately, took a slow, deep breath, and finally said something:

My, you sure must have worked hard to get all this painted.

Mattie was always known for encouraging people and making them feel good about their hard work!

When school was out in 1929, the family moved to Clovis and operated a café called Our Place, located on the main street. The family lived in the back of the café with beds in the big room, and they ate all their meals in the café. Everyone resumed their usual jobs, and the café team was back in action. No mention was made of painting the café this time – or all the furniture at home. Mattie simply had refused to panic at all the furniture being painted green.

The Santa Fe New Mexican, October 29, 1929

Variety ran the headline, "Wall St. Lays an Egg," on October 30, 1929. The article reported with a dramatic flourish, "Tragedy, despair and ruination spell the story of countless thousands of marginal stock traders." *Variety*, a major New York newspaper, October 30, 1929.

A panic of a much larger economic scale occurred in the United States on Tuesday, October 29; this date became known as Black Tuesday. It marked the most disastrous session of Wall Street to date.

Over the next three weeks, the market lost 40 percent of its value, more than thirty-five billion dollars in shareholder equity. But most Americans did not own stock. At most, four million people owned some stock – in a nation of 120 million. And although the onset of the Great Depression brought the unemployment rate from 4.6 percent in 1929 to 8.9 percent in 1930, the national average indicated that one in four Americans depended on farming or ranching for their livelihood. This average was probably higher in New Mexico since it was relatively more rural than many other states. So for Mattie and her family – like many other New Mexicans – the Wall Street gyrations were a distant noise. The ripples of the stock market crash were not felt immediately on the last frontier, the remote plains of Eastern New Mexico.

The Santa Fe New Mexican, October 30, 1929

Cloudcroft, New Mexico, about 1931. Left to right:, Paul, Lillie, Mattie, Juanita, Winnie, and Leroy in front of Juanita

Feeling virtually unscathed by the ravages of the stock market crash such as the increasing unemployment rate, the café team was on its way to Cloudcroft, a small picturesque community in the scenic Sacramento Mountains of New Mexico. They lived in a two-room house behind their café and ate in the café, where each one had a "job." Lillie said she was particularly proud of one achievement; she finished the 10th grade in Cloudcroft in spite of the fact that she and the other kids attended three different schools that year.

"Cloudcroft was fun," Winnie said years later. She pointed out that she felt lucky even to be alive considering "some of the things that happened there." She explained that one of the kids' favorite pastimes was walking across the long railroad trestle that spanned a deep mountain ravine. They were never aware of any trains using the trestle. But one day when they were about halfway across, they heard a train whistle in the not so far distance. They began scurrying across the trestle as fast as their legs could go from one railroad tie to the next. They barely made it before the train came chugging along right where they had been. Winnie said that cooled her interest in crossing that trestle. She concluded, "I was satisfied to stay closer to home after that near mishap."

"Closer to home" included a dance hall right next to the café. But Harve did not allow the girls to dance. Of course, the boys were too young to care about dancing. As for Mattie, she said even as much as she loved to dance, she never danced again after Lewis died. But soon it was time to move on and leave behind the railroad trestle, the dance hall, all the prospective boy friends, and the little café.

The family moved back to Portales, and the kids enrolled in school there. The school was only about three blocks from the house, and so at first they walked to school with a group of others once again. But Harve did not like Lillie walking with the boys, so he insisted that she drive to school. What he did not know was all the other places Lillie drove and that she would drive a lot of kids home, including the ones Harve did not want to walk with her. This was another one of the few years that the three girls and two boys did not have to change schools because of moving on to a new home.

Man struggling in blowing sand. By a photographer hired by government during the 1930s – the Dust Bowl and the Great Depression

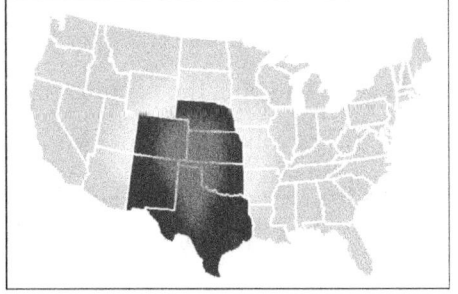

Rising like ominous black clouds on the horizon, sand storms began plaguing the West. Only worsening over the next decade, they destroyed crops, choked livestock to death, and damaged human health. Later called the Dust Bowl, these devastating storms arriving in the midst of the Great Depression shattered the dreams of many individuals and families who had high hopes for the West as their land of opportunity.

Discouraged by the farming prospects, in the fall of 1931 Harve traded the 40 acres and two-room shack on Poker Flat Road for some acreage and a four-room house north of Witts Spring, Arkansas. Because Harve was a native of Missouri, he was familiar with Arkansas. So he was very interested when a man called Mr. Jones described his place in Arkansas – it probably sounded like home to Harve. As an added lure, Mr. Jones convinced Harve and Mattie that Witts Spring would be a great place for a café because there was not one there. After loading all their possessions into a two-wheel trailer pulled by their 1928 Chevrolet, the seven-member family headed for Arkansas. The girls were teenagers while Paul was seven and Leroy was three. They stopped in Texas to pick cotton from September through November. Lillie told everyone she was moving to Missouri because, as she put it, "Arkansas was known as a state of hillbillies."

Mattie and Lillie took turns driving on the three-day trip. The family stayed in a motel in Russellville, the last town before they started up the mountains for Witts Spring. It was foggy when they left Russellville about 9:00 in the morning, and it got worse as they drove higher up into the mountains. Heavy rains had turned the dirt road into mud up to the hubcaps on the car. But the resolute family inched on.

On a particularly steep hill, the weary travelers stopped, unhooked the trailer, and everyone but Harve and Lillie got out of the car. They drove to the top to see if they could make it. Then they turned around and came back for the trailer and everyone else. Only about a mile from their destination, the trailer got stuck, leaving the shivering family members to spend a cold, rainy, sleepless night in the car.

The next morning, in contrast, was bright and sunny. A man came walking by and helped them get the trailer out of the mud so they could drive the remaining mile to their new home. Lillie said she would never forget the expression on her mother's face when she saw this "new home." While tourists in New York City in 1931 were enjoying the opening of the Empire State Building – the world's tallest at 86 stories – Mattie was shaking from the shock of seeing what was to be her new home. A big log room with a fireplace was the main part; only one window and huge double doors were at either end. There was also a loft, but it was never used. There were two porches – one at the front, and one at the back. The one across the front of the house had fallen in whereas half of the back porch had been closed in for a kitchen.

The inside of the structure had not been finished but was just rough boards. The logs did not even have mortar between them. Since the family had no other place to go, they moved in and began trying to "fix it up." First they filled all the cracks with mud, and next they papered the walls with magazines – for warmth and decoration. No one remembered where they got all the magazines. Every family member "pitched in," scrubbing what areas they could and moving in their meager belongings. A wood cook stove and an old table and nail kegs for chairs were picked up from somewhere. Martha Stewart probably could not have done much better!

The town of Witts Spring consisted of two general stores that sold only flour, salt, and some condiments but no canned or fresh vegetables or fruits. Even though Fritos corn chips, Skippy peanut butter, and Three Musketeers candy bars made their debut in America in 1932, they had not reached Witts Spring. One of the main memories the girls had about the store was staying in the car while Harve went in to buy a few of the available items – and all the townspeople staring at them. In addition, Lillie remembered seeing her future husband, Charlie, for the first time. He told the other boys that the redheaded girl was his and for them not to bother her.

Although Mattie's family did not yet know about Fritos corn chips, Skippy peanut butter, or Three Musketeers candy bars, someone gave the family a hundred-pound sack of whippoorwill peas, and a family named Compton gave them milk. Somehow Mattie made those peas last all winter, doing some creative cooking with them, including pea sausage. The famous Fannie Farmer cookbook was first published the year Mattie was born; it probably did not include a recipe for pea sausage. Perhaps Mattie's ingenious pea sausage was a foreshadowing of the great cook that she would become!

The generous neighbor, Mrs. Compton, who had given the Creeks some milk, also had a reputation of being a wonderful cook. She asked Mattie and Lillie to stay and eat one day when they picked up some milk. Mattie said, "We already had dinner." After they left, Lillie asked her mother, "Why did you say that? We could have eaten again!" In spite of dire circumstances, Mattie still had a certain measure of pride.

Even though Witts Spring was fairly isolated in 1931, it was not completely immune to the damages of the Great Depression ushered in by the stock market crash. Because the school district had run out of money, classes had been cancelled. So when Mattie's family arrived around December 1, there was no school for the children to attend.

Not many new families moved into the area, so the family from New Mexico was the object of everyone's stares when they went to Witts Springs to get the mail. In contrast, when they went to the community church, everyone was very friendly to them. Lillie "formally met" Charlie the second Sunday they attended. Spring finally came; the family planted a garden and ate much better. No more pea sausage!

"Meager" is the best word to describe the holidays that year. But led by Mattie with her characteristic grit, gumption, and grace – and the invincible optimist Harve – the family made the best of the situation. They went into the woods and found a tree; they decorated it with popcorn and red berries and paper "chains." Although the store in Witts Spring usually did not have oranges, it did get some that year. So there were oranges, candy, and nuts to put in the stockings hung for Paul and Leroy.

Recipe for the "Depression Cake," in Lillie's handwriting at age 91

Because sugar was not available, Mattie used molasses to make a cake on Christmas Day. To add to the cake and festivities, the kids picked out black walnuts from a tree in their yard. Lillie commented decades later, "That was the most delicious cake I ever ate!"

Paul and Leroy held special memories of a big German police dog named Jim. This friendly dog belonged to a neighbor but enjoyed coming to the Creek's house. The owner would come get the dog and take him back home. But the dog would be right back to play with the two young boys. The owner offered to sell Jim for $10; he said if he could get that price, he could make a crop on it. The boys laughed, but they realized later that he probably could have done just that, considering the 1930s economy and the value of $10 at that time.

Arkansas turned out not to be the "greener pasture" that Harve and Mattie had hoped for. So at Mattie's subtle insistence, Harve started thinking about returning to New Mexico. But 17-year-old Lillie was beginning to make other plans as Charlie kept coming to see her. They could not go out on a date, for Harve would not allow it. In addition, neither Harve nor Mattie was friendly to Charlie when he came to visit Lillie. One Sunday evening when he came to the house, he and Lillie were sitting on a bench when Charlie laid his head in Lillie's lap. Mattie saw this "inappropriate behavior" and said to Charlie, "If you really want to lay down, I'll get you a pillow and you can go lay down."

"Kodak snapshot" of Lillie and Charlie – their first date "outside the house"

In spite of the opposition, Charlie persevered. One Sunday he asked Lillie for a date to go "Kodaking" – a picture-taking fad at the time. The young love-smitten Arkansas guy was eager to get a date with the girl from New Mexico – the "prettiest girl he ever saw." Lillie knew Harve would not allow her go anywhere with Charlie alone. So Charlie got a friend, Drewry Lofton, to accompany them. When Lillie made a date for Juanita to go with Drewry, Juanita was furious at Lillie! To appease Juanita, Lillie said she had to "give Juanita everything she had." Charlie had borrowed a Kodak camera from Lois Lofton, and they made pictures under a big pine tree.

Lillie and Charlie decided to get married even though they still had less than friendly support. Evidently Mattie was beginning to accept the inevitable, for she made Lillie a blue chiffon dress from some fabric she had bought in Portales. Martha, Juanita, Winnie, and Pauline, Charlie's sister, went with the couple to the Justice of Peace. As Lillie and Charlie stood on his front porch, he said, "By the power vested in me by the state of Arkansas, I pronounce you man and wife." Because the Justice of the Peace wrote April 31 on the marriage license – and there is not an April 31 – he did not charge them for the short ceremony.

After the brief ceremony, the wedding party ate dinner at the home of Mrs. Johnson, Charlie's mother. The following Sunday, Mattie prepared dinner for the newlyweds and the Johnsons as well as for her own family. For dessert, Mattie prepared a favorite recipe – the "Depression Cake." The two mothers-in-law made some quilts for the newlyweds and gathered up as many other things as they could for them to start housekeeping.

In the fall, Mattie and her family anticipated returning to New Mexico. Because Charlie and Lillie planned on living in the Creek's house after they left, they moved in for a couple of weeks before the others left for New Mexico. Once again, the family possessions were loaded into the same trailer, and in 1932 Mattie was getting her wish – to return to New Mexico!

1928 Chevrolet and trailer loaded with everything the family owned – Mattie, Harve, and four children on their way back to New Mexico from Arkansas

Only this time, Lillie was left behind with her new husband. Mattie's heart was torn right down the middle. Numerous relatives recalled the devoted mother saying over the years, "That was one of the saddest days of my life."

Deserted farm house – an all too familiar sight in the 1930s. By a photographer hired by government during the 1930s – the Dust Bowl and the Great Depression

The Great Depression saw this kind of personal disappointment and separation and financial suffering by many families across the United States. Times were so tough that President Roosevelt ordered banks closed for seven days. Suicide rates peaked at all-time highs. Drought dried out topsoil in the Midwest and much of the Southwest and blew it away. Millions of acres of farmland were ruined. Their crops and lives destroyed, families left their farms in broken-down vehicles and took to the roads, desperately seeking work.

Many headed west to California, where the "Okies," as they were often called, traveled from one desolate camp to another, struggling to survive by picking fruits and vegetables for starvation wages. With New Mexico, not California, as their destination, Harve and Mattie stopped in Elk City, Oklahoma, their "home" for several months as they picked cotton there until December. Like many others, they lived in sub-standard housing albeit temporary.

When Paul's eighth birthday rolled around that 1932 December, his dad spanked him – which surprised and shocked him, for as Paul put it, "My dad never spanked me...Mother was the disciplinarian in our family." With no malice whatsoever, his dad thought Paul was old enough

Migrant family in Oklahoma, picking cotton to make enough money to continue their trek. Dorothea Lange, photographer hired by FSA during the 1930s – the Dust Bowl and the Great Depression

to get "one spank" for every year of his life, a playful but rowdy ritual people sometime carried out on someone's birthday. When Harve realized that Paul did not understand and was frightened, he explained and all was forgiven. But Paul never forgot.

The road-weary family arrived back in Portales in January of 1933. By then the population of Roosevelt County had grown to 11,109 from 6,548 in 1920; but it had actually shrunk from the 12,064 in 1910. The high hopes of countless homesteaders had diminished and they had moved on because of the drought and recession of the 1920s and the Dust Bowl beginning in the early 1930s.

Early 1940s. Taking time out of ranch work to buy US Savings Bonds. L-R: Stanley Good, Kenna, NM, Joe Wilcox, Kenna, NM, Ethel Beard, Portales, NM, Coe Howard, Portales, NM; Lewis Cooper, Kenna, NM. Photo courtesy of Jenny Cooper Clemmons

The neighboring Curry County had increased to 15,809 over the last two or three decades whereas Roswell and Chaves County had grown to 19,549. The 1910 Census indicated a population of 11,443 for Chaves County; the 1920 Census indicated 12,075; and the 1930 population was determined to be 19,549. Curry County had the railroad and numerous cattle yards whereas Chaves County had a variety of businesses supporting its economy. The cattle ranching industry suffered some hard blows during the Great Depression and the Dust Bowl, but some families "toughed it out." They were dedicated to their Eastern New Mexico land; they were hard workers; and they were excellent managers. One family stands out – the Coopers of Kenna. I remember well the impressive main gate to their ranch when traveling as a child with Grandmother Mattie to Ruidosa or Carlsbad to visit relatives. The Coopers homesteaded near Kenna in 1906, the same year Grandmother Mattie's mother and father homesteaded near Elida. Jenny Cooper Clemmons (daughter of Lewis Cooper) is the fourth generation to live on the property.

Coincidentally, Jenny and I attended E.N.M.U. at the same time – in the early 1960s. When recently talking to her, she shared information and pictures of this longstanding, well-known ranching operation. Jenny's family is a great example of the early ranchers who worked hard on their land and have continued over many decades to make a contribution to their community. Jenny and her husband, John, run stocker/steer yearlings and brand them as they arrive on their ranch in the winter months.

People such as the Coopers were one of the reasons Mattie loved Eastern New Mexico and wanted to return there. Like the Coopers, relatives of Mattie also ranched near Elida, including her brother John and sister-in-law Emelia (the couple who got married in the double wedding ceremony with Mattie and Lewis), and Mattie's sister, Mary, and brother-in-law, Floyd Holmes. Relatives of Mattie's brother and her sister still own land and/or work on the land in the Elida area.

1946. Lewis Cooper, "Tying That Steer," Roosevelt County Fair. Photo courtesy of Jenny Cooper Clemmons

Mattie was jubilant when she and her family arrived back in Portales in 1933. Nevertheless, she and her family had no house and no jobs. Winnie described their living arrangement:

1946. Bob Crosby, Roosevelt County Fair. Photo courtesy of Jenny Cooper Clemmons

We had no home and divided the time between Daddy's two sons, Roscoe, who was running a nice café in Portales, and John, who was living on a farm in Dora. We also stayed with his daughter, Ruby, and Mother's sister, Aunt Mary, who lived on a ranch west of Elida. During the week we stayed with Roscoe so the kids could go to school. We spent the weekends with various other family members.

Work day at the ranch for Floyd and Mary Holmes. Date unknown.

Franklin D. Roosevelt had been elected President in November, 1932, and inaugurated on March 4, 1933, just one day before Mattie's 37th birthday. But she had little to celebrate, for the Great Depression had worsened and foreclosures were forcing many families out of their houses and off their farms. No job and no home were the plight of many Americans, including Mattie's family.

Factory closings and bank failures increased and unemployment soared to 13,000,000. Roosevelt faced the greatest crisis in American history since the Civil War. He tried to calm Americans in his inaugural address when he said, "…the only thing we have to fear is fear itself…." He quickly lifted the nation's spirits with the rapid and unprecedented actions of the New Deal that provided funds for employment and construction of public facilities. On March 21, 1933, he instituted the Civilian Conservation Corps (CCC), the first agency of his New Deal. A few years later, Juanita would be working at the Capitan, New Mexico, CCC Camp.

Migrant family stranded on New Mexico highway. By Dorothea Lange

On a personal level, Mattie had harbored a great fear that Harve would die in Arkansas, leaving her stranded with her children faraway from her beloved New Mexico. Many families had suffered that fate. Although that fear was laid to rest, Mattie did not predict that she soon would be facing yet another calamitous crisis.

In later years Winnie remembered that emotion-packed time in their lives, "No home and no job was our life until May when Daddy passed away." Then she gave this brief account of Harve's death in May of 1933, only slightly more than four months after arriving back in New Mexico:

We were at Aunt Mary's when he got seriously ill one night after supper. They thought it was indigestion, and they were up with him all night. We came back to town the next morning.... The doctor had given him some medicine. Shortly afterwards, he got up to go to the bathroom, collapsed from a heart attack, and died.

Harve was buried at Dora, New Mexico, with his first wife and little Harvey.

Rites For Harve Creek Held Today at Mt. Zion

Rev. J. F. Nix, pastor of the First Baptist church, officiated this afternoon in funeral services at Mt. Zion, 14 miles south of Portales, for Harve Creek of Portales, former Clovis resident, who died yesterday.

Mr. Creek, a pioneer resident of Roosevelt county, worked for the Railways Ice Company here for four years prior to moving to Portales seven or eight years ago. He was about 60 years old.

Once again Mattie was widowed. She had no help mate, no home, no money, and no job. Gathering all the courage she could, the distraught widow found herself once again praying that she herself would live to get her kids raised.

"Migrant Mother," by Dorothea Lange

Mattie would need the kind of courage that, according to André Fontaine, "sustains… through the grinding attrition of day-to-day living, running a marriage, raising kids, meeting the bills, coping with sickness and emergencies, keeping the whole shebang going against the slings and arrows of outrageous misfortune." Fontaine concluded that it takes more courage to live "an everyday life." This may be particularly true when a woman is doing it on her own – just like Mattie.

One of the most famous pictures of the Great Depression was taken by Dorothea Lange, a photographer hired by the government. This picture of a "Migrant Mother" captured the despair Mattie and many others suffered during this stressful era.

With that all too familiar grief gnawing at the raw edges of her heart, Mattie knew that courage would be required to overcome her anguish and despair. Mattie grappled with the harsh reality that her generally kind, generous, congenial Harve was dead and there would be no more "moving on" for him.

Mattie would be the one "moving on" – alone.

Chapter Six:
A BEND IN THE ROAD
(May 1, 1933 - Dec. 18, 1935)

It's a long road that doesn't have a bend in it somewhere.
— Old American Saying

While visiting with Harve's relatives in Missouri, Mattie "bobbed" her hair along with Harve's sister. A few years prior to that, she raised her skirts above her ankles. Mattie had joined throngs of other women making their statement on the road to independence in those days.

When Mattie first looked at herself in a mirror with her new hair style, she cried. But not for long. With Harve's unexpected death, she had other more compelling reasons for tears. She was suddenly thrust into a desperate situation where neither hair styles nor skirt lengths mattered. When she was only 22 years old and Lewis died, her father and her in-laws were there to help her with their three little girls. At Harve's death, she was 37. This time, she had no father or no in-laws to help with her two teenage daughters and two young sons. This time the ravages of the Great Depression and the Dust Bowl were wearing away the fabric of life in

America, including Eastern New Mexico where Mattie lived. Like many other victims of this era, Mattie had no job, no income, no house.

Twice-widowed Mattie was all alone.

Until now, Mattie had never had to make all the decisions by herself. But without anyone else she had to decide what was best for herself and her children. The bobbed hair and shortened skirt length perhaps foreshadowed the independence Mattie would need to meet this new challenge.

And meet the challenge she did! First of all, Mattie fulfilled her commitment to Ruby, Harve's daughter, to "help out" when her baby arrived. Meanwhile, farm foreclosures and abandonments drove 60 percent of the population from the Dust Bowl region. Many families lost their homes after the Great Depression began. The Roosevelt Administration estimated there were 1,000 home foreclosures each day in 1933 alone. John Steinbeck captured the horror of the Dust Bowl in his novel, *The Grapes of Wrath*:

> *And then the dispossessed were drawn west – from Kansas, Oklahoma, Texas, New Mexico…families, tribes, dusted out, tractored out. Car-loads, caravans, homeless and hungry; twenty thousand and fifty thousand and a hundred thousand and two hundred thousand. They streamed over the mountains, hungry and restless – restless as ants, scurrying to find work to do – to lift, to push, to pull, to pick, to cut – anything, any burden to bear, for food. The kids are hungry. We got no place to live….*

Like the oppressed people in *The Grapes of Wrath*, Mattie needed a home, and money was scarce. So she "took the bull by the horns," as she put it several years later. With some shrewd bargaining, she traded the property in Arkansas for several cows and some furniture. In spite of it all, Mattie was able to find a place to live in Portales; for $10.00 a month she rented what was called the Price house.

 With a living room, kitchen, dining room, breakfast nook, three bedrooms, and a spacious back porch, this house must have seemed like a mansion to Mattie in comparison to her first New Mexico home – a dusty, insect-ridden dugout; her Arkansas home – a crudely-built, run-down log cabin; and her Oklahoma home – a temporary open-air structure at the very back of a cotton patch. As Mattie moved from house to house, she moved from one phase of life to another. With unceasing migrations of the human heart, she would leave the old, taking cherished experiences with her and embracing the new.

The next pressing consideration for Mattie was finding a job. Although approximately one-fourth of the labor force in America was unemployed in 1933, Mattie was able find a job in Portales, the seat of Roosevelt County. Just one year older than Mattie, Roscoe – Harve's son – ran a Portales café named the Liberty Cafe, or often called simply "the Liberty." Because Roscoe knew from experience that Mattie was a congenial, excellent worker, he hired her for a part-time job. He also was well aware that her reputation as "the best cook in town" would attract more customers to his café. According to the 1930 census, Roosevelt County's population of 11,109 had increased from the 1920 population of 6548. So there were numerous prospective

 customers for a café with tasty home cooking. Mattie enjoyed her new world; she liked the work, and she was good at it. In addition, the Liberty Café was a popular gathering place for all sorts of interesting people – and animals!

E.N.M.U. Special Collections

In the meantime, Mattie also put her cows to work. She sold their milk to Roscoe to use at the Liberty. Two of Uncle Jim's sons – Terrell and Doyal – came into town from their family ranch to stay with Mattie during the weekdays to attend school. The two nephews helped milk the cows and feed them. They especially enjoyed feeding the cows, for right along with the cows they occasionally ate some of the "cow feed"– stale bread discarded by the nearby bakery served as the staple diet for the cows. Mattie's meager income was far below the average family income of $1,348 in 1933. But she had the knack to see possibilities where others saw only stale bread.

It is not known if the two teenaged boys who ate day-old bread right along with the cows were aware of some of the new foods introduced to Americans in 1933 – including Ritz crackers, Campbell's Chicken Noodle Soup, 7-Up, and Spam. What is known is that Mattie always had enough room and sufficient food of some kind for any needy relative. Her limited resources never kept her from opening her house – and her heart – to anyone who needed a place to stay and something to eat. In those days there were proportionately more widows than there are now; approximately one out of ten women were widows in 1933. While many of these widows depended on other relatives, Mattie explored ways she could maintain her independence – and even help others.

Mattie worked hard at Roscoe's Liberty Café – two consecutive years, seven days a week, with no vacation and no "coffee breaks." This was before the days of government control over work conditions. In her "spare time" (early mornings and late evenings) Mattie worked in the fields

harvesting peanuts and sweet potatoes. Other family members also had their "jobs." Winnie and Paul delivered the family cows' milk to Roscoe's Liberty Café. A common scene during the time after Harve died – the "bend in the road" as Mattie called this trying period of her life – was Winnie and Paul pulling a little red wagon with the milk in it. Years later, Paul said it seemed like a luxury when someone else delivered milk to their house.

Paul and Winnie in later years discussed how embarrassed they felt to be seen delivering milk, but admitted that "job" helped instill a valuable work ethic in them. It also added to the increasing respect they had for their mother; even as youngsters they knew their mother was extraordinary and doing everything she could to keep the family together, to make sure the children had enough to eat, and to provide a place to live as a family. Nevertheless, that particular milk-delivery job hurt their pride. As an adult, Winnie wrote in her memoirs:

Delivering milk in that little red wagon was humiliating for a proud teenager such as I.

While Paul and Winnie's main job was delivering milk, Juanita's job was supervising Leroy, who was only four years old. She loved this assignment and spoke fondly of it long after Leroy was a grown man. Juanita also said that working together throughout all the "ups and downs" developed a strong bond among all the children and their mother. Sociologists and family life experts contend that yesteryear's view of children was that they had a responsibility to work. In contrast, the modern view of children is that they are simply to be loved. Mattie had no choice of one view or the other. She loved her children, but their working was necessary to keep the family together.

E.N.M.U. Early 1930s. E.N.M.U. Special Collections

Another familiar scene was Mattie's cows grazing on the grounds of what is now Eastern New Mexico University. At that time, the Administration Building was the only building of the fledgling college. Because it had run out of funds, the college was not operating then. "There was good grass…not worn down by the students," Mattie explained, "and they [the

E.N.M.U. early 1930s, E.N.M.U. Special Collections

administrators] were probably glad to have their grass 'mowed.'" This was another typical example of Mattie's perception; she could see available resources that others would easily overlook.

With Mattie's hard work and discipline, she and her children were adjusting to their new life after their world had been turned upside down by Harve's death. The 37-year-old widow kept up with what was going on in the rest of the world in 1933 by scanning the newspaper Roscoe received at the café and listening to the conversations of the café's customers, including bankers, businessmen, and other notables in the community. Franklin D. Roosevelt was the popular President of the United States. Arthur Seligman had served as governor of New Mexico since 1931; he died in office in 1933 and was thereafter referred to as "the Jewish governor of New Mexico." On January 30, 1933, Hitler had been sworn in as chancellor of Germany, a milestone in his infamous climb to power. And the World's Fair opened in Chicago in 1933 to celebrate its theme, a Century of Progress.

Some people across the United States celebrated in 1933 when the Eighteenth Amendment to the U.S. Constitution, which had ushered in alcohol prohibition in 1920, was repealed, making the production, sale, and purchase of alcohol legal again. But the majority of Roosevelt County's residents voted to remain "dry." They repeatedly voted to stay dry until the mid-1970s; Roosevelt was the last county in New Mexico to lift the ban on the sale of alcohol.

Mattie paid little attention to the wet-dry issue in Roosevelt County. For one reason, she never drank, but the main reason was because her focus was on Lillie, suffering miserably in Arkansas and wanting terribly to see those who had always been at the center of her universe – her mother, Mattie; her two little brothers, Paul and Leroy; and her two younger sisters, Juanita and Winnie.

Finally Lillie's new husband agreed to go to New Mexico with plans to return to Arkansas in one year. Lillie and Charlie's travel to New Mexico was not exactly uneventful. After they left Witts Spring, they had three blowouts before they got to Russellville. The newlyweds stayed there about five days, bought three new tires, borrowed $5.00 from Charlie's sister – and resumed their trip. When night came, they planned on camping out near a pool. But while they were eating their bologna, a car went "flying by," shooting at someone. The two picnickers quickly finished their meal and "hit the road."

By the time Charlie had driven all the way from Russellville to Amarillo, he was exhausted. Lillie had never driven a Model T, but Charlie told her how to "get started and off they went," Lillie recounted. While Charlie was asleep, the pavement ended abruptly and turned to a dirt road. The transition evidently was anything but smooth, for it startled Charlie so much that he insisted on driving the rest of the way! There was one important stop – in Clovis, New Mexico, where he and Lillie used part of the borrowed $5.00 to buy Charlie some shoes. Perhaps he still remembered his mother-in-law's initial rejection of him and wanted to make a good impression on her this time. Mattie adamantly denied in later years rejecting Charlie; she explained that she would've felt the same way about anyone "taking away" her "first baby." She was fiercely protective of her children – regardless of age. While some mothers' commitment to their children weakened when times got really rough, but Mattie's protective attitude never weakened nor wavered.

As for the reception Lillie and Charlie received when they arrived at Mattie's house – everyone was jubilant! Winnie wrote in her memoirs, "Now our family was complete again!" Lillie and Charlie unloaded all their possessions, moved into the Price House with Mattie, the two teenage daughters, the two young sons, and Uncle Jim's two teenaged sons. Everyone participated in the celebration of Lillie and Charlie's reunion with the clan.

But, as usual, there was work to be done. So the two travelers immediately joined Mattie in the fields harvesting peanuts and sweet potatoes. Although the work was hard and the hours long, they enjoyed being with each other. Pulling her family together, the emerging matriarch Mattie was determined to make a new start, despite past tragedies, the sheer magnitude of the windswept landscape that surrounded them, and the unpredictable vicissitudes of life in general.

One of the unpredictable threats was the infamous bank robbers, Bonnie and Clyde; they terrorized a five-state area, including New Mexico, before they were finally killed by police in 1934. While their murders of innocent people troubled people everywhere, a cold-blooded murder in the mountaintop town of Witts Spring early in the fall of 1934 "struck home" in the true sense. The message of this tragedy came by a telegram to Portales from Arkansas. Charlie's mother was attending a church service when a group of drunken bootleggers rode through town shooting their guns randomly. A bullet went through a church window, striking Mrs. Johnson in the head. Lillie commented, "Charlie's mother evidently never knew what hit her." The broomcorn had been pulled but not stacked, so Charlie and Lillie had no money. Mattie's reputation for being responsible and trustworthy evidently was somewhat established, for the bank let her sign a note for Charlie to borrow enough money to go back to Arkansas for his mother's funeral.

After staying a week or so in Arkansas, Charlie returned to New Mexico, bringing with him Pauline, his 16-year-old sister. The shock of her mother's murder and adjusting to life in new surroundings without her made this a very difficult time for Pauline. In a short while after returning to New Mexico, Charlie and Lillie rented a farm at Dora. Since Pauline had started attending school in Portales, she stayed in town with Mattie until school was out that year. Pauline always said she loved Mattie "like her own mother" for "taking her in" and being so kind to her at such a sad time in her life. Mattie, of course, was not a stranger to death. Losing her own mother at an early age, having her first husband snatched from her while in her early 20s, coping with the heartbreaking death of her first son right before his first birthday, and grieving over Harve's recent sudden death undoubtedly rallied her to help this devastated teenager.

Newspapers the world over announced with much fanfare the birth of the Dionne quintuplets in Canada in 1934, and the news frenzy continued for years. Mattie was much more excited about another birth – her first grandchild, Betty Jean, was born in 1935! All the family rejoiced with Lillie and Charlie on the arrival of this first member of a new family generation. The joy of Betty Jean's birth lightened the burden of the recent tragedies and the dire economic woes. This small baby was a new beginning and sparked a renewed sense of hope for the future.

To try to make sure her newborn survived to enjoy the future, Lillie had to wet a baby blanket and spread it over the top of her crib to keep the dust out during the horrible sand storms plaguing the area. The air in New Mexico was supposed to be cleaner than just about anywhere else. But dust storms began in earnest in the early 1930s and lasted until finally the rains came in the 1940s. Lillie remembers 1935 as the worst year.

"Dust would even settle on the fences," Lillie clearly remembered at the age of ninety-three. She went on to explain that a field near where she and Charlie owned a small grocery store in 1935 had been plowed. February brought temperatures in the seventies. With no moisture and no vegetation in the field to hold it, the dirt flew, and farmers helplessly watched their crops blow away. Lillie said dust and sand was impossible to get out of the house; she concluded, "Grit was everywhere even after the wind quit blowing…you could even feel it in your teeth." This was just one family's experience of what was happening to countless other families all over the Great Plains. The enormity of the disaster was unbelievable. More than 850 million tons of topsoil had blown away in one year, nearly eight tons of dirt for every resident of the United States.

Dust storm "blowing in"

The most infamous of the dust storms came on what was called Black Sunday, April 14, 1935, swirling up out of west Kansas. Dust even fell in New York and on ships at sea. Cattle choked and died. Ernie Pyle, one of the era's most influential writers, visited some of the hard-hit areas; he said, "If you would like to have your heart broken, just come out here. This is dust storm country. It is the saddest land I have ever seen." Many people deserted their homes and farms and moved on, blown away just like the soil they had exposed.

President Roosevelt asked why the Great Plains had blown away. What made the land die? Had it been a colossal mistake to allow homesteading on the land? The head of the Great Plains Drought Area Committee and seven agency heads presented their conclusion that the Homestead Act was "almost an obligatory of poverty." But Bennett and his colleagues did not  fault the homesteaders and settlers, for they lacked the knowledge and experience to avoid these mistakes and were mislead by the government. The Federal homestead policy, which kept land allotments low and required that a portion of each be plowed and cultivated, was recognized as having caused the immeasurable damage. Like all the other settlers, when Joseph Smith and Lewis Deatherage were working hard to cultivate their Homesteads, they were simply trying to meet the requirements of the Homestead Act.

Whatever the causes of the Dust Bowl, the Roosevelt administration responded with a billion-dollar program to aid and educate farmers in soil conservation techniques. Descendants of Isaac Greathouse, the man who bought Mattie and Lewis's homestead, now farm and ranch that land with the exception of a portion that is used for an Air Force bombing range. The descendants of Joseph Smith, Mattie's father, own the land that was his homestead. The Greathouse and Smith descendants say that the Great Depression and the Dust Bowl of the 1930s hurled hardships and harsh realities at everyone. These experiences created a way of life whose influence would be felt for generations; the lessons of the Dust Bowl have been translated into standard practice.

In addition to delighting in her new granddaughter's birth and continuing to work at Roscoe's Liberty Café, Mattie took in laundry for a few people, including Roy Simm, a single man several years older than she. One Halloween morning he dropped off his laundry at Mattie's. Later that day Charlie saw him downtown near the Ed J. Neer building.

During the conversation on Main Street, Uncle Charlie told Roy his laundry was ready though he knew it was not. When Roy came by that evening to pick up his laundry, Charlie met him at the door, pouring a bucket of water on him with shouts of "Trick or treat!"

Since Roy was dripping wet, he came into the house to dry off. In a matter of minutes, Charlie, Lillie, and all the kids at Mattie's house went to a movie, leaving Mattie and Roy there alone. Roy was a good natured fellow and the "Trick or Treat" incident did not discourage him; a good laugh was often a needed rebuttal against the otherwise depressing times. Roy and Mattie started dating after that. So everyone started referring to Roy as "Popsie" when he was not around, and Charlie began calling Mattie "Mumsie." Popsie was crazy about Mumsie, but she soon cooled the flame of romance. The only remnant left of it was Charlie's affectionate name for Mattie – "Mumsie." That name stuck for decades.

Main Street of downtown Portales in the 1930s. While Mr. Neer sold furniture, was an undertaker, and owned a pharmacy, he also sold leather horse harnesses. As a grown man, Phill Russell recalled being in the store as a youngster and smelling the rich aroma of leather as well as the pungent smell of the chemical sawdust used for cleaning the wooden floor. E.N.M.U. Special Collections

Paul and Leroy stayed busy playing with Sherman and Cotton Creek, Roscoe's sons. Even though they were a little older than Paul and Leroy, they were Paul and Leroy's nephews. This topsy-turvy kinship did not bother them at all; the four of them together were able to think of creative ways to spend their time. Although "The Lone Ranger" had debuted on radio WXYZ that year, the four boys preferred to play "Tarzan," also a popular figure in those days. As luck would have it, there were big trees and a windmill on Mattie's property – all perfect for tying ropes on to swing Tarzan-like from high places!

Sherman concluded that Leroy was not getting the "proper nourishment" and was "too skinny." Malnourishment and hunger were indeed a problem for many during the Great Depression years, 1929 – 1939. In the 1928 presidential campaign, Republican candidate Herbert Hoover promised "A chicken in every pot." This promise did not materialize – in many cities men, out of a job, waited in dreary resignation outside soup kitchen doors. Stories have been passed down through the generations, telling of families eating bird eggs and just about anything else they could find to fill their empty stomachs. Unrest increased, culminating in hunger riots in some of the larger cities.

Fortunately hunger was not a problem in Mattie's family. Mattie cooked bountiful meals for her family – home grown vegetables from her garden, eggs from her chickens, milk from her cows. There was always plenty of food for everyone – including Leroy.

During the Great Depression women were ingenious in finding ways to grow their own gardens to help feed their hungry families. Making seed beds was a common practice. 1930s photo by Russell Lee

Mattie, like many women during the Great Depression, canned the vegetables grown in the family garden. 1930s photo by Dorothea Lange

From Mattie's meager earnings she was able to buy flour, sugar, salt, and pepper from the nearby grocery store. When reminiscing about what the family ate during the Great Depression, Winnie commented, "We ate a lot of biscuits and gravy."

In spite of Mattie's family not suffering from hunger as many were during the Great Depression, well-meaning Sherman brought a goat to Mattie's place. At that time there still were no zoning regulations in Portales to restrict animals in the city limits. The goat cooperated when Sherman milked her. But when anyone else tried, the goat jumped straight up. Leroy recalled once how after trying for two hours to no avail to milk that goat, Mattie summoned Sherman to "come and get that goat." Later Mattie was teased with comments that brought new meaning to that old familiar saying, "He sure got your goat."

McDonald Grocery Store, Portales, 1930, E.N.M.U. Special Collections

Meanwhile, Mattie emphasized drinking cows' milk rather than goats' milk.

In spite of Sherman's diagnosis of Leroy as "undernourished" and "too skinny," Leroy managed to survive first grade with no middle name. But for some reason, Mattie decided he needed a middle name. Nearly everyone in those days had one; Mattie simply couldn't remember why she and Harve had not given him a middle name when he was born. So she had "William" added legally as his middle name. Because of Mattie's experience with selling her homestead and spending eighteen months in probate court, the legal paperwork required to change Leroy's name was simple for her. Paul's middle name, Norris, was in honor of Paul and Leroy's grandfather (Harve's father). So it seemed fitting that Leroy's middle name be in honor of the two boys' father, William Harve Creek.

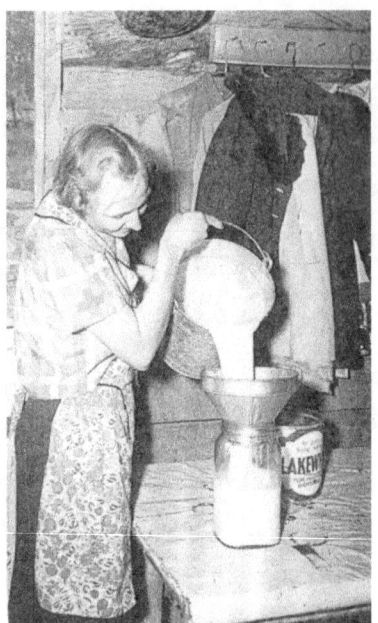

Straining milk from the family cows provided "good, clean" milk. 1930s photo by Russell Lee

Years later Leroy explained that his getting a middle name did not result in any great changes in his life. He still liked playing Tarzan, watching others try to milk that goat, enjoying the various relatives that came and went in their house – and learning to count to 100 by the time he finished second grade. He explained that this feat seemed to be of great importance to Miss Marshall, his teacher for both first and second grade. Even in his seventies, the memory was vivid of his spending hours putting numbers in the 100 squares on a special tablet. This assignment required so much time and attention that getting a middle name seemed secondary to Leroy. Other areas of learning also seemed secondary to the teacher; today's standards would not have allowed the great portion of time on only one small area of learning.

During these "bend in the road" years, Charlie and Lillie received another message from Arkansas – thankfully not as tragic as the drunken man shooting his mother. The Justice of the Peace who had performed their wedding ceremony dated their license April 31. Because there are not 31 days in April, the justice said at the time he would not charge Charlie anything for performing the ceremony. However, times "got tougher," and evidently the Justice of the Peace had second thoughts about his generosity, for he sent Charlie and Lillie a letter in New Mexico dunning them for 50 cents for performing the ceremony. Charlie did not acknowledge the request, and he never said if the Justice of the Peace asked for the 50 cents when he and Lillie returned to Arkansas 13 years later.

As for what else was going on in Mattie's world – she was surviving the death of her husband and she was coping with the devastating effects of the Great Depression. She had managed to keep her family together and at times even helped others – Uncle Jim's two sons and Charlie's sister. Her resolve to handle "the bend in the road" had strengthened her. She readily accepted the reality that "life is not fair" long before that saying became popular. She never expressed self-pity at having been widowed twice at such an early age, and she refused to let her grief turn into grim bitterness. She handled whatever fate meted out to her, and her positive attitude encouraged the family and those she interacted with on her job at the Liberty.

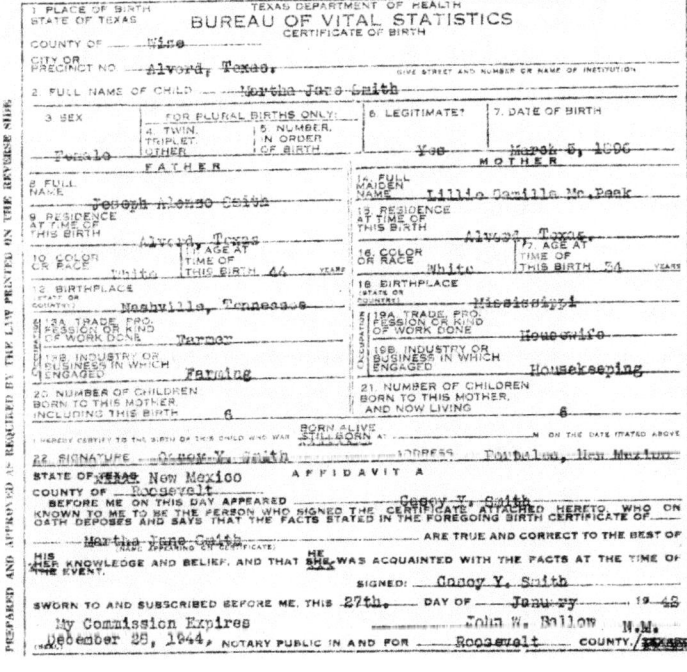

By 1935 the United States had enjoyed some measure of recovery just as Mattie had, but many bankers and other business people were growing dissatisfied with Roosevelt's New Deal program. So Roosevelt responded with a new program of reform: new controls over banks and public utilities, heavier taxes on the wealthy, an enormous work relief program for the unemployed, and the Social Security Act, passed on August 14, 1935.

Because Mattie worked at the Liberty Café, she was required to participate in the Social Security program. Enrolling in the program required a birth certificate, so Mattie contacted the county seat of Wise County, where Alvord, her birthplace, was located. To her surprise, records indicated that she was born not in 1895 but in 1896. Every woman's dream – to be one year younger than she thought she was!

The jukebox was always blaring out music at the Liberty – music helped ease the pains of economic hardship. Popular musicians in later 1934 and 1935 included Bing Crosby, Gene Autry, Fred Waring, and Al Jolson. One of the favorite songs of that era was "Time on My Hands." Evidently Elmer Kinney, a striking cowboy, had some "time on his hands," for he frequently made the long drive from the ranch where he was the foreman to eat lunch at the Liberty Café in Portales during the time Mattie was working.

"It's a long road that doesn't have a bend in it somewhere," according to an old American saying. Mattie survived several serious "bends" but was relatively happy with life. She had earned the right to be happy. Once again she had conquered the ravages of grief over the death of another loved one. While others during the Great Depression lost their homes, even as a widow, she found a way to buy a house. While other suffered long periods of unemployment, she "landed" a job because of her willingness to work long and hard and to improve her skills so that she was considered "the best café cook in town." While others went hungry all across the United States, she found ways to feed not only her family but other people as well. While many widows during the Great Depression depended on relatives to care for them and their children, Mattie took care of her children and also helped other families. Mattie refused to let the "bends" in the road she was forced to travel detour her or destroy her family.

But with the appearance of the handsome cowboy, Mattie would begin a journey on a new, untraveled portion of the "long road" of her life.

Chapter Seven:
GRANDDAD AND A NICKEL FOR A SPOOL OF THREAD
(Dec. 18, 1935 - Feb. 8, 1972)

A woman's work is never done, and happy is she whose strength holds out to the end.
— Martha Ballard, eighteenth-century writer

"Why in the world would Mattie get married again?"

This thought crossed the minds of several people attending or hearing about Mattie and Elmer Kinney's wedding on December 18, 1935, in Clovis, New Mexico. One person expressed this question aloud to several other "regulars" at the Liberty Café; they admitted wondering the same thing. Unlike her first two marriages, this time it was different – Mattie had worked hard and was financially able to survive without working the fields by day and doing laundry for others by night.

Wedding Picture
Mattie & Elmer Kinney
Dec. 18, 1935
Clovis, NM

This third marriage took many people by surprise because by that time Mattie appeared happy giving her total devotion to her family – her three daughters and two sons were her expressed reason for living. Her prayer remained constant and unchanged. Her fervent prayer after Lewis died was to live long enough to get her three daughters reared. Her prayer was the same after Harve died; she told Winnie, "I wanted more than anything to live long enough to raise my kids." Of course, when Harve died, "her kids" included the addition of her two boys – Paul was eight when his dad died, and Leroy was five.

A few friends and relatives expressed a different concern. Why wouldn't Mattie want to avoid the grief of the possible death of a third husband? But marriage was the norm for that period of time; it was generally assumed that people would get married – or remarried – rather than stay single. A woman's accepted role in the 1930s was caring for the household and the children, and a man's role was to be the economic provider for the family. A woman generally did not have any means of making a living for the family, so she needed a husband. Mattie, however, had become quite self-reliant and fulfilled both of these roles very well.

No one expressed any concern that Mr. Kinney was 13 years older than Mattie. Evidently Mr. Kinney and Mattie gave no thought to their age difference either. After all, Harve had been twice Mattie's age. Besides, Mattie liked Mr. Kinney. Simple as that. By this time Mattie knew she was born in 1896, not 1895. Otherwise she would have thought she was 14 years younger than Mr. Kinney. As mentioned in Chapter Three, Mattie did not have a copy of her birth certificate when she married Lewis; she had grown up thinking she was born in 1895. Neither did she have a copy of it when she and Harve married. But when Mattie married Mr. Kinney on December 18, 1935, she showed her date of birth as March 5, 1896.

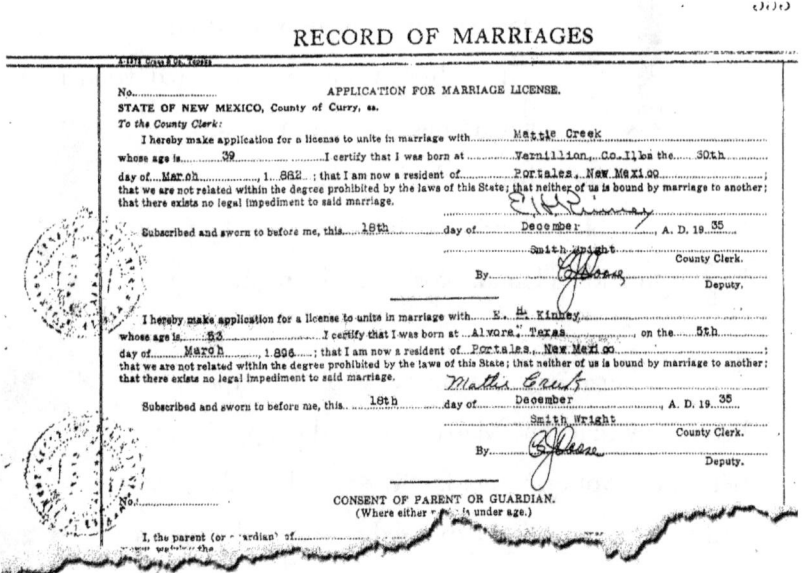

She probably had sent for what was called a "delayed birth certificate" when she signed up to pay into Social Security. The Social Security Act, signed into law August 14, 1935, required everyone to register by January 1, 1937. By the time Mattie and Mr. Kinney married, she knew she was a year younger than she had always thought.

Winnie reminisced about her mother's third marriage, "I could understand why she would want to get married again…after all she was only 39." Another consideration – Mr. Kinney was rather distinguished looking, and he "struck a good pose," as Mattie later put it. Winnie described her new step-father in her memoirs:

> Mr. Kinney was a nice-looking cowboy with striking white hair. He wore western clothes, including cowboy boots. He had a nice tan and was in good physical shape from the demanding work and long hours on the ranch.

Why everyone referred to Mattie's third husband as "Mr. Kinney" is not known. It could have been because he had an air about him that drew respect. Mr. Kinney's positions of authority and education gave him a certain aura. When Mattie met him, he was the foreman of the large Eastern New Mexico Price Ranch owned by a wealthy, notable landowner from El Paso. Before the Price Ranch, Mr. Kinney managed the well-known New Mexico Hondo Valley apple orchards located between Roswell and Ruidoso. The Hondo Valley, like Lincoln County and the town of Lincoln, was the setting for the turbulent times of the Lincoln County Wars. Historians chronicling the last of Billy the Kid Bonney's life write of the many areas and settlements along the Rio Bonito, the Rio Ruidoso, and the Rio Hondo. Mr. Kinney enjoyed learning about the colorful history of that area.

Mr. Kinney enjoyed learning not only about history but about other areas as well and was relatively well-educated, particularly for his time and for that part of the country. Portales and surrounding area were populated by ranch and farm families who thought completing high school provided a good education. There were few nearby universities or colleges. What is now called Eastern New Mexico University had just been founded the year before with only a small enrollment. The University of New Mexico, located in Albuquerque, was 230 miles away; it might as well have been on a different continent. Texas Tech was closer – only 115 miles from Portales, but few people traveled there for any reason much less to attend college. There was a college at Canyon, Texas, but young people did not venture that far from Portales. After Mr. Kinney graduated from high school in his home state of Illinois, he completed a two-year associate degree from the University of Illinois.

Maybe another reason people called Mattie's new husband Mr. Kinney was out of respect for his age. At 52, he probably was considered "old," for he had already lived 10 years beyond the life expectancy of men born in the 1880s. His striking white hair may have influenced people to consider him older than he actually was. His hand had been mangled in some farm machinery when he was 19 years old, resulting in the loss of one finger. He explained how this life-threatening accident turned his hair white "almost overnight." Calling an older person by his or her last name was just what people did in those days. Whatever the reason and all speculation aside, Martha's new husband was generally referred to as Mr. Kinney.

After their wedding, Mattie took a few days off from her job at the Liberty Café and joined Mr. Kinney for the holidays at the Price Ranch, west of Floyd. Charlie and Lillie and their new baby, Betty, also joined them, along with Juanita, Winnie, Paul, and Leroy. But after New Year's Day, 1936, Mattie returned to her job in Portales. She and her children lived in town until school was out for the summer. Looking back at Mattie and Mr. Kinney's marriage and their unusual arrangement for that era, Paul commented that his mother probably had done "a lot of thinking" about her marriage to his father, Harve. She had undoubtedly considered how "things would be different next time around." One thing for sure, she had made up her mind "not to move the kids from school to school anymore."

Mattie at the Price Ranch

After school was out for the summer, Mattie and her children moved to the ranch and began working in various capacities there. Winnie and Paul herded sheep for $30 a month that first summer on the ranch. The pay was generous for that period of time, for there was a high demand for sheep wool. Winnie and Paul both loved the money but admitted "there was no love lost" on the uncooperative sheep.

In contrast, Travis Russell, my uncle, had different feelings about sheep, especially when it came to feeding a hungry lamb.

Travis Russell helping out at feeding time. Photo courtesy of Betty Russell

Partly because they needed the money, Lillie and Charlie came out to the ranch the next spring to help during lambing season. They also wanted to help Mattie and to be with her. As for Mattie, Winnie made this observation:

> *It was a sad delusion if Mother thought she was getting out of any work by marrying Mr. Kinney.*

Mattie cooked for the ranch hands and various visitors in addition to working in the fields, raising chickens, and helping with the cattle and the sheep. The job most satisfying to Mattie (and to Travis Russell) was probably raising lambs that had been rejected by the ewes – their mothers. She would hand feed the little orphaned lambs until they could stand on their own. Her thoughts flashed back to the days when she struggled to care for her three little girls after Lewis died and her two young sons after Harve died. She used the same patient and persistent nurturing on the little lambs that she had given to her children.

At the Price Ranch in about 1939. Photo taken by Albert Moss, husband of Nellie, the daughter of Elmer Kinney.

Before moving to the ranch, Mattie had established her reputation as an outstanding worker. Her work on the ranch was no exception. Paul gave this account of one experience:

> *The first time I became really aware that my mother was something special was when we were on the ranch where she cooked for the family and hands [workers] and worked in the fields. When we were "heading maize," she took two rows and I took one. We would take in more loads than the two men working with us. I asked them if it bothered them to be "bested" by a woman and a kid.*

One of Mattie's favorite sayings was, "If it is worth doing, it is worth doing well." She probably recited this axiom to Paul in this "maize heading" situation just as she frequently called upon her extensive repertoire of other truisms when she was rearing her children.

Mr. Kinney paid the various members of the family for their work on the ranch – everyone but Mattie. This was a mistake! She soon became acutely aware that she never received any money unless she asked for it. Of course, not paying the wife for her work on a farming or ranching operation was typical. But Martha had grown accustomed to making her own money during the time after Harve died and before she married Mr. Kinney. One day she exploded to Winnie:

> *I'd gotten out of the habit of having to ask for money…and now I have to ask for a nickel to buy a spool of thread!*

One of the main reasons Mattie liked having her own money was to help her children. For instance, after lambing season was over, Lillie and Charlie moved to Kinsolvin's Ranch to work. They were furnished a house, milk, and eggs, but were paid only $25.00 a month. Charlie's sister Pauline and her husband lived in Portales near a store that was for sale, and they told Charlie and Lillie about the store. After Charlie and Lillie saw it, they decided they wanted to buy it. One problem – they had not been able to save enough money from their meager income for the down payment. Mattie didn't have ready cash either, but she signed the note to borrow $100.00 from the bank. As Lillie put it:

> *There again, Mother helped us.*

Especially after Mattie's children became adults, they realized even more fully that their mother had also given them something even more valuable than money – she had always given them kind, concerned, but firm guidance. Mattie had disciplined her children before she married Mr. Kinney, and she continued to "bring out the best in them," as she put it. Paul remembered an incident when he was a young teenager living on the ranch. Mattie had reminded him to save his "good" shirt that was clean so he would have it to wear on the weekend. He wore the good shirt in spite of the reminder. When Saturday arrived, Coke and Juanita invited Paul to go along with them into town for a movie. After he put on his "good" – but dirty – shirt, Mattie stated matter-of-factly, "You are not wearing a dirty shirt into town." End of discussion. Paul had no clean shirt to wear, so he stayed home that Saturday night. Paul admitted that his mother had taught him a good lesson – he never made that mistake again!

Back to the money issue. Another turning point in Mattie's life with Mr. Kinney was the time she did some laundry for one of the ranch hands. Not an easy chore in those days, washing the clothes took at least a half of Mattie's work day. Everything was done "by hand," literally, for electricity was not available. Although the "REA" (Rural Electrification Administration) was established in 1935, electricity was not available to the Price Ranch until 1951, according to a work order in the files of RCEC, the electric company. Mattie enlisted the help of several of the "kids," who had to carry water in a bucket from the windmill to the house where Mattie heated it in a large oval-shaped "boiler" that covered two burners on the top of a kerosene stove. Mattie used this large container to boil the white clothes after she had "rubbed them clean" on a rub board. Next she rinsed the clothes in two boilers full of water and wrung them to get as dry as possible by hand. Finally she hung the wet, clean clothes on a clothes line with wooden clothes pins in hopes the sun would dry them before the wind plastered sand on them.

Washday on an unidentified New Mexico ranch. Courtesy of The New Mexico History Museum.

After the clothes were dry, Mattie had to iron them – no wrinkle-free, no-iron clothes in those days! But first she sprinkled the clothes with clean water and folded them neatly in a large towel so the moisture would distribute evenly and they wouldn't dry out. By Tuesday they were ready to be ironed – but not with a lightweight, electric steam iron as we know it today. Heavy irons – called flat irons – were placed on the stove top to heat. Mattie used an iron until it was no longer hot enough to press out wrinkles. Then she put it back on the hot stove top and got one of the irons that had been heating. Even though ironing did not take as long as washing the clothes, it took some time and added extra stress to the back-breaking work day.

After Mr. Kinney paid the worker his monthly check, the worker in turn paid Mr. Kinney for the laundry Mattie had laboriously done. When she found out that Mr. Kinney had not passed on the laundry payment to her, she "jumped him." Mr. Kinney tried to defend himself, "Well, I thought it all went into the same pocket." Mattie retorted, "Yeah. Yours!"

Soon after this disagreement, Roscoe came out to the ranch and asked Mattie to work a couple of weeks at his café in town – the Liberty. The timing was right! Mattie willingly went to town and worked. But after the "couple of weeks" she continued working for Roscoe and eventually rented a house in Portales. Mattie was not happy living – or working – on the ranch. Winnie put it this way, "Hard work and no pay is not a good deal." She continued:

> *Mr. Kinney was soon spending more time in town than he was at the ranch. I never knew if he quit or if his boss eased him out and Johnny took his place at the Price Ranch. Either way, they were both pleased.*

In 1938 Mattie and Mr. Kinney were living in Portales in a house on South Avenue B when he was asked to manage a farm near Hereford, Texas. Mattie gave up her job at the Liberty when he accepted that offer. His job did not last long so they moved to Carlsbad in hopes Mr. Kinney would get a job in the potash mines where his son worked. In addition, his daughter and her family lived in Carlsbad. While Mr. Kinney was waiting for a job to develop, Mattie babysat in the evenings for some friends of his family. Soon she was expected to do some ironing, and then some cleaning, at the same rate of pay. Next somebody found a day job for Mattie cleaning motel rooms.

After working long, tiring hours at these two jobs, Mattie grew impatient, waiting for a job to turn up for her husband. She was determined to move back to Portales. When she wrote Lillie about her decision, Lillie and Charlie rented her a house in Portales and fixed it up. Mattie gave Mr. Kinney a choice – he could stay in Carlsbad or go with her to Portales. When Mattie left, Mr. Kinney joined her.

After returning to Portales, Mattie started working again for Roscoe at his café. But then the opportunity came for her to lease a small café. She took it – with Roscoe's blessings. Harve had always been the "PR man" at the various cafes he managed during his and Mattie's marriage. Mattie had learned a lot from Harve about making customers feel welcome, and she readily filled this role in her café. In addition, she was also a good manager and a good cook. Business thrived!

Just as Harve had various family members helping in the cafes he managed, Mattie invited some of her relatives to help her. One of Mattie's best hires was her brother, Jim Smith. The two had enjoyed a close relationship all their lives. Furthermore Jim was a good worker who quickly earned the reputation as "the best fry cook in town."

Mattie assigned responsibilities to people according to their interests and capabilities. Mr. Kinney's favorite job was counting the money and "looking after it." But he also raised vegetables and fruits to use at the café. Gigantic amounts of delicious home-made chowchow were an especially tasty contribution he made to the café's operation. But Mattie soon was obviously "the person in charge." Her customers liked her, and so did the people who worked for her. Mr. Kinney readily admitted that his wife had "an uncanny ability to 'connect' with people, and she had a 'head' for managing a business."

Soon Mattie leased another café called The Hobbs Chrevolet House Café because it adjoined a garage where mechanics worked on cars. As for what people called the new manager of this cafe, more and more people were calling her Mattie. Some people even called the newly leased café Mattie's Café. Whatever people chose to call the manager or the cafe, legend reveals that her cafe was considered "the best place in town to eat."

The Liberty Café is the fifth bulding from the corner. The Portales National Bank moved into the building on the corner in 1935. The photo was taken in the 1930s — exact date unknown.
E.N.M.U. Special Collections

The café had several booths and three stools, and served breakfast, lunch, and dinner. In addition, the café stayed open all night, serving hamburgers and other "short orders" plus Mattie's delicious homemade pies – cherry pie ala mode, lemon, and coconut cream pie. Jim moved with Mattie to the new café. Relatives on the payroll increased as Paul worked part-time wherever needed when he wasn't in school, and Charlie waited on people at the counter on the night shift. Charlie gave great service; he enjoyed the customers and they liked him because of his friendly, humor-filled personality.

Business was so good that Mattie and Mr. Kinney occasionally let the employees run the café so they could attend the local movie theater. It was on one such night – November 2, 1941 – that Charlie Johnson came to the theater to notify them of what Winnie would later call, "a heart wrenching event that changed the course of my life." First, a little background information. In Winnie's memoirs written in her early 80s, she shared how she had graduated from high school in May, 1937, and married JW Russell – affectionately called Johnny – in August, 1937:

> *I got married to my neighbor sheep rancher and moved from my mother and step-dad's ranch to my new husband's ranch. It was about 10 miles from Floyd, out on the Mesa, where one could see for miles. My new home was a two-room sheep camp. We took my new husband's two sons to live with us. Their mother, Johnny's first wife, had died an untimely death before she was even 20 years old…our only entertainment was a battery run radio which we could play only a short while at night and a wind-up Victrola with a few records. On Saturday nights we would go to the mid-night show. That was a happy time of my life, but short lived.*

The alarming news was that Winnie's husband, Johnny, had been in a horrible accident and one of the ranchers who lived near the collision had brought him to the local hospital in Portales. Mr. Kinney stayed with Johnny at the hospital while Charlie and Mattie drove out to the ranch to get Winnie and her three young children – I was the youngest, only eight months old.

Winnie and Johnny with Bob and Bill and baby Phill, in front of the Price Ranch house, about 1939

Bits of information on the accident were pieced together by various people, including the ranchers and farmers gathered at the Floyd store after that day's work. The father of a 12-year-old boy had let his son drive the tractor rig home by himself while the father stayed to recount the day's work with the other men. Johnny was returning home after leaving early that morning with a load of lambs to sell. He was undoubtedly tired, for it was about 9:00 o'clock in the evening. There was no moon so it was dark. The boy's tractor rig had no lights, and it was the days before reflectors were required on slow-moving vehicles. Johnny's pickup truck and the tractor rig collided on the curve in the highway not far from the store where the men were visiting. The impact hurled the boy out onto the field, and it threw Johnny through the windshield of his truck. This was before shatterproof windshields, so Johnny's face and entire body were pelted with broken glass. The horrific impact of the crash and the loss of blood spelled certain death. Johnny looked up at Mattie and uttered his last words as he lay dying, "I tried to miss him."

Years later Winnie wrote in her memoirs:

> *Mother and Mr. Kinney took me and my three kids in. I don't know what I would've done, for I had no money. [It was the days before anyone would have considered suing*

the parents for allowing their 12-year-old to drive an unlighted vehicle on a public highway.] We lived with them for a year. When I finally got a little insurance money, I bought a lot next to their house and made a down payment on a small house I had moved there. The house had a living room, kitchen, one bedroom, and a bathroom – the first house I'd ever lived in that had an indoor bathroom.

In later years Mattie said she never considered any arrangement other than Winnie and her three children moving in with her and Mr. Kinney. Because Mattie's in-laws had helped her keep her three girls after Lewis' death, she never gave a second thought about helping Winnie keep her three children.

Mattie led the way helping Winnie financially as well as caring for her children. Mr. Kinney also helped tremendously with myriad details – like having Winnie's house moved next door to them. Winnie commented years later:

Mr. Kinney saw to all the business details…and did a lot of the work. I'll always be grateful to Mother and Mr. Kinney for taking me and my kids in and taking care of us. And never once did I ever hear either of them mention that I should be grateful.

During this time of family crisis and dramatic upheaval, the world was also changing. The country was coming out of depression only to face its biggest threat to freedom. When World War II broke out in 1941, the airfield 20 miles from Portales was enlarged and renamed Clovis Army Airfield. B-17, B-14, and B-29 bomber crews trained there. [In 1957 this airfield was renamed Cannon Air Force Base and became one of the major jet fighter training sites for U.S. defense forces. Coincidentally, the major bombing range was placed on part of the large ranch where Johnny and Mr. Kinney had worked as foremen.]

In the spring of '42 military personnel poured into Clovis and Portales. Faraway from home for the first time and hungry for homemade food and a warm welcome, GIs flocked to Mattie's Chrevolet House Café. Mattie and her employees made sure they got generous portions of both.

By this time, Winnie was going to Benson's Business School in Clovis during the day. Still grief-stricken from Johnny's death less than a year before, Winnie could not sleep very well at night. Mattie had an idea – Winnie could help her with the café at night while the children were sleeping and Mr. Kinney kept an eye on them. Winnie said that her mother's wisdom in finding work for her helped fill an awful void in her life.

Mattie had never had to be overly demonstrative when disciplining her children and relating to other people. But Winnie said that working at the café revealed "a side of my mother I hadn't seen before." Here is one of Winnie's first memories of working at her mother's café:

> *One night was especially busy. One booth of GIs was really rowdy. They had been quieted down a couple of times, but soon they were too loud again. Mother had been cutting up chickens with this wicked looking meat cleaver [large knife]. She came out of that kitchen with fire in her eyes and that cleaver in her hand. The rowdy customers got quiet very quick. I think it was the cleaver that convinced them.*

Mattie was determined to make her café a good place to gather and to eat. She wanted everyone to enjoy themselves, but she was not going to tolerate rowdiness and unruliness. She soon established herself as "the boss." When Mattie spoke, people listened! But she still acquiesced to Mr. Kinney on some issues. One time Charlie and Paul both tried to convince her that one of the employees was stealing coins from the cash register. Because Mr. Kinney did not believe Charlie or Paul, Mattie delayed taking action against the employee. When hard evidence later surfaced, Mr. Kinney finally consented for Mattie to fire the dishonest employee.

Another time Charlie caught a waitress "knocking down" at the cash register. She would tell the customers they owed a certain amount, but she entered a lower amount in the cash register and "pocketed" the difference. Charlie was known to always give people the benefit of the doubt. But after he had witnessed this "cash register crime" numerous times, Mr. Kinney finally believed him. While Mattie reserved for Mr. Kinney the decision regarding the waitress's fate, she delivered the verdict to the waitress that she "needed to look for another job."

Who was "boss" at the café was not a big issue with Mattie, and she did not feel that she needed to speak out against the traditional view that "the man makes all the decisions." After awhile she was the one spending more time at the café, so her becoming the decision maker there evolved naturally. Both seemed comfortable most of the time with this transition in their relationship. Mr. Kinney liked gardening and was good at it, so the responsibility for the garden seemed to naturally fall to him, just as did the orchard (he grew the best fruit in town), a small dairy (for a short while), and the lawn that was the pride of the neighborhood with roses, dahlias, and carefully trimmed grass, shrubs, and trees.

Mattie always wanted things to run smoothly; she let Mr. Kinney retain his close watch over the cash register. But he stopped his work at home just in time to get to the café at closing time to "take care of the cash register." Mattie suggested to him that there were some changes that needed to be made. For one thing, he had not been leaving enough money in the register to begin the next day's business. When he did not heed her suggestions, in her usual quiet, resolute way, Mattie solved the problem. She merely began earlier in the evening counting the cash, sorting the checks (this was long before credit cards were used), and apportioning some money for paying bills and some to stay in the cash register. Before long she established that she was "taking care of the cash register." Mattie, on the other hand, was generous, for she saw that Elmer always had "plenty of money."

Mr. Kinney also still had unlimited access to his much-loved cigar supply. Access was easy, for keeping the cigar, cigarette, and candy counter stocked at the café was one responsibility that he still had. He bought these items from a particular wholesale company even after Charlie had taken a job with another company and called on Mattie's café. In spite of Charlie's best efforts, Mr. Kinney ignored him. Charlie quit calling on Mattie's café, but his boss insisted that Charlie call on the café his mother-in-law owned. This created a lot of tension in the family, but Mattie told Lillie she would "see to it that Mr. Kinney bought from Charlie." Whenever Charlie called on the café and Mattie was there, she bought from him. This change placed Mattie increasingly "in charge." It was a milestone that changed Mattie and Mr. Kinney's relationship. This role reversal established that she was the leader – the breadwinner, a role she had been "in training" for a long time.

The problem between Charlie and Mr. Kinney caused a big rift between their two families. Charlie no longer accompanied Lillie and the girls, Betty and Charlene, when they visited Mattie and Mr. Kinney. This situation kept Charlie and Lillie's two daughters from getting to know and enjoy their grandmother as much as they would have liked. Several years later Charlie and Lillie moved back to Arkansas. Charlie started attending church there and decided to write a letter to Mr. Kinney inviting Mattie and him to come for a visit. Both men put the past behind them and became congenial friends and enjoyed visiting with each other the rest of their lives.

Charlie and Lillie's two daughters, Betty and Charlene, about 1941 or 1942

Winnie with Butch, Phill, and Barbara Jo, about 1943

Charlie's writing to Mr. Kinney not only changed his and Mr. Kinney's relationship, it helped begin a change in Mr. Kinney's relationship with other family members. Many of the adults began calling him Elmer while Mattie's grandchildren called him Granddad. Because of the early deaths of Lewis and Harve, he was the only grandfather that any of Mattie's grandchildren knew. We grandchildren, of course, used the term Grandmother for Mattie; sometimes some of us called her Grandmother Mattie. Sometimes in the work setting, a few grandchildren called her Mattie. I think I just felt more grown-up calling her Mattie when the other workers were calling her that. I was one of the first grandchildren to call Grandmother's husband Granddad, and by this time I was old enough to be aware of some of the sensitive issues in the family. I remember Grandmother saying that she thought she had done all she could about "the Granddad-Charlie situation." After all, she had told Granddad that they were going to buy from Charlie because he was Lillie's husband. She lamented that if she "had it to do over again," she would have exercised "more grit and gumption."

Relatives visiting in her home were Grandmother Mattie's greatest delight, and she was not going to let rudeness ruin these special times. Over the years her example and persistent persuasion led Granddad to enjoy the times when relatives crowded into their two-bedroom house for a weekend of food and fellowship. With this change in attitude, he completely supported her plans to add two more bedrooms – and a much-needed second bathroom!

Mattie's love extended beyond her family. She loved people in general. Some of her best friends were people she met as customers of her café – Lacy and Helen Armstrong were two such people. The Armstrongs were well-respected business people, owning different businesses at various times, including a car dealership and an insurance company.

The Armstrongs' roots reached deep in the community. Helen's father was Washington Lindsey, a lawyer who had campaigned ferociously in the early 1900s for the formation of a new county in the territory of what is now New Mexico. He finally convinced the governor, and Roosevelt County was officially formed on February 28, 1903. This new county got its name from the 27th President of the United States, Theodore Roosevelt, a man Lindsey greatly admired.

Helen Armstrong's father became the first mayor of Portales after the incorporation of the town in 1909. Lindsey

E.N.M.U. Special Collections

later served as governor of New Mexico (1917–1918), only five years after the state became part of the United States.

As a child, I was too young to realize how influential Grandmother Mattie's friends were, including the Armstrongs – that is, until I went with my grandparents to the Armstrongs' home and saw the beautiful peacocks that roamed the spacious grounds of their house. Only then did I believe they must be "important people."

Former New Mexico Governor Lindsey; on lawn of Portales Courthouse; statue faces building that was the last "Mattie's Café." Photo by Phill Russell

Mattie did not limit her association and friendship to "important people." A very shy, scared woman applied for a job at her café a year or so before WWII ended. The job applicant had no experience, but Mattie sensed her desperation and hired her with a commitment to train her. Christine spoke with a strong German accent. Very soon after Christine started working, some townspeople confronted Mattie and insisted that she "fire that German Jew." Mattie would not hear of it; she told them that Christine had fled to America with her young daughter, seeking to escape the torture inflicted on her friends and relatives in Germany. She insisted that any townspeople who did not want to give Christine the respect she deserved could simply go eat at another café in town. Christine worked faithfully for Mattie for many years, joining a host of other loyal employees.

Mattie never intended for her defense of Christine to add to the growing admiration townspeople held for her. But it did. People from all walks of life and every religion knew she could be counted on to treat them with respect. During the 1940s she grew in stature as a business person, and she became even more the matriarch of her extended family. Her acts of encouragement and assistance were legend. Ruby, Harve's daughter, married and had six children. When her young husband died an untimely death, Grandmother Mattie went to her home and told her not to worry about how she would care for and feed her five young children

– Mattie would help her. And she did, in many ways, including giving Ruby a job at her café. As Ruby's children grew older, Mattie provided jobs for them at her café, always working around their school schedules. Because Ruby did not have a car, Mattie took time out of her work schedule to drive Ruby to and from work, just as she had done for Christine at first and several other employees who did not own a car.

Another characteristic about Mattie never changed. She was a strict but even-handed disciplinarian to her children. Her grandchildren were not exempted from experiencing this discipline. She believed that children should behave so that they "would like themselves" and others would enjoy being around them. She was never overly harsh, and she was not about to let anybody else overstep the bounds.

Mattie always tried to be see things from her children's point of view, and she tried to understand and encourage her grandchildren, including my two brothers and me. I remember when she bought all three of us sandals for the summer. Butch, the middle child, hated his sandals. He envisioned himself a cowboy. He did what any real cowboy would do; he got him some scissors and cut the straps of those sissy sandals. Seeing things from Butch's point of view, Grandmother Mattie bought him some bonafide cowboy boots.

Strong in many ways, Mattie seldom cried. But one special time the dam broke and the tears flowed. Wearing his Navy uniform, Paul walked out the front door carrying his duffle bag to catch his train. He was on his way to California to board a submarine headed for wartime duty in the Pacific. Watching him walk away, she struggled with the thought, "Did I do the right thing by giving my written consent so he could join the Navy as a 17-year-old?" Paul had been so insistent that he wanted to serve his country during WW II that she felt she had no choice. Eleven of his buddies from Portales were going, and he said he would say his was 18 just as some of them had.

All Mattie could think about was the awful grief over the deaths of two husbands and her first son on the day before his first birthday. The thought of possibly losing Paul was almost more than her heart could stand. Throughout WWII she worried, cried, and prayed for Paul. After seeing live combat for several years and narrowly escaping enemy ships several times, he returned home safely after WWII was over. Mattie could finally put to rest her doubts and fears. Unfortunately, some of the other mothers in Eastern New Mexico did not get to put their fears and grief to rest; their sons did not return from the war – A Roosevelt County World War II Roll of Honor lists names of 96 who did not return home from WWII.

Leroy was not old enough to fight in WWII, but as soon as he could join the service, he did just that – he joined the Army. So both of Mattie's sons began serving in the military at an early age, and she often said that she was proud that both of them were willing to fight for their country.

Martha Jane Smith. Martha Jane Deatherage. Martha Creek. Mattie Kinney. Grandmother Mattie's personality was as multi-faceted as her name. The few years Mattie was "on her own" after Harve died gave significant shape to her personality; she put into practice the many things she had been learning and became an independent individual, quite capable of making it on her own. She undoubtedly changed more during the time she was married to Elmer Kinney than she did during her first two marriages. This is understandable, for her first marriage lasted only five years and four months while her second marriage lasted about 12 and one-half years. Like her first two marriages, death ended her third marriage.

During her 37 years of marriage to Granddad, Grandmother Mattie's resolute determination also changed him. She showed him how to live life more fully and how to embrace the enjoyment of getting along with others. With her strong heart and quiet spirit she forged a marriage that developed into a gentle, caring relationship. In addition, the love of her children, grandchildren, and other relatives grew as she loved and encouraged them, and she developed many cherished friendships.

Over her years with Granddad, Grandmother Mattie improved her lot in life immensely. She owned a flourishing business and earned respect throughout Roosevelt County as an astute business person. She owned a comfortable house on a third of a city block. The lawn was lush, green grass trimmed to perfection and beautiful flowers everywhere. Her house was the first in the neighborhood to have a sidewalk at the edge of the lawn and leading up to the front door.

Mattie enjoyed buying special items for her home – such as a handsome clock that chimed on the hour and every 15 minutes. Mattie was extremely mindful of time and how it was used. She loved this clock, for its chiming served as endless reminders, not only of the time at hand, but also of moments past and the people she had spent time with.

Courtesy of Betty Johnson Huett

A large floor model Philco radio was another special addition to Mattie's living room. The last of its kind, production for this model was diverted in 1942 to making radar equipment for the war. A symbol of the Golden Age of Radio, this beautiful wooden radio occupied a prominent place in the living room. Adults listened to learn about America's involvement in World War II whereas adults and youngsters alike could hardly wait for the next radio episode of their favorite programs. That radio was at the center of many of the memorable times in Mattie's well-lived home.

Courtesy of Charlene Johnson Hutson

Mattie also bought a new car whenever she wanted. But among her most treasured possessions were a washer and dryer, several electric hand irons, and even a large cylindrical ironer. All these appliances were a far cry from the buckets, boilers, and rub board used on those back-breaking wash days she endured on the Price Ranch.

Another dramatic difference was the hall closet with deep stacks of freshly laundered and impeccably folded sheets. Between the numerous sheets she carefully placed $100 bills smoothed as wrinkle free as the sheets. She took great pride in her clean sheets – and $100 bills.

On those earlier hot, sweaty wash days on the ranch, Grandmother Mattie vowed to herself that she would never again have to ask anyone for "a nickel to buy a spool of thread."

And she didn't.

Chapter Eight:
MATTIE'S CAFÉ
(1939 - 1967)

Where I was born and where I lived is unimportant. It is what I have done with where I have been that should be of interest.
— Georgia O'Keeffe, famous New Mexico artist

Some say never go back. But it was a day for going back. Everyone knows such a day – a time to return to one's beginnings. Three of Mattie's grandchildren – now all adults themselves – did just that. The three cousins, Charlene Hutson, Phill Russell, and Lewis ("Bo") Chumbley, met in Decatur, the county seat of Wise County, Texas. Rita Russell and Marilyn Chumbley had happily accompanied their husbands to see what they could find out about the family roots of their maternal grandmother – Martha Jane, as she was called then. She lived with her parents and her brothers and sisters in the countryside near Alvord, a smaller town in that county, until they left in 1906 to homestead in Eastern New Mexico. Barely existing, they had high hopes of a better life in New Mexico.

This May day in 2004 was possibly like bygone days nearly 100 years ago when the young Mattie and other members of the Smith clan lived there – patches of white clouds floating across the blue Texas sky, birds singing in the trees, and cattle grazing on the nearby rolling, green hills. A warm sense of family history embraced the five as they strolled around the friendly little town. Then, to their delight, they saw a sign – Mattie's on the Square.

 These exact words identified the last of a series of popular cafes Grandmother Mattie owned in Portales, New Mexico, for more than 40 years! Bearing Grandmother's legendary name, this café in the county seat of her birthplace seemed to connect the present and the past.

The thirsty and hungry group – Charlene, Phill, Rita, Bo, and Marilyn – found a place to sit down in Mattie's on the Square in Decatur, Texas. As they satisfied their thirst with the cold water set before them and read the menu featuring chicken fried steak and other home-cooked foods Grandmother Mattie was famous for, they felt her presence.

 They enjoyed the food and reminiscing about Mattie's Café in Portales, New Mexico. It was a fitting tribute. After each of them later told me about the food and the fun they had enjoyed, this past and present seemed to merge for me; I cheered, "Grandmother would've loved it!"

The cold glasses of iced water took on special meaning as the five recollected how Mattie loved a good, cold drink of water. She often recounted the early days on the New Mexico homestead when water of any kind was a luxury. Many gave the Colt revolver and the Sharp's buffalo rifle the credit for taming the West while others say it was the windmills that settled the West, providing life-supporting water to the rancher and homesteader and their livestock.

Grandmother Mattie and Rita Russell getting a drink of water from the windmill on the Smith homestead in New Mexico. Photo by Phill Russell.

Prior to windmills, livestock would congregate where rain occasionally filled low-lying areas. People referred to these water-filled areas as "watering holes." This label carried over to the tanks filled with water by the windmills, and sometimes in jest people would call cafes "watering holes." This café in Decatur was obviously a favorite "watering hole," for customers seemed naturally drawn to it – just as they did to Mattie's Café in Portales. Some came in to eat, but many came in simply for a cup of coffee and a little camaraderie – and there was plenty of both.

The atmosphere of the café and the Texas town itself carried my thoughts back to the late 1940s and 1950s when I can first remember Grandmother Mattie orchestrating the many responsibilities of her various cafés.

Mattie, Mrs. Sanders, an unidentified employee, and Maxine (Aunt Ruby's daughter) in one of Grandmother's early cafes — Miller's Coffee Shop. Ted Smith, Jim Smith's son, is sitting at the counter looking toward Mattie and the others.

That period of time reflected America at its best. WWII was over, the victorious veterans had returned and settled into the tapestry of the country, and things were happening. Prepared cake mixes were introduced in 1949. Air conditioning was made available in cars in 1950. *High Noon* was named the best film of 1952, and by that year nearly half of U.S. farms had tractors. In 1953 the New York Yankees won their fifth consecutive World Series. In 1954 Eisenhower signed a bill inserting the words Under God into the Pledge of Allegiance. In 1955 the first Kentucky Fried Chicken opened. In 1959 Alaska became the 49th state, Hawaii the 50th, and the U.S. sent two monkeys into orbit. The late 40s and the 50s were interesting years. But one development was especially exciting – the cure for polio. And Mattie's Café played a role in it!

Mattie had two reasons for her special concern about polio. Linda, Juanita's oldest daughter, and Irvin Nunn, another close relative, were diagnosed with it. Her concern was well-founded – polio was particularly treacherous, tending to attack the young and healthy, and its cause was unknown. This dreaded disease was crippling or paralyzing thousands of people and killing many others. Communities wanted to support the search for a cure, and one way they did it was through "March of Dimes Saturday." One Saturday each year cafes and drugstores participated in a contest to see who could sell the most cups of coffee at the going rate of 10 cents per cup. All the dimes collected were donated to research to stop the ravaging disease or for the care of its disabled victims. Competition was always keen and often close, but Mattie won nearly every year – maybe every year.

Mattie receiving the prize for serving the most cups of coffee in the annual March of Dimes contest

Finally and fortunately Drs. Salk and Sabin vanquished the terrible disease! Although there were no more spirited March of Dimes coffee days, conquering polio was a great accomplishment. The pride lived on that Grandmother and all her Mattie's Café employees had earned in their annual feat, and they continued their warm-hearted camaraderie as the community's favorite watering hole.

How did Mattie win every year? Undoubtedly because she was an effective "team leader" long before management gurus wrote books about this topic. She set a good example of the qualities a successful business required, and she knew how to help other people do their best. She held a deep and abiding respect for all people, and she treated everyone with dignity. Several instances of her leadership and "people skills" are etched indelibly in my memory. Before the luxury of automatic dishwashers, one person washed the dishes at the café and another dried them. One time Mattie couldn't find a substitute for the regular dishwasher who needed to take some time away from her job to help her daughter with a new baby. A young dish dryer pleaded with Mattie to let her substitute for the regular dishwasher. She offered the argument that school was out for the summer, so another dish dryer could easily be found. She also emphasized how hard she had worked as a dish dryer and that she had done a good job. She promised she would work hard to earn the higher pay as a dishwasher – 15 cents per hour!

Always willing to help someone, Mattie agreed to let the youthful dish dryer try the dishwashing job. The first day was a nightmare – a special event was going on in Portales, so there were more hungry customers than usual. Dirty dishes piled in so fast and so high that the five-foot-tall dishwasher was nearly covered up by them. Seeing the dilemma, Mattie offered various encouragements: "I know it's hard, but just keep doing your best." "Don't give up…I know you can do it!" But Mattie did more than express mere words; she "pitched in" and helped whenever she wheeled another cart of dirty dishes back to the inexperienced dishwasher. In spite of her own challenging responsibilities she took the time to show the struggling novice more effective ways to get her job done.

This dishwasher survived and spent the next few summers washing dishes. After she became really good at it, she started wanting to move on up. She finally asked Mattie if she could work as a waitress. The hourly rate was higher, and the tips could add substantially to one's earnings. Coincidentally Mattie needed another waitress for the summer to fill in while others took vacation. So she agreed to try out this eager teenager. After all, she had proven herself as a dishwasher.

Frightened and trembling the first few days on her new job, the inexperienced waitress stood literally scared stiff behind the swinging doors between the kitchen and the dining area. She found being face to face with customers even more intimidating then looking at a mounting pile of dirty dishes. Before going through the swinging doors, she gulped in deep breaths to prevent her voice from cracking when she greeted her customers. Again, Mattie affirmed her, "I know you can do it!" And she bolstered the shaky teenager's confidence, "Take your time…the main thing is to be nice to the customers. Get them the food they want, and keep their coffee hot." With Mattie's coaxing, this waitress showed her mettle. She turned out to be a long-term employee, and with the tips she earned during her college days she made more money than she later made with a master's degree – simply from "being nice to the customers," "getting them the food they want," and "keeping their coffee hot."

Another reason Mattie consistently won the March of Dimes coffee day and continued her success in the café business long after a polio cure was found was her knack for helping people "do better next time" when they made a mistake or blundered. One incident involved a new waitress who initially tried to carry too many dishes of food and drinks at the same time. Mattie suggested to her several times, "Make two trips." One day she didn't heed the suggestion and dropped an armload of dishes and glasses during the worst possible time – the lunch hour when people were in a hurry and the kitchen was already busy as could be. Unflappable, Mattie demonstrated beautifully the old familiar saying, "Don't cry over spilled milk." She calmly instructed the distraught waitress to get a rush order turned into the kitchen to replace the spilled food. Next she went to the back to get a broom and a container, returned to the gigantic mess, and quietly but quickly helped the clumsy waitress clean it up. The waitress never again tried to carry more dishes than was beyond her capability.

Mattie also emphasized basic human relations principles to all her workers, but especially to one unskilled and naïve waitress. She explained to this self-absorbed teenager how every customer walking in the door had problems and worries. She stressed that the person serving them had the opportunity – and responsibility – to extend an inviting greeting and offer a hearty portion of encouragement as well as a nourishing meal or hot cup of coffee. Mattie added, "When you lift the spirits of someone else, you cannot help but feel better yourself."

How can I remember so vividly these five long-ago examples of Grandmother Mattie's extraordinary gift for lifting up people and bringing out the best in them? Because…

- That desperate dish dryer Mattie instilled confidence in and taught to wash dishes faster than anyone else on the face of this earth was someone I knew well.

- That dishwasher Mattie gave the opportunity to "move up" was someone I knew well.
- That scared waitress Mattie coached to overcome breathless fear and to voice a greeting to customers without a crackle was someone I knew well.
- That clumsy waitress who dropped the dishes but with Mattie's coaxing finally mastered the art of balancing multiple dishes on one arm was someone I knew well.
- That lucky individual Mattie taught to understand that every person has hurts and burdens and to give them ample servings of kind words, not curtness or criticism, was someone I knew well.

I knew them all well, for I was that fortunate person!

Numerous other recipients of Grandmother Mattie's ingenious gift of encouraging, mentoring, teaching, and helping could recount similar stories. Many were relatives, for Mattie refused to believe that business and relatives should not be mixed. Perhaps she remembered how Harve and she and their children were just about the entire staff of most cafes they managed. One thing for sure, she cut no slack for relatives. But she did not need to. Because she was a hard worker herself, taught people how to do their jobs, and lavished encouragement and gratitude on them, most everyone just naturally wanted to do a good job for her.

Not only did Mattie always express appreciation for a job well done, she always went the second mile for her employees – and her family members. I will never forget the chaotic summer Grandmother allowed Linda Chumbley, another one of Mattie's grandchildren, and me to split a full-time waitress shift so we both could attend classes at Eastern New Mexico University. Juggling our work and class schedules was a challenge, but the ultimate test came with transportation. Neither Linda nor I had a car. So when Mattie was not using her car, we used it to dash from place to place. Mattie had to be at the café at certain times, like the busy lunch hour, and we each had to be at our classes at exact times as well as at work at a certain times. Another consideration to factor into the transportation logistics was picking up Granddad either at the café or at the house at certain times. By then he was getting older and could not see well enough to drive. But he still liked to eat, and to do it on schedule.

One full-time waitress who provided her own transportation would've been a lot easier on Mattie. But she cared about people in general and her grandchildren specifically. In addition, she had completed only the eighth grade, and most of the people she hired had even less education. She knew first-hand the importance of a good education and was willing to do everything she could to enable her grandchildren to go to college.

Other relatives also worked for Mattie, including all five of her children and many of her grandchildren, including Charlene – one of the cousins searching family roots that day in Decatur – and various other relatives. To me, Uncle Jim was another memorable relative working for Mattie. Not only could he make the best hamburgers in the world, but he was consistently kind and gentle with everyone. Those qualities endeared him to me. But it was his "slop" job that intrigued me. In the days before food disposals, getting rid of all the scraps of food (called "slop") left on dishes was a major undertaking. When the countless dirty dishes were placed on a large chute, the dishwasher scraped leftover food from each dish through a circular hole into a large milk can under the dishwashing area. A truckload of cans had to be hauled off every day. And Uncle Jim was the man in charge. Resourceful like Mattie, he figured out how to use that slop for an economic benefit – he fed it to his hungry hogs. This was, of course, before the days of health codes that restricted such a practice. And Uncle Jim repeatedly begged the dishwashers to guard against letting silverware fall into the slop; the unmannerly hogs did not like anything that got in the way of their gobbling up or scarfing down their feast. The hogs and their feeding frenzy were not Uncle Jim's only concern. He was watching out for Mattie's business – replacing silverware could be expensive.

Uncle Jim's wife, Aunt Ola, was also an interesting relative working for Mattie. Like her husband, she was a hard worker and took her responsibilities seriously. A vivid memory of her was one Saturday when I was drying dishes for her. Aunt Ola had drained the dirty water from the three large institutional-size tubs for washing and rinsing dishes and was refilling them in preparation for the busy "lunch rush" ahead of us. Saturday lunch time was always extra busy with all the farmers and ranchers and their families in town for the day. Aunt Ola was getting impatient with the refilling of the tubs, for the tiny stream of water coming out of each faucet was not exactly "full steam ahead." Disgusted, she surveyed the three tubs filling ever so slowly and said in disgust, "I could pee faster than this!" Mind you, this was the days before language was quite so graphic or explicit, especially in Mattie's café.

Not only did Mattie discourage coarse language, she did not tolerate gossip. She unconditionally accepted everyone as an individual worthy of being treated with respect and dignity. Once Uncle Leroy heard that one of Grandmother Mattie's waitresses was not married when her two children were born. When Leroy asked his mother about it, she told him in no uncertain terms, "We will not discuss her past, private life. It isn't any of our business." Mattie added, "She is a loyal employee, does her job well, treats the customers with respect, and that's what matters." End of discussion.

Mattie not only gave her employees – and everybody else – the benefit of the doubt, she also tried to help her workers manage the many demands of their personal life. Case in point: One of her competitors tried to hire one of her best waitresses. The waitress had heard that this competitor was inflexible regarding the work schedule. So she asked pointblank, "Would you be willing to work with me so I can take off a day occasionally?" The competitor replied abruptly, "No…that's no way to run a business!" Without blinking an eye, the excellent waitress declared briskly, "I prefer to work for Mattie," and turned and walked away. Mattie was good to her employees, and they repaid her with undying loyalty.

Mattie knew how to treat people well – and she knew how to run a business! When she first started Miller's Coffee Shop in the early 40s, rats – not little wimpy rats, but very large, robust rats – had infested that area on Main Street. Mattie knew for sure that sheltering rats is no way to run a business – especially a café. Although it has been more than 55 years ago, I can still see those scary beady-eyed rodents literally coming out of the woodwork and dancing in the kitchen as soon as Mattie turned the lights off for us to go home at night. She took all kinds of drastic measures to eradicate them, but nothing worked. Being sharp at figuring out how to get something done, she soon realized that until all the businesspeople in the area took the same measures, her singular efforts would be in vain. Mattie immediately put her campaign into action! She visited each businessperson in the area and convinced them all to band together to get rid of the pesky rats.

Leading the successful war on rats added to the growing respect people held for Mattie. The high regard, gratitude, and warm affection people felt toward Mattie was clearly shown by one of her competitors the time she cut her thumb in the meat slicer at the café. Several of the employees wrapped towels around Mattie's thumb, compressing it as much as possible to stop the profuse bleeding. I hurried to get her car and was waiting at the back door with the car running. As the employees helped Mattie into the car, one of Mattie's competitors was returning to her café after going to the bank. She asked me what was going on; I explained what had happened and that we were on our way to the doctor's office. In all the chaos, Grandmother Mattie's comments showed she was obviously worried about filling the orders in her café kitchen. Nevertheless, we dashed away to get her bloodied thumb sewn back together. Soon after we got to the doctor, one of the employees called to check on Mattie and to say that all the orders were being filled and for Mattie to go home after the doctor finished with her. We found out later that the competitor had gone into Mattie's café and hurriedly surveyed the situation. Next she called her café and gave some instructions, and then she took care of the kitchen calamity at Mattie's café. When someone later asked this competitor why she did that, she said, "Well, Mattie would have done it for me." That was the kind of reputation Mattie had earned.

Trusting other people was also a well-known aspect of Mattie's reputation. John Spears, a longstanding resident of Portales, was ordering lunch one day at Grandmother's café when he discovered he had left his billfold at home. He was flustered and embarrassed, but Mattie immediately calmed his ruffled nerves by her own genuine serenity. She told him, "You go ahead and eat whatever you want to…you can pay me back later." He came back the next day for lunch, only with his billfold this time. He paid for both days' lunches. He never forgot his billfold after that, and he never forgot how kindly Mattie treated him that day he had forgotten it.

My brother, Bill Russell, lived in Portales and was struggling to support his young family and to go to college. Mattie rarely charged him for his lunch. She explained she was just glad to see him and visit with him. She had loved Johnny, Bill's father – and mine – for he had been so good to Mattie's youngest daughter – my mother. She told Bill she counted it a privilege that he would come by to see her and that she was pleased to have just a small part in encouraging him to go to college. Grandmother Mattie had a way about her that made people feel OK about accepting her generosity.

Mattie's hospitality extended beyond family. A disoriented homeless man lived in an old car shell in the alley off Main Street. His "home" was not exactly posh with grooming facilities, so he was always rather disheveled. Soon after Mattie had moved her café to a location closer to where the unfortunate man lived, he came to the back door, begging for food. Mattie told him to come on in and sit down. She gave him some food, told him he didn't have to beg for food, and explained, "It is on the house." The grateful man always ordered coffee; in those days a small pitcher of cream was provided with coffee. Mattie told the waitress to always make sure his pitcher was completely full. Furtively, he would look around and when he thought no one was looking, he put the pitcher up to his mouth and swigged down the entire pitcher of cream. Mattie did not want anyone to go away hungry from the community's favorite watering hole.

Mattie understood people of all ages, from the older homeless man to me as a five-year-old. When my two brothers, Phillip and Butch, started school, I was left with no one to play with. Preschools and day care were unheard of in the mid-1940s, and kindergartens were not a part of public schools in New Mexico until about 25 years later. So I stayed with my gandmother at the café and occupied myself behind the counter where the cash register was located. Mattie gave me a small pad of paper like waitresses used to take orders. I happily scribbled for hours on end. When interest waned, I had plenty of empty cigar boxes and coins to play with. In addition, observing the various customers coming to the cash register to pay and listening to their conversations with Mattie frequently captured my attention. Many of them talked to me while Mattie processed their bill. Mattie permitted me to talk to them only if they were truly interested in talking to me – she respected the wishes of her customers. She had a natural knack for getting along with people of all ages and connecting with them.

Most customers were like friends to Mattie. When one particular banker came in for his morning coffee break, he always offered to buy me a cup of coffee. I sat by him at the counter right across from Mattie and the cash register. When this little ritual started, I had to be helped up on the stool. My feet never reached the floor. But I have never felt more grownup in my life. The banker and my grandmother predictably made a big deal out of his paying Mattie a dime for my cup of coffee. The banker also had a lot of fun quizzing me about my coins. He used actual pennies to teach me to count to 100. I soon learned to identify all the coins and how many of each was required to make a dollar. Unforgettable people who were Mattie's friends and customers enriched the lives of many people, including mine.

But life as a kid at the café was not all play, socializing, or learning sessions. Mattie expected me even as a six-year-old – and my older brothers – to assume some responsibilities. One specific task I clearly recall was emptying and cleaning out the ashtrays. In those days just about everyone smoked, or so it seemed. Because my grandmother's café was such a popular "watering hole," numerous groups of two, three, and four people came to the café to enjoy their coffee break – which meant at least one cigarette but probably several and a cup or two of coffee. After they vacated a booth, their ashtrays would be crammed full of crumbly, smelly cigarette butts. Lots of people would even use their coffee cups or saucers to douse smoldering cigarettes. It doesn't take much imagination to understand why I never had a desire to smoke. In addition to this early job contributing to my distinct distaste for nicotine, it reinforced the strong work ethic Mattie valued so highly. Both have served me well over the years.

Life at the café also instilled a sense of family among Mattie's various workers and us kids. Employees helped supervise us wherever we happened to be playing. The alley was one of our favorite places, for it furnished a rich arena of creative opportunities – and a minimum of supervision! One of our favorite activities was throwing rocks at a large metal gate near the backdoor of the café. We tried to out-do each other in the number of rocks we could throw and the level of noise we could create when the rocks hit the metal gate. One time in my fervor I failed to "cease fire" when Phill went to the gate to retrieve more ammunition. One of the big rocks I hurled hit Phill in the back of his head. Naturally, this painful blow to the head unleashed an explosion of anger. To escape Phill's retaliation, I ran into the kitchen of the café, where Abby, one of Grandmother Mattie's longstanding cooks, hid me in a large, industrial-sized Crisco can until Phill's head quit pounding and he called off the search for me. Abby was similar to most of the other employees Mattie hired; they just naturally assumed some responsibility to help supervise us three kids – mostly out of gratitude to our grandmother. She was well known for giving people jobs and in other ways making sure they could feed and care for their own children.

Business flourished at Miller's Coffee Shop. So when Mattie asked the owner of the building to paint and do other refurbishing, he willingly agreed. When the renovation reached a certain stage, Mattie had to shut down her café operation until the project was finished. As soon as the building was ready for the café to start up again, the owner of the building told Mattie he was not going to renew her lease. Instead, he was going to operate a café there himself. Stunned, she floundered only briefly – and then she located an empty building just across the street – still on Main Street, negotiated a lease with the owner, and soon opened another café – the first one officially called Mattie's Café. It was sometimes referred to as the horseshoe café because the one long counter was shaped like a horseshoe. Whatever it was called, this new business thrived. The owner of the building where her prior café was located had assumed he would keep all Mattie's customers. But Mattie's former customers remained loyal to her, and she gained many new ones. The unscrupulous scoundrel got what he deserved – he soon was forced out of business because of lack of customers.

Mattie's employees were hard workers, but they also enjoyed the opportunity to laugh now and then. One time a surly old rancher came into the café and sat down at the counter. My mother, Winnie, went to him with pencil and pad in hand, ready to take his order. He looked around the café and then back at her and said in a voice as dry as his sun-parched skin, "With all the young, good-looking waitresses in here, why do I have to get you?" Winnie's soft blue eyes surveyed the other customers in the café and then peered at him. She said without skipping a beat, "And with all the young, good-looking customers in here, why do I have to get you?" He was bewildered for a few seconds, and then they both burst into laughter. That initial exchange was the beginning of a longstanding friendship and a continuous fun-filled contest to out quip each other.

Another time that a sense of humor provided a chuckle involved Mrs. Miller, consistently serious about giving good service. One of her customers took his ticket – handwritten in those days – to the cash register. He pointed out to Mattie that he had been charged for a B.M., and he elaborated, "I don't think it's appropriate to charge for that." They both looked at the ticket, and sure enough, "1 B.M. 10¢" was written on the ticket. Seeing the two talking and pointing to the ticket, Mrs. Miller sensed she had made a mistake. So she hurried to the cash register. When shown the ticket, she quickly explained, "B. M. is for butter milk." They all enjoyed a good belly laugh.

The cover of Mattie's menus used at the horseshoe café was brief and to the point:

"The Home of Better Foods"

Words were spelled out in the menus, possibly to avoid any embarrassing misunderstandings. For examples, Butter Milk was not abbreviated!

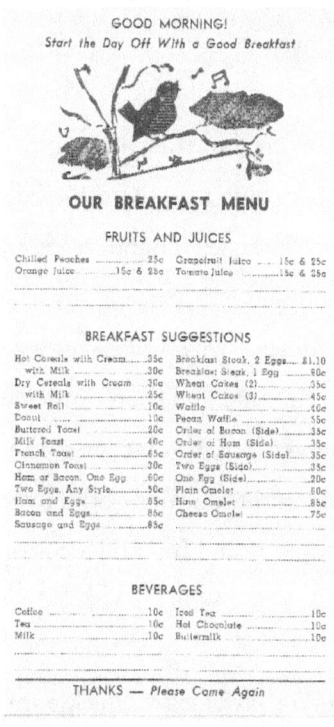

The prices seem especially inviting, particularly in comparison to today's prices.

Inside the menus were listings of the breakfast items and the evening items that always stayed the same. The lunch menu was typed new every day with four or five different specials, like homemade meatloaf, mashed potatoes (no instant potatoes in those days!), garden-fresh green beans, and a tossed salad or red Jell-O with fruit in it. A wide

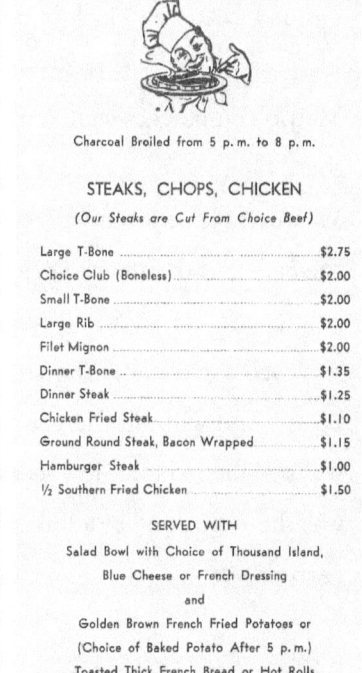

variety of homemade pies was available every day, but a special dessert to accompany the lunch special was different each day. This lunch special ranged from homemade apple cobbler to chocolate cake.

Getting someone who could type the lunch menus was always a challenge. At one time the task fell to me – after I had been in a beginning typing course for about one week. Some of my misspellings were interesting, if not particularly appetizing. For example, one day Mattie was puzzled that no one had ordered fried catfish, generally an all-around favorite. After a customer overheard her expressing her concern, he offered an explanation, "It's not on the menu." Mattie hastily opened a menu and verified that Fried Catfish was not on the menu. But to her shock and dismay a rather disconcerting and distasteful misspelling had taken its place:

Fried Cat with French Fries

No wonder there had been no orders!

A new waitress who declared she could type better than I could soon took over the menu-typing task. But she continued the tradition of funny typos and misspellings — such as her misspelling of Mayonnaise Cake. This moist, mouth-watering chocolate cake was served every four to six weeks – just long enough for her to forget how to spell mayonnaise. After about a year of creative misspellings, one humor-filled customer commented that he had never seen one word spelled so many different ways. I wish I had known then a quote I heard years later; I think it was by Mark Twain:

It's a double dumb person who can think of only one way to spell a word.

Other frequent misspellings included Desert for Dessert, French Fires for French Fries, and Chicken Fried Sneak or Chicken Fired Steak for Chicken Fried Steak.

Like Dan Quail, the new typist had a problem back in those days with the singular and plural of potato. If you would type Mashed Potatoes, why wouldn't you type an "e" in Baked Potato? Grandmother was patient with all the gallant but poor spellers who tried to type the menus, and the fun we had with the menus' creative spelling added to the congeniality of the community's favorite "watering hole."

Liquor was not an item you would find on the menu at Mattie's Café. The main reason was that Roosevelt County was voted "dry" in 1909 and stayed that way until 1975, when a community vote ended prohibition after 66 years. Mattie did not protest prohibition as most other café owners did, for she believed that excellent food and service should be the main attraction in a café. In addition, she simply didn't care for alcoholic beverages herself.

However, Mattie did have a much-used whiskey cake recipe that was a family favorite – she never served it at any of her cafes. The combined memories of several relatives say this is Grandmother Mattie's Whiskey Cake recipe:

3 cups sugar
1 cup shortening
6 eggs
3 cups flour
1 cup sour milk (1 cup milk + 1 tablespoon lemon juice)
1/4 tsp soda
2 - 4 tablespoons whiskey
1/4 to 1/2 cup of chopped walnuts

Cream shortening and sugar. Add eggs one at a time, stirring thoroughly after each egg is added. Add flour and milk alternately. Add chopped nuts and mix only until well distributed. Put in greased and floured Bundt pan or 9x13 cake pan. Bake 1 hour at 350. Allow to cool slightly before removing from the Bundt pan or cutting. Sprinkle with powdered sugar.

Although our grandmother's Whiskey Cake was a far cry from a family secret, she still hid the bottle of whiskey in the bathroom closet behind the clean washcloths. We often wondered why she bothered to hide the bottle because the hiding place was well known. She once explained, "It's just the principle of it." That was just the way she was – a very principled person.

Also as a matter of principle, all Mattie's cafes had some things in common. Mouth-watering, home-cooked food could always be counted on as could "Service with a Smile." Her cafes were always sparkling clean; she required standards higher than those imposed by the county health department. Serving a customer a cup with lipstick stain or a glass with water spots on it was considered right up there with the worst of sins. Another predictable feature – you could always be sure there would be pots of ivy – lush, deep green, beautiful heart-shaped philodendron. I can remember several large decorative containers at one time on a long shelf; the ivy covered a large portion of one wall and grew all the way to the ceiling. Grandmother nurtured that ivy as carefully as she did her children, her grandkids, her customers. The plants were watered continuously and ceremoniously – with the leftover tea from each day, and the leaves were cleaned before they actually started showing the dust and grease (or whatever collects on ivy leaves). The leaf-cleaning ritual had to be carried out on Sunday afternoon when the café was closed because it required standing on the cabinet top to reach the leaves. In addition, cleaning each leaf individually was extremely time-consuming.

Mattie was willing to spend the time and effort – down to the last philodendron leaf – to create a place people enjoyed gathering and eating. Because she worked in her café six days a week, visiting friends and relatives ate at the café. Mattie loved nothing better than having the back booth or two full of relatives ordering from the menus whatever they wanted. Of course, they didn't pay, for Mattie considered her café her extended home kitchen. She was known to say on occasion if a relative offered to pay, "It's on the house."

Mattie's customers were also like her extended family. While she worked hard to make sure her café provided good food and good service, she gained a deep sense of satisfaction from pleasing others and being surrounded by fun-loving, happy individuals. The good money she made in the café business was important to her – she didn't want to ever again have to ask anyone for a

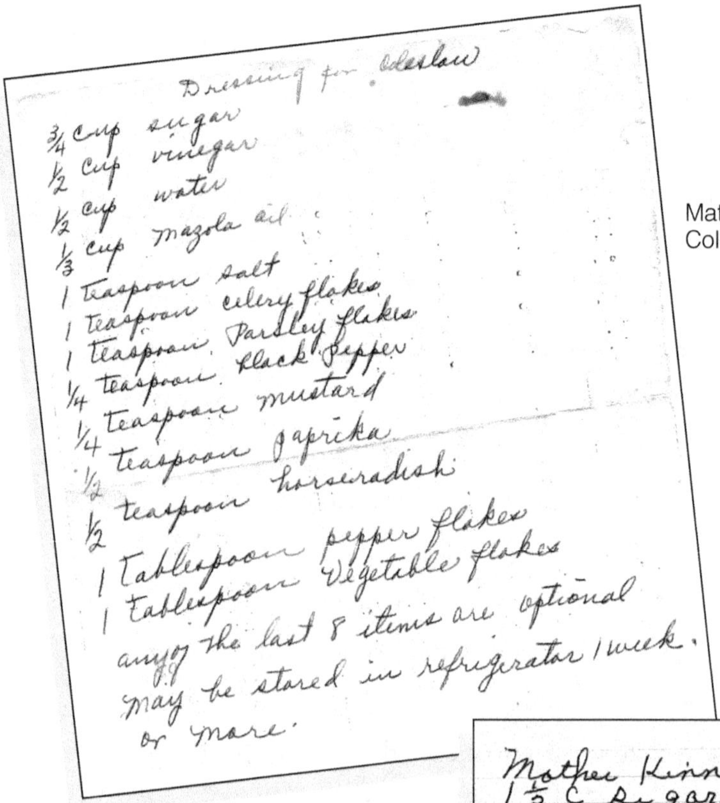

Dressing for Coleslaw

3/4 cup sugar
1/2 cup vinegar
1/2 cup water
1/3 cup mazola oil
1 teaspoon salt
1 teaspoon celery flakes
1 teaspoon parsley flakes
1 teaspoon black pepper
1/4 teaspoon mustard
1/4 teaspoon paprika
1/2 teaspoon horseradish
1 Tablespoon pepper flakes
1 Tablespoon vegetable flakes

the last 8 items are optional

may be stored in refrigerator 1 week or more.

Mattie's large quantity recipe for Coleslaw dressing in her handwriting

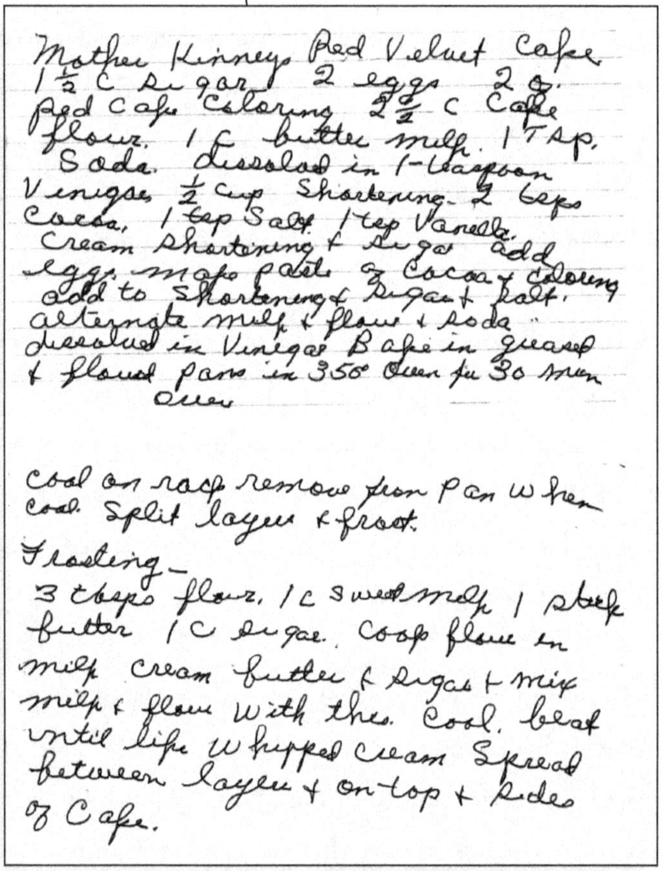

Mattie's Red Velvet Cake recipe

Mother Kinney's Red Velvet Cake

1 1/2 C sugar, 2 eggs, 2 oz. Red Cake Coloring, 2 1/2 C Cake flour, 1 C buttermilk, 1 Tsp. Soda dissolved in 1 teaspoon vinegar, 1/2 cup Shortening, 2 tsps Cocoa, 1 tsp Salt, 1 tsp Vanilla. Cream shortening & sugar add eggs, make paste of Cocoa & Coloring add to Shortening & Sugar & Salt. Alternate milk & flour & soda dissolved in vinegar. Bake in greased & floured pans in 350° oven for 30 min.

Cool on rack remove from pan when cool. Split layers & frost.

Frosting—
3 tbsps flour, 1 C sweet milk, 1 stick butter, 1 C sugar. Cook flour in milk cream butter & sugar & mix milk & flour with this. Cool. beat until like whipped cream Spread between layers & on top & sides of Cake.

nickel for a spool of thread! But people were the most important. She truly cared for people, and their affection and respect for her met a deep, heartfelt need.

St. Augustine used a beautiful phrase, *ordo amonrum*, the order of loves. The most important thing you do in life is choose your loves and prioritize them very carefully. Even though Mattie loved her café – the work, the people, the money – her children were her first love. Leroy recounted the time he got sick as a young teenager and could hardly walk up the stairs to the doctor's office. The doctor quickly diagnosed his problem and prescribed extended rest as well as medicine. Never giving it a second thought, Mattie gave up the lease on her café to stay at home to take care of Leroy. As Leroy put it, "That's the kind of mother she was."

After Leroy's recovery, Mattie opened a new café. Her former customers and many new ones flocked there to enjoy the good home-style cooking, including mouth-watering homemade pies as usual. She kept her commitment; her café was once again "The Home of Better Food in Town."

As the three grandchildren and their spouses looked at the menus at Mattie's in Decatur that day in May, 2004, the slogans on the menu reminded them of all the reasons their grandmother's cafes were always successful – "the best home-style cooking," "the best coffee," "the friendliest service," etc. As the family researchers enjoyed their meal, they summarized Grandmother Mattie's intriguing café history, starting with The Little Brick Front Café she and Harve established in 1929 in Portales.

This small cafe was an inauspicious beginning of the legendary reputation she built over the next nearly 40 years. Although she was "second in charge" to Harve, she got plenty of on-the-job training that served her well in the subsequent years. She instinctively was a good cook, and her basic personality reflected qualities needed to manage a business – she was a hard worker and congenial, and her warmth attracted people. She continued to learn as she and Harve managed additional cafes, including Our Place in Clovis and a small café in Cloudcroft called the Café on Main Street.

The tallest building was our grandmother's last café — Mattie's Café, located on Second Street across the street from the Court House. Photo by Phill Russell

After Harve died, Mattie worked several different times for Harve's son, Roscoe, owner of the Liberty Café in Portales. She then leased a small café and did quite well. In early 1941 she leased what was called the Chevrolet House Café located where the Roosevelt County Telephone Cooperative parking lot is now located. Next, she leased Miller's Coffee Shop, located on Main Street two stores down from where the First National Bank was located at that time. In 1951 she lost the building lease on Miller's Coffee Shop but soon opened the first café that was officially called Mattie's Café; it was also on Main Street, just across the street from Miller's. Business was so good that within a couple of years Grandmother needed a larger building; in 1953 she found just the place.

The Second Street location was home of Mattie's Café for nearly 15 years – until she closed the café and retired in 1967. In 1999 the Roosevelt [café] opened in the same location as Mattie's last café.

The Grand Opening of Mattie's Café on Second Street. From left to right, Nellie Moss, Winnie, and Mattie.

While Mattie closed her café, she did not "retire" the heartwarming memories or the values and lessons learned in her various cafes for nearly 40 years. In 1979, friends, relatives, and former employees helped our grandmother celebrate her 83rd birthday party at the First National Bank in Portales.

Everyone was reminded of the fun-filled "café days" when every Mattie's Café was the favorite "watering hole" of the community. A nephew, O. J. Smith, put a Mattie's Café sign up for all to enjoy, and someone used a crayon to write on it: "Free Coffee."

MATTIE AND FAMLY: Sons and daughters of Mattie Kinney help her celebrate her 83rd birthday. From left, Mrs. Lillie Johnson, Paul Creek, Mattie Kinney, Winnie Luttrell, Leroy Creek, and Juanita Chumbley.

Mattie's Cafe reopens in Portales for an 83rd birthday celebration

The cousins and their spouses in Decatur savored the memories of that birthday party – Charlene had traveled as far as 1600 miles to join the birthday celebration. Someone at the party asked Mattie why people still remembered her and cared so much for her. Taken back a little by all the fanfare, she modestly mentioned how blessed she had been and how thankful she was for all her friends and relatives.

Someone else asked the question a different way, "What do you think the secret for your success has been?" She considered the question a moment and then replied; her answer truly reflected her life – at home and at every café she worked at, managed, or owned:

Because I always tried to treat people right.

Chapter Nine:
HOW ABOUT A CUP OF COFFEE?
(1940 - 1980s)

Family stories reveal our family values, character, and personality.
They connect our past to the present, and they can shape the kind of person we become.
— Helen Armstrong
Successful businesswoman, political activist, daughter of first mayor
of Portales, New Mexico, and first governor of New Mexico – and Mattie's friend

Sitting around Grandmother Mattie's kitchen table or in the assorted chairs and sofa in her cozy living room and hearing the rich chords of stories spun by various family members are among my most treasured memories. As I think of some of my favorite stories of growing up with my grandmother, other memories from the past come rushing back. The scenes, sounds, and smell of these memories always include each adult sipping a cup of freshly brewed coffee. So kick back with a cup of hot coffee and enjoy these rather random recollections that reveal the remarkable flavor of who Mattie was, what she was like, and why she endeared herself to everyone who knew her.

THE WAY GRANDMOTHER MATTIE LIKED HER HEROES

Mattie was a hero to many, but she declined to accept accolades. In contrast, she loved talking about her heroes. And she had some. Anyone who had overcome great hardships to search out a new and better homeland was her hero. She recounted how the Deatherages immigrated to America. She shared stories her mother passed down of the McPeak clan immigrating from Scotland. Mattie fervently believed that America was the greatest place to live, and she was grateful for her ancestors and those of Lewis who had braved the treacherous unknown and made their way to America. Her father and mother were also her heroes; they moved from Mississippi, to Arkansas, to Texas and then struggled to homestead in New Mexico in hopes of a better life for themselves and for their children.

Anyone who served in the military was Mattie's hero. Defending America was a noble legacy, according to Mattie, and she said she would be forever grateful to all the people willing to risk their lives to serve their country and whose acts of bravery permitted the rest of us to live so bountifully. Mattie heard stories from various people about the atrocities in other countries including a scared refugee she had hired to work at her café in spite of criticism from some of her customers. Mattie loved the many military people from the air base near Portales; they flocked to her café for homemade food and a friendly family atmosphere. Knowing Christine and numerous military people made WWII even more personal for Mattie. She urged them all to tell their stories so that future generations might learn from them.

Mattie was especially proud of family members who served in the military – her two sons, Paul and Leroy, and several grandchildren, and she considered them heroes. She loved their courage, their dedication to ideals, and their commitment to our country. But neither of her two sons nor any of her grandchildren saw themselves as heroes. They had a deep and abiding gratitude for our country, and all of them considered serving it a privilege. Grandmother Mattie concluded,

I like that in a hero.

ART APPRECIATION

In the days before leash laws, dogs ran freely through the neighborhoods of Portales. This was also before the days of food disposals, so trash barrels were used for all household discards, including food. Searching for tasty morsels of food, dogs often turned over the trash barrels, scattering the barrel's contents all over the alley. The wind helped spread the contents even more.

Dogs also often left their gnawing bones in Mattie's grass, causing an awful commotion when the lawn mower hit them. Mattie was particularly perturbed when she found an old sun-bleached, weathered cow skull in her front yard. Along with other unseemly items left by the roaming dogs, she promptly tossed the skull in the trash barrel in the alley. I remember her commenting, "I wonder when the dogs will drag up the rest of the bones from that dead cow!"

A few days later an article appeared in the local newspaper. It featured a local artist whose most recent artistic accomplishment was his newly landscaped lawn in a Southwestern theme, replete with desert rocks, desert plants, and sun-bleached bones. The proud owner-artist reported that the centerpiece of his masterpiece – a sun-bleached skull – had had been stolen by some "rotten, lowdown cow thief."

Incredulous, Mattie hurriedly retrieved the skull from her trash barrel and returned it to its rightful owner, who lived only a few blocks away. She explained to the grateful artist that the "rotten, lowdown cow thief" was actually a dog who had delivered the skull to her lawn, and she was returning it.

"Besides," she commented, "I lack the art appreciation that such a valuable artifact like that deserves."

Mattie was really good at diplomacy.

DRESSING THE CHICKENS

Brenda remembers the time something happened with Grandmother Mattie that reflected both a communication gap and a generation gap. When Brenda and Janet were quite young, Mattie decided she was going to raise some chickens. Back then fresh or frozen chickens were not as readily available in stores as they are now.

Grandmother Mattie feeding chickens on the Price Ranch in about 1936

Mattie had a lot of experience with chickens; she grew up raising them with the ultimate goal of feasting on luscious fried chicken, savory chicken and dumplings, and tasty chicken pot pie. Mattie ordered several large boxes of little chickens – tiny chicks with soft, fluffy, yellow "down" all over them. The girls were ecstatic when grandmother told them they could help her raise those baby chickens and dress them when "they get big enough." Brenda thought, "Nothing is cuter than a baby chicken!" She and Janet looked forward to their trips to their grandmother's house so they could check on how those baby chickens were growing.

Mattie kept the chicks in the boxes until they outgrew them, and then she rigged up a fence on the back porch to keep them. Eventually the chickens grew too big for the back porch, so Mattie moved them to the cellar. Brenda said, "Those chickens made the biggest mess down there…I wasn't as excited about them as I was in the beginning. But when Grandmother reminded us that we were going to get to help dress them when they got big enough, we helped feed and water them with renewed enthusiasm."

Eventually the chickens outgrew the basement, so Mattie transferred them out to the little room built onto the garage. With each move, the girls wondered when the time would ever arrive when the chickens would be "big enough." Finally, the time arrived! Mattie invited Brenda and Janet to spend the night with her so they could get an early start the next morning to dress those chickens.

Janet, Grandmother, and Brenda

Brenda described what happened that long awaited day:

> *Grandmother grabbed those chickens, and she'd wring their necks until their heads pulled off. Then she'd throw them over in a basket…they were jumping around and some of them flopping clear out of the basket and flailing around and plopping into each other.*

> *The next challenge was plucking off their feathers. Janet was really getting tired of it all and could hardly pluck any feathers at all. Grandmother finally said to her, "Now you told me you'd help me dress these chickens."*

> *Totally perplexed, Janet replied, "I thought you meant we were gonna' put some clothes on them."*

I never knew whether to classify this incident as a communication gap or a generation gap – or both! Whatever, Janet, Brenda, and Grandmother Mattie laughed with each other about it for years afterward.

SOUND CAREER COUNSELING

Mattie took great pride in "turning off a lot of work." Examples of her phenomenal skill and speed were legendary. For example, she held the record for cutting up chickens – wielding a sharp knife, she cut up a flock of chickens in an unbelievable short time. I don't know if she set the record with the same chickens that Brenda and Janet thought they were going to dress or not. Years after Grandmother Mattie's record-setting feat, I offered to cut up a chicken in preparation for dinner. My grandmother's disappointment in my poor performance was superseded only by my sense of relief that she assigned me to some other work I was more fitted for.

I don't remember what that other "work" was, but I do recall when a few years after my cutting-up-a-chicken fiasco Grandmother Mattie was helping me with my college human anatomy class. To assist me in learning the names of all the human body parts – muscles, bones, organs, etc. – she would hold up a flash card and I would try to match appropriate bits of information. She expressed her amusement that a collar bone couldn't be called just that but rather had to be called a scapula, and that "your sitting down place" (a phrase she used when threatening to use a willow switch to encourage better behavior) had a variety of names, depending on the specific area, like gluteus maximus.

Feeling quite pompous after one study session, I announced that with my great mastery of all these medical terms, I might just become a surgeon. My grandmother took one skeptical look at me and made her own kindhearted, kidding analysis, "You might know all these highfalutin words, but if you couldn't cut up a human body any better and faster than you can cut up a chicken, I believe I'd find me another surgeon."

Mattie was always good at using practical application to make her point. I took her advice – I did not become a surgeon.

MAKE DO, OR DO WITHOUT

Mattie and her five kids saw a lot of changes in their lives. They grew up before every family had one or more television sets in their home. They grew up without pantyhose, credit cards, facelifts, tummy tucks, and hair transplants. Grandmother and her family wouldn't have been able to afford many of the new developments anyway. So she taught her kids to *make do or do without* – one of her favorite sayings. Mattie said she sometimes wondered if all her well-intentioned teaching was "soaking in."

But one time when Winnie was grown and working for Grandmother Mattie at the café, she knew Winnie had learned one lesson well. It was 1952 when Christine Jorgenson had a sex change operation. Everyone at the café was talking about it, freely expressing their various opinions. Noticing that Winnie was intent but had said nothing, Mattie asked her daughter what she thought about the first-ever sex change operation. Without altering her somber facial expression, she turned her head from side to side in wonderment and commented, "Well, I wouldn't even consider having it done." She then concluded, "You always taught us to *make do or do without.*"

SWEAT IT OUT

Mattie earned a medical degree from personal experiences treating five children and numerous grandchildren to adulthood. She prescribed sassafras tea in the springtime to "thin your blood." She prescribed black draught in the fall to "build up your blood." She prescribed castor oil any time of the year to "clean you out." But the wonder drug of all seasons was a cure-all toddy. She squeezed a lemon until every smidgeon of juice had dripped to the bottom of a large coffee mug. Then she carefully measured two tablespoons of honey into the mug. Then not so carefully, she poured in a plentiful portion of whiskey. She waited for the hottest water she could get from the faucet and added enough of it to fill the cup to the brim.

As Mattie gave her full attention to getting the remedy ready, she also instructed the patient to get ready for bed. After swigging down the hot, stinging concoction as fast as humanly possible, the patient got in bed and covered up – and sweat it out!

I sweat it out many times, and always felt better in the morning. I think the love and concern Grandmother Mattie served with her cure-all toddy was a vital ingredient of the miraculous cure. I still use this tried-and-true toddy on occasion. When I think about my grandmother's tried-and-true love and concern, the toddy works even better.

CLIMB EVERY MOUNTAIN

In 1963 I continued to carry out Grandmother Mattie's dream for all her grandchildren – to get an education! After graduating from Eastern New Mexico University in June, I headed for Oakland, California, where I would do graduate work at Mills College. Grandmother went with me to "make the trip," as she put it, and to help me "settle in." On the way to Oakland, we stopped in Fresno to visit friends, who took us to see the giant redwood trees in Sequoia National Forest. We enjoyed the drive on The Generals Highway, which climbed over 5,000 feet from chaparral and oak-studded foothills. My grandmother and I were in complete awe as we began driving among trees larger than either of us could ever have imagined; they were beautiful and impressive. Having come from the high wind-swept, treeless plains of Eastern New Mexico, we both were amazed.

Judging the size of the giant sequoias was difficult because neighboring trees were so large. But the largest of the sequoias are as tall as an average 26-story building, and their diameters at the base exceed the width of many city streets. The ages of the General Sherman, General Grant, and other large sequoias are unknown, but a park ranger told us that these giants are between 1800 and 2700 years old. They had seen civilization come and go, survived countless fires and long periods of drought, but continued to flourish. They were tributes to determination, persistence, and the sheer will to survive. Inspired by the beauty and the tenacity of these giant trees, we joined the group in excitement to climb to even greater heights – to a favorite lookout. A little past halfway up, Grandmother Mattie said breathlessly that she would sit on one of the benches and wait for us on the way down. After all, she was 67 years old at the time.

Finally the rest of us reached our destination, and the view was breathtaking! We could see for miles – layers of mountains and even the tops of some of the giant redwoods. Absolutely exhausted, I was relieved that everyone wanted to enjoy the view for awhile. As I was still grasping for breath, we heard a lone hiker coming around the bend and up to the lookout. It was my grandmother! She was walking slowly but steadily. When she realized that everyone was looking at her in complete surprise, she offered this explanation, "I just had to stop a minute and get my second wind." Captivated by the magnificent view, she chimed in with the group, "This view made the climb worth every step."

This example of Grandmother Mattie's gumption came in handy to me the next several years as I met the challenge of living more than 1000 miles from my hometown, learning my way around the San Francisco-Oakland area (a far cry from my small, friendly New Mexico hometown of Portales, population, 15,000). Even more gumption was required to cope with the academic demands of a very competitive graduate school and launching into the scary job market. Sometimes I wanted to give up, stop, and turn around and go back home.

Every time I would get discouraged, I thought of my grandmother climbing that mountain. Like her, I simply stopped long enough to get my second wind, knowing that the climb to the top would be worth every step.

Grandmother Mattie's grit and gumption in various situations throughout her life also inspired countless others.

THE TELLTALE COW CHIPS

Mattie and Charlie had a special relationship. Reasons might have included Charlie's enthusiasm for life, his sense of humor, and his knack for figuring things out, for Mattie admired these traits in anyone. One of her favorite stories demonstrating these characteristics in Charlie happened on Crow Mountain, Arkansas, when someone ran over Charlie and Lillie's new mailbox and demolished it. Charlie had a suspicion who the guilty culprit was, but he called the sheriff to handle the case. When the law

Charlie and Mumsie

officers concluded they did not have enough evidence to pursue Charlie's lead, Charlie showed them the clues that would solve the crime – some cow chips.

The law officers hooted at Charlie, the self-appointed detective. But their disdain was short-lived. Charlie picked up various pieces of cow chips scattered all over his front yard; he reasoned that the impact of the vehicle hitting the mailbox had thrown them from the truck bed. The officers and Charlie drove to the home of Charlie's suspect. Sure enough, the very distinctive cow chips Charlie had collected from his front yard "matched" the cow chips remaining in the suspect's pickup. It was obvious Charlie's cow chips had to have come from the suspect's pickup. Mystery solved. Key clues? Telltale cow chips.

Grandmother Mattie shared this telltale-cow-chips story whenever a good laugh was needed or whenever a person was struggling with a problem and needed a reminder to look at all the possible clues to a solution. Usually the only prompting required was Mattie's simply saying, "Telltale cow chips…."

QUEEN FOR A DAY
Uncle Charlie's cow-chip tale reminds me of another cow-chip story – a story Mattie never tired of telling. Aunt Ruby was only 16 when her father, Harve, and Grandmother married. Aunt Ruby was a congenial, likeable person, and she always said that Mattie was the best step-mother in the world. The two became close, life-long friends. When Aunt Ruby retired from cooking for Mattie's Café, she moved to California to be near several of her children who had moved there from New Mexico.

Aunt Ruby's children nominated her to appear on the popular program, "Queen for a Day." Her story was indeed heart tugging. Her mother had died when she was a young teenager, and her husband died an early death, leaving her with five children to rear. She had struggled to keep her fledgling family together. Out of countless applicants and nominees, she was selected to appear on the show; she told the host that what she wanted most was a new "cook stove." She described how her old one was worn out and required a stick to keep the door closed. She also told him about her early cooking experiences, including cooking on the kind of stove that used cow chips for fuel. The California city-slicker show host was astonished; he asked her what she would do if a piece of the burning cow chip landed in whatever she was cooking. In her slow, easy-going manner, she explained, "Why, I'd just take my spoon and flick it out." Simple as that! Aunt Ruby won out over all the other contestants that day and was proclaimed "Queen for a Day!" She went home with a new "cook stove" and many other prizes.

Mattie always enjoyed seeing deserving people receive something they wanted, and she particularly liked this cow chips-to-glory story.

DON'T ASK TOO MANY QUESTIONS

Like Mattie, I loved Aunt Ruby. I am convinced that Aunt Ruby and her Creek clan had immense influence on my husband's decision to ask me to marry him. Let me explain. During the summer of 1965 I had gone to Orange, California, to teach at Chapman College there. Del was stationed at nearby El Toro Marine Corps base. One of my Eastern New Mexico University professors had retired and moved with her husband to La Jolla, California. She invited me to visit her and her husband. While I was there, she described her husband's nephew as a handsome Texan, an intelligent University of Texas graduate, and "on the road" to a promising financial future as a Marine Corps officer. She asked if I'd like to meet him. Being 24 and single, I tried to avoid appearing overeager as I said, "Yes."

The first date with the nephew, Del, was very enjoyable, so he asked me out again – for the same evening I had told Aunt Ruby I would come to dinner at her house in nearby Pomona for a mini-family reunion. Or, as she put it, "to see all her kids and her kids' kids." I knew I would enjoy visiting with Aunt Ruby and her family. I had grown to like all of them in New Mexico before they moved to California. In addition, I knew Del and I both would enjoy the good home cooking the Creeks were well known for. So on our second date, we went to Aunt Ruby's.

It was love at first sight! Del loved the Creeks, and they loved him. And for anyone who liked good food, well, that was simply a bonus. Del had just returned from a year's military assignment in Japan, so the home-cooked food was "a sight for sore eyes," as he put it. The mounds of delicious fried chicken, mashed potatoes (the real thing), rivers of gravy, fresh green beans, crisp tossed salad, and tantalizing desserts to choose from went straight to his heart.

For years Grandmother Mattie enjoyed teasing me about taking an eligible bachelor to Aunt Ruby's on our second date. Being an extraordinarily good cook herself, she commended me for recognizing the truth in the saying, "The way to a man's heart is through his stomach." Del and I have been married more than 40 years, and he has always said it was love at first sight. I have never asked Del if he is referring to me – or to Aunt Ruby and our family of good cooks.

Mattie always said, "Don't ask too many questions."

Del and Barbara in 2005 when they celebrated their 40th wedding anniversary

HITTING THE ROAD

Before Uncle Jim assumed the responsibility for hauling away the cream cans full of "slop" from the café, Granddad hauled them away in his early 1930s Chevy. How a hole appeared in the floor of the back seat of this old car, no one ever knew. And no one knew till years later why Phillip and Butch kept wearing holes in the soles of their shoes. But the truth finally came out. The boys admitted they were always eager to ride with Granddad so they could make great sport of sticking one leg at a time out the hole and bouncing a foot along the pavement. Fortunately, Granddad drove only about 15 miles per hour. The boys also enjoyed poking a tree branch through the hole and dragging it along the pavement. When Grandmother Mattie heard about the stick, she heaved a sigh of relief. "Well, I'd rather you wear out your shoes than use a stick…that stick could've hit something and ricocheted into your eyes!"

Our grandmother had a refreshing habit of finding something good in every situation.

A BAR BOUNCER

Paul told this story about Grandmother Mattie: *Mother's niece was married to a fellow from Elida, and he was bad about drinking. This fellow and his wife had their first baby at the hospital in Portales, and he came into town to take his wife and baby home. However, he had been celebrating just a little too much. The inebriated new father turned his car over on the curve at Lilac Park about two blocks from where we lived in the Price house. Carrying the new baby, the new mother walked the two blocks to our house. She handed the baby over to Mother, who had been heating flat irons on a big, red-hot pot-bellied stove. The new father said he was going to take his wife and the new baby home. Very drunk, he grabbed for the baby. Mother hit him with the flat iron and knocked him back into stove butt-first. I can still smell his scorched pants!*

Saloon in early days of Portales, Tye Terrell Collection, E.N.M.U. Special Collections

Believe it or not, after that, Mother was always one of his favorite people.

People liked Grandmother Mattie because she had a special knack for helping them do the right thing – whether they wanted to or not.

FORGIVE AND FORGET

Leroy tells this story: *My friend, Bob Sparks, and I decided that we'd take a trip to Hobbs. We got down there and ran out of money. But we wanted to stay another night or two and were considering hitchhiking over to Carlsbad. I thought, "I'll send Mother a wire and ask her to wire me a couple of dollars so we can have a little eating money."*

Paul, Mattie, and Leroy

Our country was in the midst of WWII, and Paul was in the Navy and somewhere in the South Pacific in a submarine. Mother had not heard from him for nearly three months. Someone told me later that when she received my telegram, she nearly fainted – someone else had to read it to her. She just knew it was bad news from the government. Well, I lucked out – it was a good thing I wasn't in Portales, for she was so mad at me that she would've killed me!

Like many teenagers, I didn't even consider what her reaction would be when I sent that telegram. All I knew was that I needed $2.00 to get home on.

Leroy added, "I'll never forget how bad I felt about hurting Mother…I've regretted it all my life."

Even though Leroy never forgot this incident, his mother forgave him – completely. That's the way Mattie was; she was never one to hold a grudge.

JUST CALL ME GRANDDAD

"What's in a name?" a famous poet once said. "That which we call a rose by any other name would smell as sweet." But could a boy named Leo Elmer be happy with his name? My youngest brother was given this name at birth, but he has always been called Butch. Many of my cousins were called by nicknames – for examples, Linda was called PeeWee, Charlene was Noonie, Lea Norris was Norcie, and Lewis was called Bo. My nicknames included Jody Blond, JoJo, and B.J. These nicknames seemed to fall away as we all grew older and we assumed our "real" names, at least outside the family.

That is, every nickname but Butch. As a little boy when Butch asked Grandmother Mattie why he was named Leo Elmer, she explained that the Leo was after his father's brother who had died as a young man and the Elmer was after Granddad. Not favorably impressed by being named after a young dead man and an alive older man, Butch asked in as grown-up voice as he could muster, "Why didn't you just name me "Granddad"?

Always with a chuckle, Grandmother Mattie loved telling that story. No one ever asked, "What's in a name?" But Mattie, like everyone else, continued to call this grandson by his nickname, Butch. He just wouldn't be the same if called by the name Leo Elmer – or Granddad.

A TOUGH BANKER

Harve was a very generous man. Even though at times he, like many men in the 20s and 30s, had little cash, he would help out a person who asked for a loan. One particular man was known to play on Harve's sympathy, and he owed Harve money when Harve died. This borrower recovered financially, and one day Grandmother Mattie reminded him of his debt. He replied, "Harve loaned me that money, not you." Grandmother retorted, "…and you didn't pay Harve either."

Mattie was also willing to help people if they needed a little cash to make it to payday. One time she commented that not once had any of her employees failed to repay her. Unfortunately, this was neither true of the scoundrel that owed Harve money nor of a few relatives. One particular relative asked Mattie for money with the promise that she would pay it back. But she did not repay it. Then she asked for another loan. Mattie gave it to her. Again, no repayment. When the relative asked for a third loan, Mattie did not give it to her, and she told her why. Mattie was generous, but she was not going to let anyone take advantage of her generosity.

"Besides," she commented, "not holding people to their commitment to repay a loan is not really doing them a favor. People need to learn to honor their commitments."

Another one of Mattie's invaluable lessons.

A TENDER HEART

When it came to kids, Mattie admittedly had a tender spot in her heart. When I was in high school, an organization I belonged to planned a recognition service for outstanding members. My responsibility was to arrange for the awards. So I selected some pretty sterling silver trinkets, or charms, for the award winners to wear on their charm bracelets. "Woody" Woodward, owner of the longstanding, popular Woody's Jewelry had them engraved soon after I told him the award winners' names and initials. As treasurer, another girl was responsible for collecting a small fee from the membership to pay for the awards and engraving. I asked her several times for the money, but finally it was time to pick up the engraved trinkets – and to pay for them. Still no money from the club treasurer. Finally she told me she didn't have the money but offered no explanation.

When I told Grandmother Mattie about the situation, she said we would drive me out to her house to get the money. I told the girl of our plans, and she was visibly shaken but said nothing. When we arrived at the house, Mattie and I were astounded. The house was a shack, and the surroundings matched it well. The mother answered our knock on the door. Although she seemed embarrassed, she graciously invited us to come in. My schoolmate was setting the table; the food was meager and the dishes austere. Both mother and daughter searched for something to say. The mother finally broke the awful silence. "Thank you for being my girl's friend," she said to me.

This comment left me speechless. So the mother turned her attention to Mattie; they talked just enough for us to recognize that the mother did not realize why we had come to their house. Mattie and I both had almost forgotten. The mother then said, "I understand you have a café…do you need a good hand? I can wash dishes."

With no hesitancy whatsoever, Mattie said, "Yes, I do. When can you start?"

The woman replied, "As soon as I can figure out my transportation."

"If you can find a way to get to work, I can give you a ride home after the café is closed," Mattie offered.

Before we left, Mattie had a much-needed dishwasher. When we got in the car to return home, I asked her, "What about the money?"

With her eyes intent on the narrow, unpaved road to the main highway, Mattie said matter-of-factly, "I will pay for the charms." Then she gave me a sideways glance and advised, "Next time – get the money up front."

The older I get, the wiser Grandmother Mattie becomes. Hardly a day goes by that I don't remember or rely on something she taught me – money-wise and heart-wise.

THE BEST FATHER I NEVER KNEW

I was only eight months old when my father was killed. Yet, it seems I knew him, because his memory reflected forcefully from the memories of those who did know him. Grandmother Mattie, Mother, and other family members who knew Johnny – as he was affectionately called – made it clear to me that if you love people and continue to talk about them, even in death, they are never out of your life.

Johnny in his customary cowboy clothes

When Mattie married Mr. Kinney and moved to the Price Ranch, Johnny came into the life of my mother's family. Johnny's family lived in the area, and he worked on the Price Ranch. "Those times when we lived on the Price Ranch run deep in my memory," Mattie recalled. "And Johnny was a catalyst of those times, those memories."

Completing her junior year of high school, my mother, Winnie, moved to Price Ranch for the summer. When school started in the fall, she lived in town to work but returned to the ranch for weekends. She soon was smitten by the handsome cowboy and his "two darling boys" (her words). Johnny was a widower – his wife had died tragically before her sons were even old enough to gather memories of her.

Winnie was especially struck with how kind and encouraging he was with his two motherless sons. But Mother soon discovered that Johnny was kind and encouraging to everyone – even the less than motivated unskilled ranch hands he was given charge over. He taught by example that people come first in this world and you should treat others the way you would like to be treated. Be fair and honorable – not because you will get something out of it, but – just like Mattie, because it is the right thing to do.

Kindness had always been easy for Johnny, he explained, but it became easier after his first wife died. He valued life and relationships even more, knowing how fragile life is and how quickly relationships can be ended. Mother said he always spoke with reverence and affection for his wife, and he tried to tell his sons about their talented and beautiful mother. After Johnny was killed, my mother said she tried to follow his example. In addition, Mattie made a special point of telling us about all the qualities that made him special to them and to many others.

Johnny loved music. Although money was scarce – almost non-existent, he and a brother together bought a Victrola, an old-fashioned windup record player. He played the limited number of records with great enjoyment, coaxing everyone to sing along with the words of favorite ballads such as "Strawberry Roan," "When the Work Is All Done this Fall," "Riding Free on the Old SP," and "Tumbling Tumble Weeds."

Love of music was matched only by love of reading. Johnny's passion for reading was a little easier to nurture than was his love of music, for books were prized and passed around from one family member to another. To have one's own books "for keeps" was a special treat. Bob, Johnny's older son by his first marriage, remembers well his father getting him some books, including *Billy Goat Gruff Goes to the World Fair*.

Talking about the books he'd read – the people in them and the ideas – stirred Johnny up, as Mother put it. And when Johnny was "stirred up," people just naturally wanted to join in the discussion and to explore why people did what they did, how they could've done it better, what the important things in life are, and other significant issues.

Johnny also revered nature – the whole encompassing gift of the world of soil and grass, and trees, and sky, and animals. Once Grandmother Mattie took me riding out near the ranch where Johnny grew up, worked, and died. I just wanted to see the views my father saw in his last days on earth.

My mother, Winnie, was no stranger to death when she married Johnny. His two little boys reminded her of how her own father had died before she could remember him, and the two little boys reminded her of her two half brothers, Paul and Leroy, who were only slightly older when their father, Harve, died. Mother marveled how Johnny had been able to put the pain in the past but at the same time try to keep the memory of the boys' mother alive for them. Then after he was killed, Mother tried to do the same. On the 50th anniversary of my father's death someone asked Mother, "How long did it take you to get over Johnny's death?" Mother wisely replied, "You don't ever 'get over' the death of someone you dearly love; you simply learn to go on living…."

Grandmother Mattie had taught Mother the importance of passing on good memories but also finding new meaning in life after the death of a loved one. Mattie had learned this wisdom through experience, for she was only 11 when she suffered the death of her mother and only 22 when Lewis died; her first son died the day before his first birthday, and her second husband died before she was even 40.

In years past, people pointed out how I look a lot like Johnny, especially our large, dark, brown eyes. I am glad I resemble my father, and I am glad my brothers also have similar features. These resemblances send a rush of kinship through me. But I am especially grateful that my grandmother and mother passed on stories about him, for these stories demonstrate how I also have his way of seeing things, of looking at life…the power of kindness, the delight of music, reading, and nature, and accepting that grief is part of life and not letting it destroy the joy of living…I am my father's daughter. I am truly grateful for the best father I never knew.

SNAKES ALIVE!

Mattie had a deep-seated fear of snakes. Her reason was well-founded. Except for an indomitable will to live as a young girl, she would probably have died from a rattlesnake bite. Because she was so unflappable, many enjoyed doing anything that would "get a rise" out of her, including startling her with snakes, real and toy ones. Here is the account Winnie gave of one such time:

> *I was not an active part of this trick. Pearl, Vera, Nita, and I were tramping the pasture at John and Ora Creek's when we found two little baby snakes. Someone said, "Let's take them home." So Nita and Pearl picked them up, and each one put a snake in the pocket of the jackets they were wearing.*
>
> *"We walked into the kitchen where Ora and Mother were sitting at the table. Pearl threw her snake on the floor, and Ora and Mother jumped up in the chairs. When they saw the second snake that Nita threw on the floor, they jumped up on the table.*

Winnie did not go ahead and tell "the rest of the story," as Paul Harvey would say. But from my own experience, I can guarantee that Mattie made it clear they should not ever do that again. My participation was much like Winnie's – that is, I didn't take an active part, but I can remember with great relish how Phillip and Butch bought a couple of toy snakes made from clay hardened on a long, thick string or cord. Just holding the snake in one's hand and shaking it around created a rattle not unlike that of a rattlesnake.

Mattie was sitting at the café counter once when the two partners in crime nonchalantly walked up behind her and shook their snakes. The thrill of seeing Grandmother jump and scream was short-lived, quickly snuffed out by Grandmother's twisting her fingers through my hair and lifting me off the floor. I had not been alert enough and quick like my two brothers; they had run away before Grandmother hit the ground the first time.

Grandmother always emphasized learning from your mistakes. All three of us were quick learners – never again did we subject Grandmother to our snake antics or any other frightful teasing.

WHAT YOU DON'T KNOW WON'T HURT YOU

Winnie said her mother, Mattie, taught her many useful things, like how to work. And work itself sometimes revealed some interesting insights. Winnie told about her early work experience and what she learned much later – and her philosophical conclusion:

> *My first responsibility came when I was about four years old, and that was bringing in the chamber pot at night and emptying it every morning. We had a windmill that pumped water into a big overhead tank that sat up high on a platform. It was under that water tank – where we got our drinking water – that I emptied the pot. Years later when I learned about recycling, I concluded that was most definitely recycling at its worst.*
>
> *I also hoped that it is literally true: What you don't know won't hurt you.*

THE BAD AND THE GOOD

"What was the hardest thing you ever had to do?" was one of the questions in a family heritage book I asked my mother to fill out. Here is her response:

> *When we came back from Arkansas in 1933, we were destitute. We were living with relatives, first one, then another. In May, my step-dad died suddenly. Mother went to work for my step-brother in his café at $8.00 per week.*
>
> *Mother traded our car for two or three cows.... We milked the cows and sold the milk to the café. There were not health rules then, and we sold raw milk. Juanita did most of the milking while my job (and Paul's) was delivering the milk in a little red wagon.*

Can you imagine how embarrassing that was for me – a proud 15-year-old teenager pulling a little wagon down the street?

Winnie said that while their being fatherless resulted in poverty that created some embarrassing moments throughout the years, Mattie tried to make up for it in other ways. She tried, for example, to find ways to make her children feel special. Here is another account by Winnie:

Mother always made us feel special on our birthday. Cakes in those days were not an everyday thing. But Mother always made us a cake. We always had some kind of present – maybe a new dress or a pair of stockings or socks. My gift was always stockings, for my birthday was in November.

SIGNING OFF

Sharing stories was a favorite pastime in my family, and my mother, Winnie, always had a good story. Her pleasant personality and dry wit made even a mundane experience interesting. Here is a story Mattie loved for Winnie to tell:

When I was about 13, some of the members of my Sunday School class were also in my English class at school. Once when we were studying letter writing – salutations, endings, etc. in English class, one of the girls was asked to pray in Sunday School. When she finished her prayer, instead of ending with the customary "Amen," she said, "Yours truly."

JUST IN CASE

Mattie was a fairly cautious person, and she tried to teach her children to avoid taking risks and to use good judgment. She issued warnings like, "Be sure to always wear clean undies…just in case you have to be taken to a hospital." Betty Jean remembered how Grandmother showed her how to hang clothes in a closet so you could get them out in a hurry…just in case of a fire, etc.

"Just in case" was a phrase Grandmother added to many ultimatums. Winnie said that she may have learned the lesson too well. When she was 13, the family moved to Witt Springs, Arkansas. It was wintertime and in the Great Depression. "Church was about the only activity we could afford," she said, "and during the summer a revival would be going on all the time." Winnie said she accepted a holiness preacher's invitation to be baptized, and she was immersed in a "swimmin' hole" in the river. She continued, "Later a Baptist preacher came along, and I was baptized again." With a wry look on her face, she added, "Just in case."

NOT JUST AN ORDINARY "PUMP HOUSE"

Lewis ("Bo") Chumbley spent a career as a top-knotch chemist with Dow Chemical Company. Foreshadowing this illustrious career – and the varied uses of Grandmother Mattie's "pump house" – was Bo's Civil Defense responsibilities in 1966. Here is the story in his words:

> *Grandmother's pump house enjoyed numerous uses, especially with childhood imaginations. But it once was actually a licensed storage site for nuclear materials. Right after Marilyn and I got married and I was teaching physics at Clovis High School until she finished her college degree, I took a course to become a certified "Radiological Monitoring Instructor." It was the 1966-67 school year, the age of fall-out shelters, and in the event of Nuclear Holocaust, each fall-out shelter was supposed to have at least one person trained to use a Geiger Counter to make sure the shelter was "clean," or not contaminated with radioactive fall-out.*
>
> *The course I took was designed to train these Geiger Counter operators. Part of the training course involved hiding radioactive source material (small capsules of Cobalt-*

60) around the classroom and have the students use Geiger Counters to find them. In order to possess the radioactive source material, instructors had to identify a storage area which could be "secured" (locked up) and which was separate from any living quarters. As newlyweds, we were living in a little rental house with no suitable spot for storing nuclear materials.

As so often she did, Grandmother came to the rescue! She let me designate her old pump house for my storage site. In my certification, it was actually licensed as a storage site, complete with the black and yellow decals. Even as a young child playing in and around that interesting old pump house, I knew it was not just an ordinary "pump house"!

LIFE ACCORDING TO GRANDMOTHER MATTIE

The ancient philosopher Sophocles said, "A short saying oft contains much wisdom." And Ralph Waldo Emerson, the great American philosopher and writer, said, "Next to the originator of a good saying is the first quoter of it." I doubt that Mattie had read much of Sophocles or Emerson. But had she read their works, she would have agreed with them, for she quoted short time-proven sayings a lot.

Mattie liked people, and they liked her. Here are some of her favorite maxims or sayings that capture the reasons she got along well with people:

1. You can catch more flies with honey than you can with vinegar.
2. The best way to cheer yourself up is to cheer up somebody else.
3. Pretty is as pretty does.
4. Don't judge another person until you have walked in his shoes.
5. You can make more friends with your ears than with your mouth.

If only one word could be used to describe Mattie, it would be character. Here are some of the adages or sayings she lived by:

1. If you don't stand for something, you will fall for anything.
2. Honesty is the first chapter of the book of wisdom.
3. The trouble with stretching the truth is that it is apt to snap back.
4. Your wrong doings will find you out.
5. The smallest deed is better than the greatest intention.
6. Just do what is right; nothing else matters.

Mattie was well known for her strong work ethic. She believed strongly in doing "an honest day's work." She recited these familiar sayings as the occasion called for them:

1. Idleness is the Devil's workshop.
2. Anything worth doing is worth doing well.
3. Sleepy head, sleeping in the sun. How do you expect to get your day's work done?
4. Shake a leg!
5. Get yourself in high gear and get with it!
6. Up and at 'em!
7. Don't let any grass grow under your feet.
8. You sure got a good scald on that.
    This was considered the ultimate compliment from Mattie — it meant simply that you did a really good job. Lillie explained where it came from: *Mattie made up this saying. She killed and dressed so many chickens in her life… you scalded them before you picked the feathers off. If you got the water just right, they were easy to pick. Too hot, and the skin might come off too. Not hot enough and the feathers wouldn't come out. But if you got the water just right, you could do a good job picking off the feathers. Soon this saying generalized to other jobs.*
9. Whatever your hand finds to do, do it with your might.– Ecclesiastes 9:10

10. If a task is once begun,
    Never leave it till it's done.
    Be the labor great or small,
    Do it well
    Or not at all.

Here are some of Mattie's sayings that reflected her optimism and acceptance of the ups and downs of life:

1. When one door closes, another one opens.
2. You are between a rock and a hard place.
3. You made your bed, now sleep in it.
4. Beggars cannot be choosers.
5. Things may have to get worse before they can get better.
6. It's a long road that doesn't have a bend in it somewhere.

Mattie liked to plan ahead and to be organized. She was often heard sharing these sayings:

1. A penny saved is a penny earned.
2. Don't put all your eggs in one basket.
3. A place for everything, and everything in its place.
4. A bird in the hand is worth two in a bush.
5. Look before you leap.

Here are some other maxims, proverbs, and old sayings relatives and friends remember Mattie using as circumstances called for them:

1. *Let sleeping dogs lie.*
2. *I could stretch a mile if it wasn't for walking back.*
3. *A whistling girl and a crowing hen always come to no good end.*
4. *A watched pot never boils.*
5. *It will never be noticed on a galloping mule.*
6. *I feel like I was sent for, couldn't go, went anyway, and wasn't needed after I got there.*
7. *Make do, or do without.*
8. *Birds of a feather flock together.*
9. *You can lead a horse to water, but you cannot make him drink.*
10. *You have to stay awake to make your dreams come true.*

Although Mattie was quick to quip a good quote, she was never preachy or pedantic. She simply recognized the time-proven wisdom of well-selected quotes. One of her favorites was "We need to know where we have been to know where we are going." I for one am profoundly grateful that Mattie learned from her past experiences and wanted others to benefit from them as well. As a very principled person, she cut to the heart of a matter to affirm, chasten, encourage – whatever the circumstances required.

 Like many who knew Mattie, even now when in an uncertain situation and wondering which way to go, I find myself embraced by her presence. Hearing her recite one of these sayings nudges me in the right direction. All these memories – and many more not recorded in this chapter – encourage me to speak for myself and many others:

"Thank you, Grandmother Mattie, for a golden legacy of grit, gumption, and grace!"

Chapter Ten:
ROOM FOR ONE MORE
(1950s - Early 1970s)

Let there be kindness in your face, in your eyes, in your smile....
Don't only give your care, but give your heart as well.
— Mother Teresa

Mattie could have written an intriguing, fast-moving book about the experiences she shared with the countless and diverse grandchildren living with her to attend college or work – or both. If she had written that drama, Mattie would undoubtedly have told about the time a man held Carolyn Creek at gunpoint in the driveway of her home. Here is the story in Carolyn's words:

It was 1972 and the spring semester of my sophomore year in college. When I went to an evening class, it had been cancelled. So I went to Doc's for a soda and then left to go back to Grandmother's. Along the way I noticed the same pair of headlights following me. I thought it was someone I knew. But as I pulled up in front of Grandmother's house and parked, the vehicle – an older model blue pickup truck – turned and went up the street to the side of the house. I turned my car off and gathered my books. Then the driver made a U-turn and came back to Grandmother's house, pulling up by the arched rose trellis. By this time I had walked to the back of the house to go in.

The man in the pickup motioned to me. It was too dark to see his face clearly. So still thinking it was someone I knew, I walked over to his pickup and opened the passenger door. The man had a gun! He pointed it at me and ordered, "Get in." I screamed, slammed the door, turned around, and started running for the back door of Grandmother's house, fully expecting to feel a bullet come through my back.

Fortunately, the stranger did not fire his gun at Carolyn! Here is how she continued the saga:

Obviously, I did the "right thing" because the man peeled out, throwing gravel as he sped away. As I got my key into the lock of the back door, Grandmother was right there – she had heard me scream.

Grandmother must have called the police; I do not remember my calling them. I do recall the detectives asking a lot of questions – one of them was, "What kind of gun was it?" It was the first gun I had ever seen up close, so all I could tell them was that there was a big hole at the end of the barrel!

Grandmother Mattie insisted that Carolyn call her parents, who at that time lived in Roswell. By the time the ordeal was over, it was late. Not wanting to worry her mom and dad, Carolyn asked if she could wait until morning to call. Mattie agreed, and then she asked Carolyn if she wanted her to sleep with her. Carolyn replied, "No, Grandmother. I will be OK." Carolyn described what happened next:

I turned off the light and got under the covers, thinking about the night's terrifying events. Then I heard footsteps! It was Grandmother, who announced in the darkness, "Well, I am going to sleep with YOU!" So Grandmother crawled into bed, and as we lay there, the rose bushes outside the window scratched across the window screen – screech, screech, screech – a sound so many of us know well from sleeping in that room. Grandmother demanded, "Why didn't you tell me about those bushes?" The next morning the first thing she did was trim those scary rose bushes!

Here is how Carolyn related "the rest of the story":

> *The next morning I called at 7:30 to let Mom and Dad know what had happened. Dad had already gone to work, so I described the frightening experience to Mom. I went to my 8:00 class and my 9:00 class. By the time I got back to Grandmother's a little after 10:00, Mom and Dad were sitting at the kitchen table drinking coffee with Grandmother.*
>
> *It's great to be loved!*

Carolyn's story captures well the love and concern Grandmother Mattie gave to all her children, grandchildren, and great grandchildren – and to everyone, for that matter. No one else at Mattie's house ever suffered a gunpoint threat from a stranger, but she expressed sincere interest and provided helpful guidance to anyone who shared a problem – large or small.

Carolyn's graduation — one of several degrees she earned at E.N.M.U.

Grandmother Mattie's love was felt throughout all the ordinary happenings of life as well. Every season and holiday were special at her house. Relatives gathered from miles around to enjoy the fun and the food. Mattie's house was a place for celebrations, a place for savoring, a place where friendships among relatives were forged. Relatives of all ages enjoyed being with each other there.

Summer time at Grandmother's

Martha was a regular visitor at Mattie's – summer and winter – since she lived only about 20 minutes away. As an adult, Martha shared some of her warm, homey memories. Her recollections are similar to those of many other grandchildren who frequented Mattie's house:

- *The sound of the screen door slamming on the back porch*
- *The tantalizing aroma of Grandmother's canning grape juice and grape jelly*
- *Eating Sunday dinner (as the noon meal was called) – oven fried chicken, mashed potatoes, homemade rolls, and apple pie with cinnamon red hots*
- *Sitting out on the back porch at the card table – the kitchen was reserved for the grownups!*
- *Grandmother's homemade chicken pot pie and apricot cobbler. I can still smell and taste them.*
- *The pungent smell of the cellar*
- *Grandmother's beautiful yard – it seemed huge to me as a child. The colorful roses that covered the trellis near the backdoor, the daisies that grew by the street, the crepe myrtle that grew by the kitchen window, the row of grapevines, the plump, red cherries, and the giant weeping willow trees.*
- *The adults sitting around the kitchen table drinking coffee and talking and laughing – lots of laughing. Grandmother's house and her family were a happy bunch.*

Happiness was indeed a central part of life with Mattie and the family culture she created, and so was food. For example, memories of Mattie canning fruit span many years. In later years she did some freezing. But the memories of canning are the most vivid, especially to Bo. Here is one of his recollections:

Grandmother canned fruit every year – jars and jars and jars of fruit. The fruit would never all be used and the remaining jars would ultimately "turn bad," as Grandmother put it. She would throw out the spoiled fruit to reclaim the jars to use for the current year's crop. One year when I was staying with Grandmother, a family living in the nearby little white house (always referred to as Winnie's house) was boarding about a dozen dogs of all sizes. The dogs barked constantly; those of us with bedrooms in Grandmother's house nearest the dogs found them a noisy nuisance. One day when I was helping Grandmother empty the jars, I took the dishpan full of spoiled fruit to the fruit trees; she was sure it was good fertilizer. But instead of spreading the smelly fruit around the trees, I tossed it to the dogs. They yelped but ran away from the strange, anesthetizing castaway – no more barking! When I turned around to return to the house, there was Grandmother, laughing her head off. The dogs did not have a sense of humor. But Grandmother did.

Here is another one of Bo's accounts; this one involves a cousin's culinary creation:

When Butch came back from the Army and started college at Eastern, he started something else – a unique concoction in a gallon jar kept on Grandmother's kitchen cabinet mostly for convenience, but it also served as an intriguing conversation piece. Butch filled the glass jar with peppers and vinegar. Then he added boiled eggs, Vienna sausages, carrots, and sundry other ingredients. The more courageous members of the family would eat various delectables out of the jar, always waiting with great anticipation for the explosion of taste. When the savory items were almost depleted, Butch simply added more of the same – vinegar, peppers, or whatever.

Bo offered this conclusion about the hotter-than-fire, ill-fated mixture:

> *It got to looking pretty gross after awhile, particularly after the fumes ate through the lid. Granddad fussed about it and then one day he threw it out. Butch was hotter than the brew!*

Years after the peak popularity of this concoction, Del and I took Grandmother Mattie to visit Butch and Penny where they lived on Maes Ranch near Las Vegas, New Mexico. For a day's outing, we all went into Santa Fe. Of course, eating some Mexican food was on our agenda. When some pickled vegetables prepared Mexican style were served, Mattie took a few bites and commented matter of factly, "Butch's brew tasted a lot better than these." Had we all known more about marketing – and had Granddad not tossed out Butch's taste-proven tidbits, grocery stores and fancy restaurants everywhere might not be stuck with the wimpy items available today. Instead, they could be enjoying world-famous "Butch's Brew."

Mattie did have a knack with food, and she spent a lot of time in her kitchen. But only reluctantly did she acquire a freezer and install a dishwasher and a food disposal. Once she got accustomed to these "modern conveniences," she loved them. But she sometimes simply expected too much from them. She thought, for example, any food put in the freezer was preserved in perpetuity. Case in point. Once when Phillip was visiting her, she asked him if he knew how to grill a steak. He was a fairly accomplished steak griller, so he answered with confidence, "Sure." When Mattie retrieved the steak from the depths of the freezer, it looked like it had been there since the beginning of the Ice Age. Being the kind, considerate person Phill is, he did not want to say anything to offend our grandmother. So he proceeded to do the best he could with a freezer-burned hunk of beef. When Mattie took her first bite, she quipped, "Hooomph…you're sure not much of a griller!"

In contrast, Glenna Chumbley remembers Mattie's "magic touch" in the kitchen. One of her favorite memories is how Mattie saved the turkey gravy one Thanksgiving:

The turkey gravy had been made, but everyone in the kitchen tasted it and agreed it had no taste whatsoever. Grandmother said she knew just what to do, and she got the yellow food color and put three drops in. Paul raved and raved about how that was the best-tasting gravy he ever had. Grandmother just died laughing. She always emphasized the importance of how food looks.

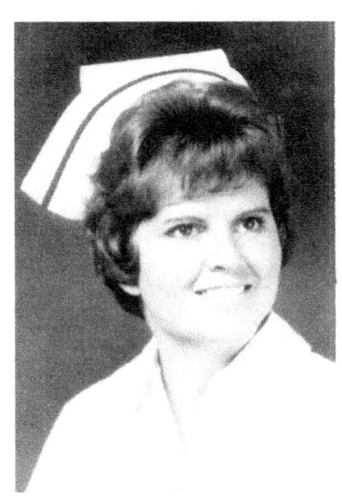

Lea Norris Chumbley remembered an incident about appearance, but it has to do with hair, not food. She was about 13 or 14 when her family moved to Artesia. Lea rode the train back to Portales to spend the summer with Grandmother Mattie so she could wash dishes at Grandmother's café to make some money. Here is one of Lea's many memories from that summer:

That summer I learned to curl my hair. I was in Portales only a few days when I asked Grandmother to curl my hair for me. She said, "Why?" I told her that I did not know how because Mother always did it for me. Grandmother said, "It's about time you learned how." She sat down and gave me instructions the first few times. She never did it for me, but she helped. I finally learned to put in rollers. I remember how surprised and pleased Mother was when I went home...and could "do it myself."

Ironically, Grandmother Mattie did not fix her own hair. She had long hair until she was grown and admitted that after she cut her hair, she never could get the curlers to stay in well enough to do their job. One of her "luxuries," as she called it, was to have her hair done every week by Dood Davis, a good friend and hair stylist and owner of one of the nicest shops in Portales.

Mattie did not want Lea to feel as inept as she had felt about doing her own hair. Furthermore, she was a good teacher even when she could not perform the feat herself!

Still reminiscing about the summer she spent with Mattie, Lea provided a thumbnail sketch of this compassionate woman who was always concerned about others:

> We would get home from the café about 9:00 and sit and talk for awhile before going to bed. She always came into my bedroom to tell me goodnight. One night when it was storming, she came in to see if I was afraid.

Butch explored another unusual business and outlet for his creativity while living with Grandmother Mattie during his college days. Here is Bo's account of it:

> Butch had an interesting piggin' string business. He had a bunch of parachute cord and would braid it into piggin' string. Butch's "factory" was on the back porch of Grandmother's house. He had cord and piggin' strings strung among the ironing equipment and clothes hanging over the cellar door. Getting into the kitchen through the back door amidst the large spider web of piggin' strings was an interesting entry.
>
> Butch would dye the piggin' string different colors and then braid nooses and splice the ends and wrap leather around parts of them. His piggin' strings were real fancy. Some distributor started buying them to sell through western wear stores. So a good demand was being created for them. But all too soon, Butch ran out of parachute cord and could not get any more. This ended a promising enterprise!

When quizzed about this unusual enterprise, Butch gave a mini-education on the historical background of the piggin' string:

> Back when pigs ran wild on the New Mexico prairie, ranchers wanted to catch them to identify them so they could "own" them. After the pig was caught, a piggin' string was used to hold the pig still. The pig's skin was too thin to withstand branding, so an ear

was marked in a unique way to distinguish the pig as belonging to that particular rancher. Ranchers then began using a piggin' string to hold a calf still while being doctored or branded. Although the practice of catching wild pigs went by the wayside, the use of the piggin' string with cattle remained, and so did the name piggin' string.

Butch helping Christi and Jesse learn to ride a horse

Although Mattie was quite supportive of Butch's entrepreneurial pursuit, she consoled him when he experienced difficulty getting more parachute cord. She emphasized, "Get an education first!" And that is what he did; he stayed with Mattie and completed his college degree at Eastern New Mexico University with a rodeo scholarship. After college he continued his longstanding love of horses. One of his favorite things was teaching young people how to ride horses.

Other familiar memories include how Granddad would sit intent and motionless listening to baseball games blaring from the large floor-style radio sitting by the front door of the living room. Everyone also remembers the requirement to be quiet, especially when something exciting was about to happen – which was most of the time during a ballgame. The same rule applied when Gabriel Heater's deep, booming voice announced the world news. But by the time Ronny and Bo were staying at Mattie's to attend college, Granddad's choice of radio and TV programs had changed drastically. For instance, Granddad had always been a big Detroit Tiger fan. So when this team was playing in the World Series and it looked like the team had the final game in hand, Bo assumed Granddad would be watching the game. He skipped out of a college chemistry lab early to get to Mattie's to watch at least the winning celebration. When Bo arrived, he found Ronny already there – fuming! He also had anticipated watching this important World Series game, but Granddad had switched channels from the ballgame at about the sixth inning to watch the then all-time-favorite soap opera, *As the World Turns*. For the most part, Mattie "took up" for her grandchildren. But not always, not when she also preferred watching *As the World Turns*.

One time Grandmother Mattie did "take up" for me in a different way was the year before my senior year in college – 1962. The World's Fair was in Seattle, and several of my friends and I decided to drive there to see it. Grandmother put her stamp of approval on the plan. So for weeks ahead of time, I carefully selected clothes and pressed them impeccably (These were the days before wrinkle-free fabrics and certainly before wrinkles were fashionable). I carefully placed each outfit on a card table near a window in my bedroom. Always one to plan and prepare ahead of time, I wanted to be perfectly attired for this once-in-a-lifetime trip. The evening before we were scheduled to leave, I went into my bedroom – and horrors of all horrors! The window had been opened about six inches, and Grandmother had turned on the sprinklers to water the roses and grass at that end of the house. Not only had the thirsty plants received a dousing, so had all my perfectly pressed clothes. Mattie heard my blood-curdling scream and came running. I do not know which one of us felt worse. She apologized profusely and then worked half the night with me to salvage my World's Fair wardrobe. With about three hours of sleep, I was on my way to Seattle the next morning at the break of day and Grandmother was at the café, doing the work that made the trip — and nice clothes — possible.

Always encouraging and rarely critical, Mattie was also known to "call a spade a spade." For example, I selected some shows for us to see in Las Vegas on our trip to get me settled into graduate school in California. I had always heard of Pearl Baily, so I chose this show — with Mattie, of course, paying for the tickets. A once world famous boxer was featured along with Pearl Baily. The bright lights of Las Vegas and the marvelous food dazzled us. But Mattie was not particularly impressed with the show. "Pearl Baily was OK," she admitted, "but that boxer had been hit in the head one time too many."

Mattie always made room for any relative who wanted to spend a semester or two to attend college or even "a night or two." For example, Rita and two sons, Phillip Alan and David, spent quite some time with her while Phill was making a transition in an assignment from the Navy. Mattie loved family members staying with her and getting to know her grandchildren. She said, "I'll always 'have room' for them."

Phill's career in the Navy took him and his family all around the world, including two assignments in Hawaii. Although the faraway places they lived were interesting, all Phill's family members said visiting Grandmother Mattie's was extra special.

David and Phillip Alan in Hawaii

In contrast to Mattie's love for her grandchildren, she never cared too much for animals, saying, "There's not enough room for them." But at one time after Granddad died and there were no college-age grandchildren staying with her, Mattie had this little bird. I cannot remember if she bought it or if someone decided she needed some company and gave it to her. She was convinced that she and "birdie" could communicate. Looking fondly at the little feathered creature, she would say something like, "How in the world are you doing this morning?" Surprisingly, the downy thing would make noises that indeed sounded like "answers." The two could carry on a "conversation" for several minutes. Satisfied that enough had been said, the little bird would tuck its head under its wing, or Mattie would terminate the social exchange by telling the little bird she had work to do.

Once when Mattie went out of town for a few days, she entrusted the care of "birdie" to Winnie, who tried to replicate the feeding ritual as well as the conversations. What Winnie did not anticipate was a cold front that hit the area. When Winnie entered the door of the enclosed back porch where "birdie" lived in her cage, she gasped and then shrieked. Grandmother's "birdie" was on its back, feet curled in the air, and "stiffer than a poker." Winnie dreaded having to tell her mother she had let "birdie" freeze to death; she cried until Mattie came home. Of course, Mattie cried, too, when she got home and saw the defenseless, dead bird.

But she looked Winnie straight in the eye and said, "Don't feel bad. You didn't mean to do it. You did the best you could." That was Mattie.

Although Mattie was kind and compassionate, she was also a strict disciplinarian. Everyone just knew what she expected, and they did their best to live up to those expectations. As a young child, you did not want Mattie to wrap her finger around a lock of your hair and lift you off the floor. As an adult, you wanted her approval. However, Granddad was always considered the "bad guy" who issued the mandates, often referred to as "Granddad's rules." Everyone growing up around Mattie and Granddad remembers his rules:

- *Do not climb on the high chicken fence. (You could fall off and kill yourself; worse, yet, you could do damage to the chicken wire.)*
- *Do not climb up on the top of the garage.*
  (There were low hanging electric wires there.)
- *Do not climb in the fruit trees.*
- *Do not pick cherries. (I never understood this rule, for the tree always produced more cherries than were ever eaten.)*
- *If you do pick cherries, be sure to spit the evidence (the seeds) in the garbage can in the alley, not right under the tree.*
- *Do not play hide and seek under the grape vines.*
- *Do not try to smoke the grape leaves. (If you do smoke grape leaves, never get more than 2-3 of Granddad's matches. Otherwise, he would notice – which you did not want to happen.)*
- *Do not taunt or tease the large, less-than-friendly collie dogs of the renters in the house across the alley. If the dogs didn't get you, the junkyard-mean owners would.*
- *Do not throw rocks at each other near anything glass, especially car windows.*
- *Do not play in the middle of the street.*
- *Do not slam the screen door on the back porch. (I never realized how annoying slamming that screen door endlessly throughout the day could be to the adults until I was grown and found myself annoyed by it.)*
- *Do not walk on the Bermuda grass after Granddad burns it (a late fall ritual).*
- *If you do walk on the burned grass (reduced to blackened ash), be very certain you do not walk in the house until you've walked vigorously in the street for an hour or so. Otherwise you'll make black footprints in the house – another no-no.*

- *Remain completely silent once Gabriel Heater's deep voice comes on the radio to give his version of world news, invariably announcing, "Ah, there's good news tonight!" no matter how direful the report.*

Even to this day – some 55 years later – I somehow feel compelled to remain totally silent during the news broadcast. Of course, I don't play in the middle of the street, throw rocks at cars, or smoke grape leaves either. But I often wonder in what other insidious, subtle ways life with Mattie influenced me and the many others fortunate enough to grow up around her.

Mattie was the world's best pie baker. It was a toss-up whether her egg custard pie or her coconut cream was the best. And her cherry pie was also a favorite. She made pie baking look easy. So when a cherry pie baking contest was announced in a college food science class I was taking, I signed up. The county contest was only weeks away, so I began immediately to practice. Mattie had canned some cherries grown in our orchard so I retrieved a jar from the cellar. My first cherry pie was not exactly a winner. I had not taken into account that Mattie had canned the cherries with the pits in them, anticipating she'd get rid of the pits when she used each jar. As for the crust, it was about as tough as the pits in the cherries. The first cherry pie went in the garbage.

In spite of a dismal beginning, I had caught the cherry pie baking fever. The second pie was only slightly improved; at least I had taken out the pits, which was no small accomplishment. Mattie had also offered her suggestions for making some much-needed improvements. For example, she noticed how unattractive the shriveled home-canned cherries were so she suggested using frozen cherries. She emphasized that food must look good to taste good – an important lesson!

With each "practice pie," Mattie critiqued the pie and my performance – a significant aspect of the contest. By the time of the county contest, everyone in the family had eaten about as much cherry pie as they cared for. When I showed up for the big contest, I discovered it was not such a big contest – I was the only contestant in the county! But the judges insisted that I bake my pie and show off my Julia Child skills. After I finished, they agreed that I qualified to go onto the state competition to be held in about a month in Los Alamos. Not wanting me to be an embarrassment to our county, the judges provided a lot of hints for improving my performance and culinary flair – like not scratching my nose no matter how distracting the itch.

Barbara Jo and a practice cherry pie

Mattie's input and encouragement, my practice, and the family's enthusiastic consumption paid off – I won the state contest, which was a legitimate "win," for nearly all 33 counties in New Mexico had sent a contestant. Although I didn't win the top national prize, I did receive several other awards and placed third in the cherry recipe contest, which, of course, Mattie had helped to concoct.

In addition, I had a great time riding the train to Chicago. Another highlight was meeting some interesting girls from other states – even one celebrity from Las Vegas, Nevada, the daughter of Betty Grable and Harry James. None of this would've happened without Grandmother Mattie's steady support and "I-know-you-can-do-it" attitude, her help at each stage of the recipes, her insistence that everyone help eat the "practice pies," and her paying for a zillion frozen cherries.

When I stood on that stage of the famous Palmer House Hotel in Chicago and the awards were handed to me, I was the one who took them in my hands. But it was Grandmother Mattie who had really won the awards.

Mattie was smart in so many ways, not just in knowing how to concoct and bake award-winning recipes and how to help others hone their skills, but in other ways as well. For example, none of the bad mother-in-law jokes ever applied to her. All Mattie's in-laws loved her, and she loved all her in-laws. Rita, Phillip's wife, said she loved Grandmother for she always made her "feel like family." Weesie, Leroy's wife, put it this way:

In-laws in 2005 enjoying the tradition of love and acceptance Grandmother began generations ago. Left to right back row: Del Chesser (Barbara Jo) Ron Singleton (Martha) Ron Egan (Brenda) Ann (Ron Creek). Left to right front row: Patty (Darren Chumbley) Marilyn (Bo Chumbley) Rita (Phill Russell) Weesie (Leroy Creek) Penny (Butch Russell)

> *Mattie made me feel comfortable and at ease from the first time we met. I considered her to be a good friend.... She was not a judgmental person.*

Penny was only 19 when she and Butch married in March of 1972. She said she was surprised that so many of Butch's relatives took time out of their work schedules to travel to their wedding. Leading the family group was, of course, Grandmother Mattie! Penny had heard a lot about Mattie from Butch, so she was somewhat intimidated by this remarkable person – but not for long. Penny explained:

> *She made me feel important just by her taking the time and the trouble to come to our wedding so far away. But she also made me feel very comfortable. She did not want to be the center of attention – she made others the center of her attention.*

Ann did not get to know Grandmother Mattie, for she died in 1988 before Ann and Ronny married in 1989. But Ann said she soon felt that she knew this grand matriarch. She told why:

> *Everyone in the family spoke of Grandmother with so much love – and the various family members seemed to reflect this love with each other. Other qualities they said Grandmother had, they also had. So it was like her presence was felt even though I didn't have the privilege of knowing her. This unique woman created a tremendous family culture that transcends life and death...it will live on in the lives of her descendants....*

Although Leroy and Weesie's daughters, Judy and Kathy, never lived with Mattie, they visited regularly. They both said Mattie made them feel special even though they did not stay long periods of time with her like many of the other grandchildren did. Leroy and Weesie talked aften about Mattie, and they talked occasionally on the phone with her. Judy and Kathy said they were reminded often of Mattie and their parents' love for her. So when they saw Mattie in person, they felt perfectly comfortable with her.

Judy said she respected Mattie for many reasons, including her accomplishments. But she admired her especially for how she treated people:

> *I was very lucky to end up with a grandma like Mattie. She was an excellent example to all of us.... I remember quiet talks with her when she came to visit us in Durango.*

"Quiet talks" and listening were indeed among Grandmother Mattie's vast array of "people skills." She truly listened when you talked to her; she was never self-absorbed but made you feel like she considered you and what you had to say the most important thing in the world at that moment.

As a fairly young person, Kathy shared her memories of Mattie. Her recollections captured the mood that we all enjoyed there:

We always enjoyed going to see Grandma. My family would pile into the station wagon…and we'd get there about noon and pull alongside her house and start the unloading process.
A special part of this was going through the rose arbor to greet Grandma for the first time. She was always in the kitchen, fixing something good to eat or drinking a cup of coffee and talking with one of the many relatives.

We'd get a big hug from Grandma and then put out suitcases in the designated bedroom that was in the back of the house. Getting to this room required going through the living room (more fun-loving relatives!), passing the greatly appreciated "swamp air cooler," into another hall, through the sewing room, another hallway, and finally to the big bedroom. My sister and I preferred this bedroom because it had several beds and our cousins could spend the night with us.

These cousins – Brenda and Janet Luttrell – might already be at Grandma's, or they would arrive soon after we got there. Once we got acquainted again, we were off to play, which included checking out the fruit trees and getting on top the chicken house to share our secrets. The willow tree was a welcome part of that setting, for it helped hide us from any adult who might see us and tell us to get down. We'd soon get bored and head to the big bedroom to jump on the beds.

Soon a meal would be served. Grandma had been in the kitchen most of this time along with my mom and aunts preparing the best country fried food one could ever ask for. My sister and cousins and I always ate on a card table on the back porch where everyone considered a "kid" was assigned to eat. Of course, we preferred to eat there – we could talk with our mouths open and not worry about interrupting anyone, etc. Another big bonus – we got to fill our plates first. Someone would say the blessing, and we would dig into the long-awaited delicious food, being careful to leave some room for the great desserts.

Under the back porch was the basement where Grandma stored things. It was dark down there, and we never attempted to go there. This place was a mystery; I remember one of our conversations at dinner when someone told us that there was acid down there that would eat your skin right off. We wanted to know more, but never asked because it was just too scary. We tended to view objects retrieved from the basement with great caution.

Filled with good food, we were off again to explore other adventures – including asking our older cousin Carolyn to take us to get a soda at the drive-in. She generally said yes. We stayed with the adults a little while to hear their conversations, but soon we'd retreat to our bedroom to tell ghost stories.

Later Kathy summarized her feelings toward Grandmother Mattie:

The days at Grandma's were always very pleasant. Life there was good.
It was a joy to know such a strong woman. I have often thought of how she raised her family practically on her own…she was truly a good example for women today!

Carolyn Creek provides some additional insight into Mattie's personality, including her belief that "Actions speak louder than words":

In my memories of Grandmother, I cannot recall her having said out loud that she loved me. But there has NEVER been a doubt in my mind that I was loved very much – as much as any other grandchild of hers – because of how she treated me. It showed through every time I was with her. She was loving, yet stern. As a child, I knew not to get on her "wrong side" not because I had ever seen repercussions; it was just something I knew. Grandmother balanced love and discipline so well. When I think of Grandmother now, I think of her sitting in her rocking chair by the window in her living room, with handiwork in her lap, a cup of coffee on the table next to the chair, and her laughing at some story someone told – laughing so hard that tears come to her eyes.

Linda Chumbley remembered best the quiet talks she and Mattie had. Linda emphasized, "Grandmother always had time to listen." Late evenings seemed to be the time Grandmother could relax from the demands of her café. Linda recalled how she and Mattie would talk a while and then go to a drive-in for ice cream to finish off the evening. It was a good thing they did not have a flat or any other problems that required they get out of the car, for they more often than not went in their nightgowns and robes. Linda pointed out, "Grandmother was not a stuffy person."

Viki Russell Crawford is a great grandchild who has good memories of Grandmother Mattie. Although Mattie had plenty of workers when Viki told her she'd like to work and that she was a "good worker," Mattie found a place for her, saying, "There is always room for one more good worker." Here is Viki's memory of working for her great grandmother:

I worked only a week or two in the summers. Even though I was quite young, Grandmother Mattie would let me work the register, and that is how I learned to count money and give change to customers. When I was 14, I applied for a job at the Mustang Drive-in at Mountainair, New Mexico. The reason I got the job was because of the experience I had at Grandmother Mattie's cafe and I could give change back correctly – my boss was really impressed! I worked as a waitress until I was 17, and then I got a job at Rust Tractor – I was very proud to be able to put Mattie's Café on my application. I am just one of many fortunate relatives that Grandmother Mattie "made room for" at her home and at her café. She helped us all develop a good work ethic and to get a good start in life.

Reminiscing about Mattie, people would often say she was extraordinary. Some of Butch's memories explain a little more about this remarkable lady:

Butch and Brenda reminiscing about their "chicken" experiences with Grandmother Mattie

As I try to remember some extraordinary things that Grandmother did, I found it hard to remember any particular thing that would be representative of her character. As I considered why that was so, it came to me that she was constantly so extraordinary that having grown up around her, the very extraordinary things she did every day seemed very ordinary. She got up very early nearly every morning, went to work hours before lots of people got out of bed, and worked all day long and into the night nearly every day. She ran her business very efficiently and made a good profit.

Grandmother did all sorts of money-saving things, such as making her own lye soap. With that lye soap, she did all her laundry, personal and for the café – tons of "counter rags" and dishtowels for drying dishes – it was the days before automatic dishwashers....

One of her money-saving projects was raising "fryers" to use at her café.... When the chickens were big enough, she put on a huge iron pot of water to boil. Enlisting the help of us kids and whoever else might be around, she proceeded to "process" these tasty birds.... The way I remember it, several of us kids would catch the fryers with wire hooks and deliver them to her. She might have a chicken in each hand, wringing their necks and jerking their heads off both at the same time. Then we plucked as many of the feathers off as we possibly could. Next, Grandmother dunked them in the scalding water so we could pick off the remaining feathers.... Within a very short time, we would have "processed" an entire flock of chickens....

I never thought about this being an extraordinary feat until I had occasion as an adult to do the same thing myself. When Penny and I were working at Maes Ranch, one of our nearby ranching friends offered to buy and feed a bunch of chickens and split the eggs if we would keep the chickens on our ranch. This was the beginning of our chicken herd, which grew and grew, until I decided to butcher some for fryers.

Calling on my childhood memories of how Grandmother easily performed this simple task, I got me a pot of boiling water and captured several roosters and proceeded to wring a rooster's neck. After what seemed like an hour, my arm felt dead – the rooster was probably in better shape than I. But he was not dead. By this time, my fire had gone out and the water had cooled off.

I found me a hatchet and put the roosters and comrades out of their misery. I built my fire again, got the water boiling, and proceeded. After about a half day I succeeded in accomplishing what Grandmother did in a matter of minutes. Furthermore, I did not do it as well – I ended up skinning the chickens more than "picking" their feathers.

I am sure if I had tried to do many of the things Grandmother did with such apparent ease, I would find, as I did with my "chicken effort," that they were not nearly as easy as she made them appear to be. Of course, it took physical strength to do these kinds of things, but what impressed me was her mental strength and the can-do attitude she had. As I hear again the stories of her past, it is easy to understand why she was like she was – except that in addition to doing all these demanding tasks with ease, she also for the most part took pleasure in doing them. That, to me, was perhaps her most outstanding trait – if it needed to be done, she did it one way or another, she did it fast and well, and she took pride in the process.

Hearing Butch's memories and revisiting the past in general only deepens my admiration and gratitude for how Grandmother helped so many people over the years. I want to hold these memories close to my heart for as long as I live and to be grateful for them, for what I am today came from the past.

This is true for me and it is true for each generation, descendant, and friend linked to Mattie. People expressed their gratitude to Grandmother in various ways, including giving pieces of china dishes to her over the years. One of the most unusual gifts – and tastiest – was in about 1965 when a group of friends expressed their gratitude in a large cake they gave to Mattie.

Bo and Marilyn enjoying with Grandmother and Granddad their "friendship" cake

The picture of that cake reminds me that we all need to be more grateful and to guard against carelessly disregarding our past. We need to recognize that life is a braided cord of love, valor, encouragement, and other powerful influences stretching down from time long gone. We need to be reminded what it was that went into our making. We need to appreciate that the life within each one of us cannot be defined by one single cord but many threads woven.

Even those descendants who never met Mattie are touched by her life through the various threads of gold she spun into a lasting legacy – that cord of grit, gumption, and grace that connects all of us, in large ways and small for generation after generation.

Chapter Eleven:
RED SILK PAJAMAS
(Early 1900s - 1980s)

*The best and most beautiful things in life cannot be seen
or even touched…they must be felt with the heart.*
— Helen Keller

randmother Mattie did not make a big deal out of clothes. Yet the stories family members shared about her and clothes reveal a lot about her personality and her character – just to mention a few…

Her emphasis on being a good person, not just looking good;
Her treatment of all people with utmost respect, without regard
    of their social standing, of their appearance, or the clothes they wore;
Her ability to "make do with what you have" and
Her desire and determination to create something beautiful in a
    situation robbed of its loveliness and beauty.

Some situations involving clothes even show Mattie's ability to laugh at herself. I remember well one amusing experience. That dark morning Mattie jumped out of bed before 5:00, threw on her clothes, swiped on a little lipstick, powdered her face (as usual, more powder landed on the dresser than on her face), and dashed out to her car, fearing she would be late to the café to help with the early morning breakfast rush.

With a winsome expression on her face and a twinkle in her blue eyes, Mattie – like Paul Harvey – sometime later told "the rest of the story":

As I lifted my leg to get into the car, I felt something brush against it. Thinking it might be one of the neighborhood cats, I gave a big kick. The brushing feeling was still there. When I looked down, I saw my pajama legs hanging out from under my dress.

In haste to get to work, Mattie had put on her dress but failed to slip off her red silk pajama bottoms! Because she discovered the pajamas so soon – no harm done. But she had more to say about it:

I often think how embarrassed I would've been if I had walked into the café with those red pajama bottoms flapping. Those guys at the café would've never quit laughing, and they would've never let me "live it down."

Another memory comes rushing from the past – a different dress, a different era, a different setting. This jaunty picture of Grandmother Mattie and Maggie Davis was taken in 1919 when Mattie was 23 years old. Maggie was Lewis' niece – the daughter of Will, Lewis' only surviving brother. Lewis, the "love of her life" (as Mattie sometimes referred to him) and the father of her three daughters, had died only a year before. When someone said to Mattie that she did not look like a grieving young widow in this picture, she answered quickly and matter-of-factly, "I was good at covering up my sadness."

This picture reflects yet another contrast. While Mattie was quite stylish in this picture, the memories she shared of those first years after Lewis died in 1918 were of digging potatoes and doing other field work as well as taking in laundry for other people. Aunt Lillie explained that Lewis' parents provided some nice clothes and fabric for their beloved son's widow as well as "helped put food on the table" so she could keep her three young daughters. How Mattie sometimes dressed did not accurately reflect her meager existence or her broken heart. The dresses Mattie and Maggie had on in this picture were both evidence of Mattie's skill in making patterns and transforming them into stylish dresses. The fancy, intricate beadwork –the picture does not do it justice – was also evidence of Mattie's ability and artistry. Moreover, these lovely dresses reflect Mattie's desire and determination to create something beautiful in a life that had been cruelly robbed of its loveliness and beauty.

Too young to be aware of the bleakness of the days after their father's death, the three little girls, however, remembered the good times as they grew older living near their grandparents as well as how pretty their mother looked when she was "dressed up." In Winnie's book for recording life's memories, one of the items said, "Describe your mother in her 'best dress.'" Winnie flashed back to her childhood and described a time after her mother and Harve had married:

> *The first recollection I have of Mother being "dressed up" in her best dress I was about four years old. We had gone to town in our Model T Ford and parked on South Main. My mother and daddy had gone to the grocery store – Piggly Wiggley's. They were coming across the street, and I can still see her – she was in a dark red dress, the top embroidered in black beads. The skirt came to the top of her high-top, buttoned-up shoes. Her hat was flat-topped with a wide, wide brim. I thought how elegant my mother looked!*

Winnie also held a distinct opinion of her own clothes as she grew up:

> *Being the third girl, many of my clothes were hand-me-downs. But Mother was a good seamstress, and every year before school started, we all had two or three new dresses…the only complaint I had was that Mother made my dresses longer than I liked. Her rationale was that I was a growing girl and soon would outgrow them. But by the time they got short enough to suit me, they were well-worn and faded.*

Mattie's exceptional sewing skills remind me of the old saying, "She could make a silk purse out of a sow's ear." Using patterns created and cut from brown paper, she transformed colorful flour sacks into pretty little dresses. She even made at least two wedding dresses. Lillie recalled her mother's making her wedding dress from some blue chiffon fabric she had bought in New Mexico and taken with her to Arkansas, where she and Charlie were married in 1932.

Grandmother Mattie also made a wedding dress for my mother; here is what Winnie said about it:

> *A fancy wedding was out of the question – money was scarce in 1937. But I did have a new dress. I bought a navy blue remnant of two yards for $3.00, and Mother made me a pretty dress. It was very neat. Mother was a good seamstress.*

Winnie's wedding trousseau was also a product of Mattie's sewing expertise. Winnie delighted in teasing her mother about it in later years:

> *My mother made me two pairs of pajamas. Can you believe it – pajamas for a wedding night!*

Passed onto Lillie was Grandmother Mattie's love of sewing – and her skillfulness at it. When Mattie left Arkansas, she took her Singer sewing machine with her. Even though Lillie had no sewing machine, she wanted to make herself a new dress with some fabric she had ordered. So she asked a neighbor if she could use her sewing machine. The neighbor willingly obliged, and Lillie completed her dress. Soon after that she and Charlie left Arkansas, at Lillie's insistence, and came to New Mexico to join Mattie and the rest of the family. Mattie still enjoyed sewing for her adult daughters even though they had learned how to sew; the daughters in turn enjoyed sewing for their children. While Mattie "passed on" many intangible qualities like a solid work

ethic and love for family and friends, she also encouraged the development of useful skills like sewing and cooking. In the photo at left, Lillie is wearing the dress she made with the borrowed sewing machine and the skills her mother had taught her.

Perhaps the pajamas in Winnie's wedding trousseau were a foreshadowing of fashions to come. In the early 1940s during World War II many women joined the work force outside the home and began wearing pants, or trousers, as they were called back then. This was a dramatic change, for only men had worn pants until then. Mattie, of course, had been working outside the home for decades – "wearing the pants in the family," figuratively speaking. So she welcomed the comfort and convenience of wearing pants. She definitely preferred wearing pants over short dresses or skirts that showed the knees. She was not prudish; she simply thought knees were not a particularly pretty part of the body – anybody's body.

Facing no opposition from her mother, Juanita wore trousers to accommodate her active life style. Even as an adult, for example, she could do handstands and stand on her head, feats unmatched by anyone else in the family. Mattie's encouragement of Juanita and her other children to "do what you want to do" and "follow your heart" began early and continued throughout their lifetimes whether it dealt with clothes or standing on your head. Like Mattie, Juanita did not like working on the ranch; Mattie encouraged her to take advantage of the opportunity to work at a camp near Capitan in the mountains of New Mexico. A picture taken there shows her in her customary attire.

Winnie also began wearing pants before many women did in the early 1940s. While December 7, 1941, dramatically changed countless lives forever, only weeks before – November 2, 1941 – Winnie's life had already been drastically changed when her husband was killed. Widowhood, three young children, and no money forced Winnie into the work force. Although she wasn't a "Rosie the Riveter," she did become part of the effort that won WWII – she packed parachutes at the airbase near Clovis. There was a great demand for parachute packers because parachute packing was vital to the safety of all wartime pilots and air crewmen. It was estimated that 90 percent of all parachutes used in WWII were packed and inspected by women. Winnie started out as a parachute packer and worked her way up to a parachute inspector. The job itself required wearing trousers, but sometimes Winnie's position also required flying to Dalhart, Texas. Winnie once quipped, "Wearing trousers was a plus when getting in and out of a large cargo plane."

Winnie soon found that trousers were also an added plus in other activities.

Lillie did not start wearing trousers as early as her two younger sisters did. Her daughter, Charlene, said that her mother even wore a dress when she worked on their farm in Arkansas. Charlene said her mother's reluctance to wear trousers may stem back to her experience when she was a junior in high school and all the family members were picking cotton. Not wanting her daughters to wear their dresses in the field, Mattie bleached some cotton sacks and made them some bell bottom pants with a blue stripe up the side like Navy pants.

Whatever the reason and whatever the time, Mattie and her three daughters were all practical and started wearing trousers long before most other women did.

Mattie and two of her three grown daughters wearing the women's new 1940s style — pants! Leroy (in background) said it was not easy being a teenaged boy with an independent mother and three older, self-reliant sisters.

"Clothes should be practical – but pretty," Mattie once said. Granddad neither shared nor applied the "pretty" part of my grandmother's belief as it applied to me. When I started to school, Granddad took me to the barber shop and told the barber to give my wind-blown topknot of blond hair a Buster Brown haircut. Granddad also bought me a pair of plain brown oxfords. Admittedly, I was a rough and tumble tomboy and needed some "cleaning up" before beginning school.

Left: Barbara Lee (looking pretty as usual) and Barbara Jo (looking like a ragamuffin as usual) on the front porch of Mattie's house. Right: Ronny with two fashion plates — Barbara Jo and Carolyn with stylish saddle oxfords — and Carolyn wearing a dress designed by Mattie

Nevertheless, with my new "practical" haircut and shoes, I felt like the ugliest duckling in the entire class. Just as she came to the rescue of many other people, Grandmother Mattie came to mine. As soon as my unruly hair had grown out just a little, she took me to her hair stylist. No more men's barbershops for this girl! As for the shoes, I don't remember ever having to wear another pair of those hideous brown oxfords. By the third grade I was wearing snazzy red and white saddle oxfords. Having a more attractive hair cut and shoes was important to me – even at a young age I considered them like my second skin. Mattie's ability to understand other people's feelings and what was important to them was a beautiful gift. My grandmother's keen sensitivity and larger-than-life heart captures one of my favorite sayings; I saw her live out this saying many, many times throughout her lifetime:

The best and most beautiful things in life cannot be seen or even touched.... They must be felt with the heart.
— Helen Keller

Soon after Barbara Lee married Uncle Paul, she expressed interest in learning to sew. When Uncle Paul returned to New Mexico from serving in the Pacific Theater during WWII, he enrolled in college, like more than two million other war veterans taking advantage of the GI Bill the first few years after the war was over. Money was scarce in 1947 when he got married, especially for "store bought" clothes. After all, a new dress from the store might cost $7.00 or so, and you could sew a homemade one for about $3.00. Barbara Lee was a very pretty young woman who didn't really have to try very hard to be extra pretty. She was selected as one of ten most beautiful coeds (called Yucca Blossoms) for the Eastern New Mexico College yearbook.

Although Barbara Lee was very pretty and intelligent, she didn't know how to sew. Her sewing experience was limited to making a grass skirt for one of many appearances in musical presentations – she was an accomplished pianist and had a beautiful voice. Always willing to help someone, Mattie agreed to teach Barbara Lee to sew. As an attentive and encouraging teacher, Mattie's favorite phrase – meant to be diplomatic – was, "If I were doing that…." One time when she prefaced a suggestion to Aunt Barbara with that short expression, Aunt Barbara replied something like, "But *you* are not doing it." Aunt Barbara – generally as kind as she was pretty and talented – said she immediately felt awful about her response, for Mattie was just trying to be helpful and diplomatic.

A similar incident happened when my mother, Winnie, was washing clothes in the early 1940s at the family "laundry mat" – the garage. Mother was sorting clothes in preparation for washing them when Mattie came home from the cafe. As she was chatting with Mother, she noticed how Winnie had sorted the clothes and quickly concluded that she knew a better way. So she softly uttered her favorite phrase, "If I were doing this…." My mother recounted how she blurted out before thinking, "But *you* are not doing it…." Mother said she would forever regret her thoughtless reply because Mattie had been so good to her, especially helping her with us three kids. Neither Aunt Barbara nor Mother ever said what Grandmother Mattie's reaction was. I will always regret not asking.

Mother and Aunt Barbara's anguish was obvious when they bemoaned how horrible they felt about their infamous "If I were doing this…" incidents. So when Mattie was helping me with a dress design course in college and prefaced her well-founded suggestions with, "If I were doing this…," I kept my mouth shut. One example: I had designed a dress with the sleeves extending from the bodice with no seam around the arms. When Mattie said, "If I were doing this…" I listened to her explanation that even as attractive as the top of the dress looked, as soon as I lifted either arm, the fabric would rip. Never one to criticize without offering a possible solution, Mattie suggested putting a diamond-shaped piece of fabric "cut on the bias" under each sleeve. Incorporating this feature into the design worked beautifully – a gusset, as it is called, allowed full movement of the arms and also provided for the distinct design of the fabric to be uninterrupted by seams around the arms. Keeping my mouth shut when Mattie said, "If I were doing this,…" paid off handsomely for me. "We" made an A in the dress design class!

As I reminisce about Mattie's helping me with that class, I do not remember as a 20-year-old marveling at the fact that she so willingly took the time to help me. But now as an adult with many years in the work world I marvel. The rigorous demands of her café did not give her the privilege of an eight-hour day. She left the house before 5 a.m. six days a week and worked until 9:30 or so each evening with only several short breaks throughout the day. As the years go by, I respect Grandmother Mattie even more for the precious time she spent helping people – including me.

Sometimes before her afternoon catnap, and sometimes afterward, Mattie watered flowers or the grass — or both. In every situation, she wore nice shoes (bought either at Turner's Department Store or Ken Hubbard's Modern Shoe Store, both longstanding stores "on the square" in Portales). Although she would inevitably step in mud while changing the sprinkler's location – this was long before automatic sprinkling systems were common, she was always in too much of a hurry to change into older "gardening" shoes. One of my self-appointed jobs was to occasionally line up all her shoes and scrape off the dried mud. One time my knife slipped, scratching the leather heel of one of Mattie's favorite pairs of shoes. Kindhearted as she was, she didn't scold me. But she made her point. Holding the shoe up to eye level to inspect the scratch more closely, she said softly with a thought-provoking smile, "I'd rather have mud."

Mud on Mattie's shoes seemed somewhat inconsistent, for she loved few things better than clean clothes. Only as an adult did I learn that my grandmother had not coined the hallowed phrase, "Cleanliness is next to Godliness." Similar to her dedication to cleanliness was Mattie's propensity for hard work, having a system for everything she did, and never wasting time – or anything else. For example, Winnie had a fur coat made and there was a little of the "fur" left over. Mattie immediately saw the possibilities of this little "scrap" to trim a hat. Winnie recorded this early observation of her mother:

Mother sewed all our clothes and kept the washing and ironing done. Washing was done on the rub board in a wash tub. The ironing was done with heavy irons heated on the stove. And there wasn't wash and wear material then. Mother cooked three meals a day. Her days were long.

The memories of Mattie held by Betty Jean, Mattie's first grandchild, are admittedly not extensive, for she moved with Uncle Charlie, Aunt Lillie, and Charlene from New Mexico to Arkansas when she was in the sixth grade. But one of Betty Jean's vivid memories was how Mattie always had a system for doing things, for example:

I remember her telling me how to hang clothes hangers in a closet the right way, just in case your house ever burned down.

Because there was a greater possibility of a house burning down back then was probably Mattie's rationale for giving careful thought to the "best way" of hanging the clothes. Moreover, there was a lot of work to do so she gave careful thought to the "best way" of doing everything. She lived by the creed, "If it is worth doing, it is worth doing right," and she offered this advice to her children, grandchildren, or anyone else she believed needed it. My earliest memory of the "right way" for "doing the laundry" conjures up in my mind's eye Grandmother Mattie feverishly sweeping the concrete garage floor in preparation for sorting the laundry – a pile for colored clothes, a pile for Butch and Phillip's Levis, a pile for Granddad's khaki pants and shirts, one for white clothes, and another for wash cloths and towels (and maybe dish cloths and dish towels). The washing machine was a large, white container with soapy water and clothes stirred by an agitator in the center and a large, metallic tub for rinsing the clothes. After the washing and rinsing were completed, the water was drained with a long hose to the nearby flowerbeds or lawn. This systematic setup was a vast improvement over the primitive rub-board washdays on the ranch in years gone by. No more hauling heavy tubs of water!

Flinging myself all over the piles of dirty laundry was a favorite pastime. Perhaps to distract me from doing this (washing clothes was serious business to Mattie!), she would occasionally give into my begging and let me put a few small items through the "wringer," a rather ingenious device consisting of two long rollers. Wet laundry was "fed" between the rollers to squeeze out the moisture – quite a technological advancement over wringing out the water by hand. Mattie predictably admonished, "Watch what you are doing." One washday she left the garage to go into the house, probably in search of more dirty clothes – she loved looking throughout the house and finding more things to wash. I seized this opportunity to run something through the wringer. That "something" inadvertently turned out to include my hand, for I held onto the piece of clothing too long and let my small fingers get too close to the wringer. I screamed bloody murder! By the time Mattie came running to my rescue, the monster had "swallowed" most of my hand. There must have been a safety latch or release that allowed the two rollers to separate.

After that tortuous wringer escapade I never again shared – much less understood – Mattie's great delight in washing clothes.

My childhood memory may exaggerate the size of it all, but it seems that Mattie's clotheslines behind the garage covered an area as large as the entire backyards of most other people – I cannot remember anyone having more clotheslines than Mattie. Furthermore, she used every inch of the wires stretched between sturdy wooden poles to hang out clothes with sun-bleached wooden clothes pins. Another image etched indelibly in my memory is the countless dresses and khaki pants and Levis hanging on the clothes lines. The wind always blows in Eastern New Mexico – sometimes only gently and sometimes fiercely. But nearly always there was enough breeze to inflate the dresses hanging on the lines to make them look like numerous headless, hefty people standing at attention in military formation. The starched-stiff pants waving back and forth looked almost as bizarre.

Mattie rejoiced at the smell of clean laundry dried in the New Mexico sunshine and arid climate; she savored the aroma of the dry clothes as she took them off the line. Although in later years she had a washer and dryer on the closed-in back porch, if the weather was just right, Mattie still hung out sheets and pajamas on the clotheslines to take advantage of the refreshing sun-dried smell. "Makes you sleep better," she declared.

A stinky, misshapen hunk of lye soap was Mattie's solution to cleaning the rags used on the café's greasy grill, the institutional-size ovens and range tops, and the barrel-size "frylator" that fried to golden perfection the bushels of fish sticks and French fries. The greasy aprons worn while cleaning the grill were added to the wash for good measure. The rags had originally been clothes worn by various members of the family; it was fun even as a youngster to match the rags with the original owner. Mattie was big on "making do with what you had." She would never have used the good counter cloths or dish cloths for heavy duty cleaning; it would have ruined them. Using worn out clothing was the logical thing to do. A commercial detergent might have been available at that time to clean greasy rags, but why buy soap when you could "make do with what you had"? And she had plenty of grease left over from the café because just about everything was fried back in those days.

A large wooden spoon was used to stir the steaming, eye-stinging stuff in a huge, heavy, oblong cast iron pot in the garage. Gallon cans that originally had held green beans and other vegetables for the café contained the grease, waiting its turn to be stirred into the lye soap-making pot. I remember wondering how grease could possibly be a vital ingredient of a concoction that would "cut the grease" from the cleaning rags Mattie brought home from the café. I still wonder about that.

Another reflection of her penchant for practicality was Mattie's immediate attraction to a 1950s development – nylon fabric that could be washed, dried quickly, and required no ironing. Mattie made a lot of clothes from this 100 per cent nylon fabric before she – along with everyone else – discovered this fabric "couldn't breathe" and was insufferably uncomfortable, especially working at the café. Granddad's shirts, however, did "breathe" after a few wearings. That is because he'd lean back in his recliner and smoke his RoiTan cigar, ashes falling down the front of his shirt and burning numerous little holes. Luckily the fabric did not flame; the pieces of ash simply melted enough of the nylon to make ugly little black holes in the fabric. Mattie got rid of her nylon dresses a lot faster than Granddad quit wearing his holey shirts.

A different "sewing project" turned out to be much more popular – squaw dresses! Portales seemed too far away from the Indian population of New Mexico to be influenced much by it. An exception was this clothing craze that hit Eastern New Mexico in the mid-1950s. While "squaw dress" was the original name of this new fashion craze, the name was changed to "fiesta dress" in later years because some people thought the term, "squaw dress," was derogatory. But Mattie would never have intentionally been disrespectful of anyone; she would have changed the name herself had she thought it belittled anyone or any group of people.

The whirr of her cherished Singer sewing machine is one of those long ago sounds I will always remember. You could hear it the second you entered the house – Mattie sewing endless yards of colored or gold or silver metallic rickrack or "braid" onto the full skirts of pretty fabric. If the

Mattie and Aunt Mary wearing their matching "sister" dresses

whirr of the sewing machine was punctuated with numerous starts and stops, you knew she was sewing decorative rickrack onto the sleeves and across the front of a blouse. You could always predict that Mattie would be in an even happier mood than usual, for she loved creating those colorful skirt-and-blouse ensembles.

These fiesta skirts might also be called broomstick skirts today, but generally the fiesta skirts back then were heavily starched and put on a board where tiny pleats were painstakingly put into place for the skirt to dry. In spite of the uniqueness of Mattie's creations and a fortune of decorative rickrack and braid sewn onto these pretty skirts, no one but Charlene still has hers.

Perhaps Charlene's not getting to see Grandmother Mattie as much as the grandchildren living in New Mexico did was the reason Charlene treasured her beautiful fiesta dress. Maybe the rest of us took Mattie too much for granted, carelessly casting off or losing track of something that she had invested heartfelt love in.

Other items of clothing that female family members remember Mattie giving to them as children include pretty lacy panties. Martha and Brenda recall that as youngsters they could always count on Mattie's giving them some for special occasions.

Barbara Lee and Carolyn wearing their matching "mother-daughter" dresses

Sweaters for grandchildren were also one of Mattie's favorite gift selections. But it was not just the gifts per se, it was the heart of the giver; Grandmother Mattie had a special way of affirming people and making them feel special. Rescuing me from the unbecoming Buster Brown haircut, then the hideous brown oxfords, and making me about the first one in the eighth grade to wear a fashionable fiesta dress are among my treasured clothes-related memories.

Barbara Jo at age 14 wearing her fiesta skirt

Charlene at age 16 wearing her fiesta dress

More than 50 years later, Charlene showing her skirt to her grandchildren. Left to right: Meredith Walden (on the floor), Katherine Weber, Charlene, Austin Weber, and Nikki Walden

Charlene says her pretty fiesta skirt Grandmother made especially for her is also among her treasured clothes-related memories. Just thinking about them warms our souls now more than 50 years later.

Charlene was Mattie's second grandchild. Named after Grandmother, Charlene's name is Charlene Jane. Here are some comments Charlene made about her namesake:

Even though I didn't get to see Grandmother much when I was a child, I always felt close to her because I was named after her, and our birthdays were close – mine was March 4 while hers was March 5. Later in life she also gave me a ring that had been her wedding ring…she had made it into a birthstone. She probably gave it to me because our birthdays were both in March.

Neither fashion nor beauty but function was Mattie's standard as purses go. By the time I was old enough to be aware of how she handled her money, her confidence had been restored in banks and she kept most of it in a bank. But she always carried a purse that looked more like an overnight suitcase than a purse. She needed this large, sturdy purse – or bag, as she often called it – to put "a little change in" (her words). Her large purse was loaded down with various coins, including silver dollars, until "it weighed a ton" (my words). Silver dollars were Mattie's favorite, I believe. When café customers paid their bills with silver dollars, she methodically saved them.

Mattie with a large purse — her purses became larger as the years went by.

Periodically Mattie let me clean out and straighten the intriguing contents of her purse. In every instance, I knew she would have a bank-full of silver dollars! She had always liked silver dollars, but after the Coinage Act of 1965 was designed to reduce or eliminate the amount of silver in coins, her fervor for them increased. Coins minted after this date were composed of lower percentage of silver or contained none. Therefore, Mattie – like many other Americans – began stashing away silver dollars minted before 1965. When Mattie's purse grew intolerably heavy, she would allow me to take out the coins and stack them on the Formica table in the kitchen and put them in paper wrappers. Then she would deposit the rolls of coins in the bank. With the exception of the silver dollars, of course!

Mattie also had a treasure trove of jewelry – it reflected the richness of her multifaceted personality. Here are just a few of my favorites:

- *A beautiful reddish natural oval stone surrounded by a beaded outline of shiny sterling silver*
- *Sparkling handset aurora borealis gems set in a dressy pin*
- *Pretty pink pearls in a long, attractive necklace*
- *Hand-painted, multicolored enamel ear screws (In the 1940s the earrings were actually secured by turning a little screw behind each ear.)*
- *Tiny antiqued bronze beads strung with many strands to create a clunky necklace*
- *Multiple layers of shimmery glass beads suspended on delicate transparent chains*
- *Striking black beads coupled with lustrous crystal shapes*
- *A dainty, old-fashioned gold locket attached to a ribbon-bow pin*

Although Mattie's jewelry was pretty and some pieces even elegant, she usually based her choices on practicality because she wore her jewelry to work the long hours at the café. Her favorites for wearing to work were matching necklaces and earrings. She never wore bracelets, and the only rings she wore were her wedding rings.

Granddad was one of Mattie's most ardent admirers. He summed up his feelings about her by saying on more than one occasion, "She is a grand lady…a lady with class." Granddad showed his affection and admiration by buying Mattie very nice dresses, jewelry, and other accessories. I still enjoy wearing a pair of pink leather gloves that were hers; inside one of the gloves is printed "Genuine Piccary Pigskin." Granddad bought them for her in Chicago when the two of them went to Illinois to visit his relatives. The couple spent a weekend in Chicago, staying at the luxurious Palmer House and shopping and sightseeing. There was an inexplicable aura about Mattie that made expensive clothes and accessories – like the pretty pink gloves – seem appropriate. On the other hand, she looked classy in most any clothing, for her sense of presence spoke even more eloquently than the clothes she wore.

Whatever Mattie did, she struck an arresting pose – whether it was stirring lye soap in her steamy garage, chatting with her customers as they paid their bill at the café, or discussing business with her banker in his office. About 5 feet 4 inches, she probably weighed about 130 pounds – neither too lean nor too heavy, but just right. She carried herself with disarming sincerity and friendliness but persuasive authority; she "held her head high," following the advice she often gave to encourage others to "do your best" and "take pride in yourself." Even in her early years of marriage, caring for three little girls under the age of four, she "held her head high" and "did her best" and "took pride in herself." Her demeanor lead people to have confidence in her, and it somehow made others feel good about themselves. Like anyone who knew Mattie, Charlene took great pride in her feelings toward our grandmother:

When Grandmother came to Arkansas to see us, she always brought a gift; it was usually material to make a dress, complete with buttons and thread. My friends had grandmothers who lived in our area and cooked Thanksgiving dinner, but they were stay-at-home grandmothers. I was always proud that my grandmother was a business woman who operated her own café which was named after her. And she carried a big purse, drove a nice car herself, had her hair done at the beauty shop, and wore pretty clothes and lots of jewelry. I was proud of her because she was a business woman when we didn't know any others…she looked and acted different from my friends' grandmothers.

Another admirable feature about Mattie and clothes was that she welcomed all people to eat at her café regardless of how they were dressed. Of course, back in those days, no one would even think of entering a café without a shirt and shoes. But I am talking about the laborers, the workers in the surrounding stores, and casually dressed weary travelers – they all were welcome right along with the store owners, bank executives, university professors and administrators. The customers at Mattie's Café were truly a cross section of society; they came from all walks of life, and Mattie treated each one of them as a valued individual.

Judging other people by their clothes was simply not Mattie. Nevertheless, she liked pretty clothes – and functional purses – for herself. She even occasionally liked a special "up-do" hair style. But she placed greatest importance on actions. One of her favorite sayings was…

Pretty is as pretty does.

Her life clearly and consistently demonstrated this time-proven adage.

Photo taken by Steve Huett

Mattie often said red was her favorite color. Warm, friendly, and vibrant, the color red is often also associated with courage. So Mattie's choice is fitting – she was all of these. All the sweaters I remember her giving as gifts were red; red was the preferred color of the lacy panties she gave her young granddaughters. She loved roses of any color, but red was her favorite. She often said, "My next car is going to be red."

The dream of a red car was never realized, and Mattie never wore much red. Dignified ladies just didn't wear bright colors back then – and red cars were a rarity. As dignified as Mattie was, her red pajamas were an exception. As I was sharing some anecdotes with relatives to include in this book, I told about the time she failed to take off her red silk pajama bottom after putting on her dress.

Yet another relative interrupted with a chuckle, "That story about Grandmother and the red silk pajamas made my day!"

Mine too.

Chapter Twelve:
A GOOD CAR
(1913 - 1970s)

A good car can get you where you want to go.
— Mattie

My grandmother had a longstanding love affair with cars. I learned about it after I found this picture among some other old pictures at her house. Like most teenagers, I was interested in cars, so I bombarded Mattie with questions – "What exactly was this old-fashioned contraption?" "Who was this quaint looking couple?"

In her early 60s, Mattie was instantly drawn into the past. With a faraway look in her thoughtful blue eyes, she replied indignantly to my first question as though I should have known the answer, "Why, that is a Model T Ford!" Ownership of this car, she explained, helped put Aunt Alice and Uncle Mitt among the elite of Portales, New Mexico, and the surrounding area. Even though by the early 1920s the automobile was well on its way to becoming an integral part of American life, the dream of owning a nice car was not a widespread reality in Portales.

Yet these relatives were the proud owners of this sleek, shiny Model T Ford; it probably was a 1920 or 1921, for it had "aired up" tires and all the other styling features of those years. Regardless, it provided not only status in the community but mobility and independence. Mattie recollected how she renewed her commitment the first time she rode in Uncle Mitt and Aunt Alice's car that she herself would someday own a good car.

Traveling even further back into her memories, Mattie described the exhilaration of her very first ride in a car; that experience ignited the sparks of her infatuation with cars. It was the day she and Lewis got married – May 22, 1913. A friend drove Lewis and her – along with her brother, John, and his bride-to-be, Emelia Eminger – into Portales from Kentucky Valley. As a young girl and teenager, Mattie had made this grueling day-long trip in a horse-drawn wagon several times; a car reduced the bumpy, dusty trip along wagon wheel ruts to a few hours. In later years Mattie could recall only the friend and car owner's first name – Bill. But she remembered well the thrill of her very first ride in a car. The warm, wonderful feelings of young love and a wedding had woven themselves inextricably with the spirit of freedom and independence that a good car gives. Although the marriage was tragically ended by the global Flu Epidemic of 1918, Mattie's love for Lewis and for cars would last a lifetime.

Before realizing the American dream of owning a car, Mattie encountered plenty of experiences that only deepened her desire. When filling out her "Write-your-life-story" book, Winnie responded to this question: "What childhood memory first comes to mind when you think about winter?" Here is her answer:

> *One winter memory stands out. Lillie and Juanita were in school, but I was too young to go to school and was at home with Mother. After lunch a fierce snow storm began. It still was like a blizzard when it was time for school to be out. Since we lived only about a mile from school, the girls didn't routinely ride the bus but walked to school. We didn't own a car so Mother thought she'd better walk to meet the girls. She built a good fire in the big kitchen range, fixed me in a chair, and told me to stay in that chair. She bundled up, and then left me by myself. That was probably the first time I had ever been alone. I had all kinds of visions! I was so happy when they all three came home.*

Wrestling with the weather with no car also made an indelible impression on Lillie. When in her early 90s, she could still remember this childhood stormy experience decades ago and how relieved and thankful she was to see her mother trudging through the snow to meet her and Juanita. She explained how the threesome were covered with frozen snow when they burst through their front door, eager to enjoy the ice-melting warmth of the fire their mother had started before she left on the rescue mission. A good car would have lessened the severity of the situation.

Uncle Jim and Grandpa Smith with Uncle Jim's early 1920s Ford Model T Touring car and dog after a duck-hunting trip. Photo courtesy of Louise Smith

Mattie's father, affectionately called Grandpa Smith, stayed with Mattie after Lewis' death to help with the three little girls. As time passed and he was needed by one of his other adult children, he would go there. The only contingency – someone had to come and get him, for he never owned or drove a car. Even though many people of Grandpa Smith's generation depended on horse and carriage, he did not own this means of travel either. Grandpa Smith's reliance on others for his transportation reminded Mattie of the self-reliance a good car provides and intensified her determination to own one someday.

When the young widowed Mattie met Harve, she was impressed first of all by his kindness, congeniality, and generosity. She also took notice that he owned several farms – and a good car! Looking back, Paul Creek – Harve and Mattie's oldest son – said he realized as a young man that his mother married his father mostly for financial security. After all, she was left with three young girls to care for and no way to make a living. This does not take away from the affection that grew between the two as they had children, enjoyed some good times with the children they already had, and eked out a living through some tough times along with many other Great Depression survivors.

Like a duck takes to water, as an old phrase puts it, Mattie loved driving Harve's car. She was a quick learner and easily mastered the tricky art of "starting the car" and shifting gears – no "automatics" back then! Very comfortable handling a car, she became the main driver. Although Harve made a lot of the decisions, he seemed perfectly happy for his new, young wife to be in the driver's seat of his car.

Soon after they married, Mattie and her new husband took their combined families to Buffalo, Missouri, to visit Harve's father. Mattie did most of the driving and proved her mettle in more ways than one on this road trip that required three days; here is one of Winnie's recollections:

> ...the water was over the road in one place. All the passengers had to get out and walk across a railroad bridge. Only the driver stayed in the car to drive across. Some men were directing the traffic; they said one of them would drive the car across the water if the driver was afraid. Mother said if anyone could drive across, she could do it too – and she did!

Lillie's most vivid memory of this part of the trip was the insistence of the men directing traffic that Harve "take the wheel." He was more insistent than they were; Lillie recalls her step-father saying emphatically, "No, let her drive. She can drive better than I can."

More than ever, Mattie realized that a car enabled one to go places, see things, and meet new people. She said she loved visiting with Harve's relatives; they were fun-loving and treated her as very special. Winnie also enjoyed taking road trips to Missouri and interacting with the extended family. But she had another positive memory related to this Model T Ford; she said she always enjoyed looking out "the little round window in the back of it." She recalled that Harve traded it for a four-door Model T that had square windows. Although Winnie was glad the newly-acquired car had interesting windows, she was most grateful that her mother was a good driver; here is what Winnie said about it:

This car had belonged to the town drunk. I heard the adults telling how he had turned it over. I was afraid to ride in it, for I was afraid it might turn over just driving down the road. Floorboarded, it could get up to 45 miles per hour, shaking and rattling… thank goodness Mother was a good driver.

One trip Mattie took that she did not enjoy was the move to Witt Springs, Arkansas, in the fall of 1931. No one but Harve wanted to go. At least Mattie had some help driving there, for by then Lillie had tackled the challenge of the car's reluctant "starter," the "choke," clutch, brakes, and "foot feed." She and her mother drove the family's 1928 Chevrolet as it pulled a two-wheeled trailer loaded with all the family's earthly possessions. When the disgruntled group arrived, Lillie recalled one pleasant surprise:

Although we were as poor as could be, the people of Witt Springs, especially all the kids, thought we were rich because we had a car. We liked that.

This faulty perception their car created was little consolation to Mattie. She did not like the new destination the car had brought them to, for it failed miserably to live up to the great expectations! Harve had anticipated starting a thriving café in this little mountain town. But too late he discovered the reason there was no café was probably because nobody had any money to buy food even if a café had been located there. Of course, at that time economic hardships were widespread, and they would get worse before they got better. The ravages of the Great Depression affected people everywhere. Mattie hung on to her hopes that the family car would somehow get her and her beloved family back to New Mexico. Lillie said she thought her mother secretly feared that her aging husband might die and leave her and her children stranded in this isolated mountain town. That fear was put at least partially to rest in the fall of 1932 when Harve agreed to return to New Mexico.

A new dreadful emotion, however, took its place. By then Lillie had fallen in love with Charlie and married him; she would be staying behind. "Leaving Lillie in Arkansas," Mattie was known to say many times over the decades, "was one of the saddest days of my life."

In spite of being inconsolable over leaving Lillie behind, Mattie and her clan "hit the road." The 1928 Chevrolet proved road worthy; it got the travel-weary family back to Portales, New Mexico, in January, 1933. Harve died in May. Desperate to provide a way to feed her fatherless family, Mattie traded the car – and the Arkansas property – for three cows and a few pieces of furniture. The cows were milked and the milk sold to the Liberty Café, owned by Harve's son, Roscoe. Money from the milk put food on the table! Again, a car had come to the rescue albeit in a rather roundabout way.

When Roscoe offered Mattie a job at his café, she quickly accepted, grateful for an opportunity to increase the meager family income. With no family car, Mattie walked to work at the café – and undoubtedly resolved again to someday have a good car.

Mattie and Mr. Kinney in front of the ranch pickup – Winnie in the background

Before she got a good car, Mattie got a new husband. She and Mr. Kinney (as he was usually called) got married in December, 1935. As foreman of a ranch, he drove a red pickup. Mattie drove it some whenever it was available, but Mr. Kinney was accustomed to having it constantly at his disposal for the work on the ranch. She soon tired of working on the ranch for little pay (and no good car!) and eagerly accepted Roscoe's second invitation to work for him. Then Mr. Kinney took a job in Texas, where he was provided a pickup. After that job ended, Mattie and he went to Carlsbad in hopes his son could help him get a job in the New Mexico potash mines. Working odd jobs there and waiting for a job to develop for her husband "grew old," as Mattie put it. So she returned to Portales and resumed working for Roscoe, who always welcomed her with open arms because she was such a congenial person and an excellent worker.

No one remembers exactly when Mattie bought the car the family referred to as "the old green Chevy." It may have been in Carlsbad, or it might have been when she returned to Portales. This picture of a 1931 Chevy is what "the old green Chevy" looked like as a new car. But it was well worn by the time Mattie bought it. Nevertheless, it was a stepping stone to her longstanding goal of owning a good car. When someone stole it, she commented, "I cannot believe anyone would steal that old car." Whoever stole it wasn't totally satisfied with it either; it was soon mysteriously returned.

A 1931 Chevy much like the old green Chevy used to carry discarded food from the café to feed the pigs. Alan Burkett is "at the wheel" of the family car; picture taken on ranch two miles South of Dora, New Mexico. E.N.M.U. Special Collections

Philosophical about the car, Mattie concluded, "It is better than nothing." At least she was not walking. In fact, she was "moving on up." She had started her own café! While Mattie managed her café, Mr. Kinney used the old green Chevy to haul large cream cans of discarded food to the pens where he raised hogs. As the café business operation expanded, so did the "slop" operation. To accommodate the increasing number of cans of discarded food, the seats were taken out of the back of the old green Chevy. The lids did not always fit securely on the cans, or perhaps some cans did not even have lids. Somehow discarded food spilled onto the floor. Not cleaned and dried sufficiently, the floor of the old green Chevy developed rusted spots. Why we kids called it "the slop bucket" is completely understandable.

In the early 40s "wear and tear" increased dramatically on the "slop bucket." After my mother, Winnie, my two brothers, and I moved in with Grandmother Mattie and Mr. Kinney, we added to the list of those dependent on the old car – three adults, three young children, various and sundry employees, and 22 hogs!

Insult was added to injury to the old green Chevy; Mattie recalled, "You soon could see little glimpses of daylight through the rusted floor." This was simply too much temptation for two energetic little boys. Phill and Butch used sticks to knock out little pieces of the corroded floor to see even more daylight. Soon the hole was large enough to thrust a foot through it. Skipping the sole of one's shoe over the dirt street below was great sport. According to my brothers, I soon insisted on taking a turn. All of us were cautious to a degree – before we let the sole of our shoe make contact with the street, we waited until the driver – Grandmother Mattie, Granddad, or Mother – slowed down in approach to the house. Visiting cousins also joined the glee; Bo remembers how bold and adventurous this "game" was. It is amazing that we did not break a bone or at least badly bruise or scrape a foot. The adults were mystified for awhile about the enlarging hole in the car floor. Neither could they figure out why the soles of our shoes were wearing out in an incredibly short time. They soon put all the pieces of the mysteries together – and our fun-filled rides in the old "slop bucket" were ended.

Mattie grew exasperated with this old car; it had served its purpose, and "then some," as she used to say for special emphasis. Because she was a hard worker, a good manager, and applied everything else she had learned about the café business over the years, Mattie was making good profits from her café. She started looking at the various new cars others were driving in Portales. When she looked at Hudsons, she liked what she saw.

Mattie was finally ready to buy her first good car! The Hudson Motor Car Company had come to life in the winter of 1909. By the close of WWI, the leaders realized they needed a competitor to the Ford Model T, which was the dominant vehicle of the era. By 1922, the Hudson Essex was introduced and enjoyed some popularity. Then in 1951 the Hudson Hornet came on the scene and quickly became the car of choice. Mattie counted the money in her big purse and her growing bank account and paid cash for her first good car!

The owner of the local Hudson dealership, Lacy Armstrong, was one of Mattie's "regulars" at her café; this relationship probably influenced her choice. She respected Lacy as did most other people – he was a fair and honest business man, very pleasant, and also a distinguished looking fellow. His wife, Helen, was the daughter of New Mexico's former governor Lindsey. It was unlikely that Mattie was unduly persuaded by the fact that the Hudson was considered "one of the hottest cars on the road." She probably was not even aware that Hudson won 27 of 34

NASCAR Ground Nationals in 1952 – an incredible accomplishment. My grandmother presumably chose a Hudson because of the car's luxurious comfort and reliability on the road. Finally she had fulfilled her enduring dream of owning a good car, and she had chosen one with comfort and class!

After that first beautiful, black car, Mattie owned two other Hudsons – one was a Commodore, known far and wide as one of the best cars around. As for colors, one Hudson was a striking pink, and one was a handsome gray. While most family memories focus on the gray Hudson, the pink one was the most memorable one to me – it was such a remarkable contrast to the black cars and other dull colors of cars during that time. Lillie liked the pink one too, for her pastor on Crow Mountain (Arkansas) owned a car just like it, pink color and all.

Mattie's car was vital to the operation of her café, for she routinely provided rides for some employees. She needed the workers, and they needed the jobs. Her providing rides was a practical solution for both. Workers frequently included relatives – for example, Harve's daughter Ruby. Sixteen when Harve and Mattie married, she loved her new step-mother, who was only a few years older than she. When Ruby was in her early 30s, her husband, Frank, died, leaving her with five children to rear. Like Mattie's earlier plight, she had no special training or experience to make a living and she did not own a car. Furthermore, there was no public transportation system in Portales. Mattie knew Ruby was a good cook, so she provided her some on-the-job training and a paycheck until she became one of the evening cooks. Mattie also made sure Ruby had a ride to work, and she herself took the well-appointed cook home at the end of the evening when the café closed.

An unusual wreck happened once on Mattie's way to pick up one of her dishwashers. Mattie had a big, heavy Hudson; I cannot remember if it was the black, grey, or pink one or a Hornet or a Commodore. What I do distinctly recall is sitting in the back seat, seeing the tree tops and the sky zipping by with astonishing speed. Seat belts were not yet required – probably not even available. I was not standing behind the front seat, which I much preferred, but seated in the back seat as Grandmother usually insisted. The scenery stopped abruptly when we collided with someone who failed to honor a stop sign at an intersection. The impact knocked me into the front seat; I toppled onto the defenseless worker. Mattie jumped out, ran around the car, and yanked open the door to see if we needed help. Next, she checked on the other driver. Since there was no evidence of injury to anyone, Mattie put the car seat back into place, pulled the shaken worker upright, hugged me and put me "back in place," jolted back into the driver's seat, and dashed back to the café. After all, the dishes were piling up. She later commented, "It was good thing that we were in a good car!"

When the popularity of Hudson cars faded away, Mattie brought a very pretty blue and white Plymouth, paying cash again, of course. Carolyn was most impressed that it was "an automatic." The gears were changed by pushing buttons – P for Park, R for Reverse, N for Neutral, and D for Drive. I was – and still am – particularly fond of this car, for it was the one I drove as a teenager to get my first driver's license. That car also is a heartwarming

One of Mattie's two Plymouths; with Carolyn and Ronny

reminder of how Mattie put people above material things. As much as she loved a good car and took good care of every car she ever owned, she still let me – a young, inexperienced driver – drive her new Plymouth. She knew how much it meant to me to be able to call one or more of my girl friends and invite them for a drive, which always included encircling Max's Drive In, the favorite place for teenagers and college students to "get a Coke" in the late 1950s and 1960s.

Though Mattie liked this sporty blue and white Plymouth, she wasn't as attached to it as I was. She couldn't resist buying a bigger car when the new Pontiac came out in about 1962 or '63.

Mattie's other Plymouth, with Carolyn and Martha — and their dolls

She bought a sleek, new grey one – "the prettiest Pontiac on the lot," as the proud new owner put it. Soon after Mattie bought her new Pontiac – paying cash, as usual – she decided that she and Granddad would go to Wink, Texas, to spend the weekend with Paul and Barbara. Bo was living at our grandmother's at the time, working and going to college. Here is how Bo related what happened:

I was off work, so I went with them. We got to Wink about noon Saturday to find that Paul and Barbara had gone to El Paso to spend the weekend with Leroy and Weesie. So we ate lunch in Wink – and turned around and came home to Portales. [Even though phones were widespread – only ground lines, not cell phones – people often did not call before "dropping in" to spend a day or so with relatives. In Grandmother's family, everyone was welcome any time!]

On the way home we had a flat in this new car with new tires, only to discover that the new jack was defective. After about an hour, a guy with a well service truck came along with a winch on his truck. He just backed the truck up to the car, attached the cable from his winch, picked up the whole end of the car, and changed the tire for us.

Needless to say, Grandmother had another new jack by Monday evening – a new jack that would work!

Another incident occurred on a trip to Arkansas in this new Pontiac – also Bo's words:

> *Grandmother asked me to go with her, Granddad, and Mother (Juanita) to Arkansas to spend Easter with Aunt Lillie. I had done almost all the driving, but Grandmother decided on the way home that she would drive through Amarillo. As we were stopped at a light, a police officer walked up to her window and told her that she had run a red light a block or so back and he was pulling her and the "guy in the Plymouth" over. She understood him to say for her to follow the Plymouth to the side of the street and park. The officer left as quickly as he appeared, and Grandmother sped along, trying to find "the Plymouth." In a few minutes the officer caught us from behind with the fanfare of lights and siren – the Plymouth following behind. When Grandmother pulled over, the officer explained the situation from the beginning. We had been stopped behind the Plymouth at the light in question. The driver had gotten tired of sitting, so he just started up and pulled through the red light. Grandmother assumed the light had changed and simply followed him through the red light.*
>
> *We thought we were all going to jail. The officer thought it was funny. Nevertheless, he gave Grandmother a mail-in ticket. And I drove home.*

Years later Mattie recalled the Amarillo situation. She said from that day on she "did her own thinking" and never relied on "what the other guy is doing" regarding lights and other traffic regulations. That practice paid off; Mattie was a law-abiding citizen and driver, never getting another traffic citation. She encouraged others to take this same approach.

Late one night when Mattie was driving home after closing the café, a different kind of mishap occurred. A wide, deep ditch had been dug earlier in the day in what was originally called Priddy Street. Later when most all the streets were renamed in Portales, this street was called South Dallas Avenue. Unaware of work on the sewer system on her home street, Mattie turned off the Arch highway, headed for home – 821 South Dallas Avenue. She was going fast enough that her car straddled the ditch before it came to a halt. These were the days before the wide usage of cell phones, so she walked to her house and promptly – and vehemently – called whatever officials she could find that time of night – probably the Portales police. She was furious, for there were neither warning signs nor any reflectors or lights to alert approaching drivers. Before this ordeal was resolved, the city had put into place new regulations about detour signs and other ways to warn drivers of impending danger. She was gratified that her indignation would guard others from such accidents in the future. She realized how fortunate she was not to have been hurt, and her large, heavy Pontiac virtually unscathed. Again, Mattie expressed her appreciation, "It was a good thing that I was in a good car."

Leroy as a young boy. Although Paul is only half-way in the picture, he also fully "inherited" his mother's love of a good car.

Just as Mattie insisted that the city officials enforce good laws to protect drivers, her appreciation of a good car seemed to be passed on to others. Her sons, Paul and Leroy, for example, had a natural affinity for cars from their earliest days. Someone remarked that Leroy had also inherited Mattie's "love for life, everybody, and everything – including dogs." The warm affection between a boy and his dog does seem strong in this picture. Yet the dog was a chalk dog!

Love of that chalk dog and "for life, everybody, and everything" did not extend to all cars – Leroy would not drive just any old car. Like most teenagers in that era, he did not own his own car. But unlike most teenagers he never asked to drive the family car. His not asking was understandable. When he was a teenager, the family car was the old green Chevy, nicknamed "the slop bucket." Leroy explained his reason clearly and bluntly, "I wouldn't be seen in that old thing." He admitted that he was somewhat embarrassed that he did not know how to drive a car when he went into the Army. He elaborated, "I was the only person I knew in the Army who didn't know how to drive."

Leroy made up for lost time when he got out of the Army; he bought a brand new '49 Chevrolet. Just as his mother had easily learned to drive his father's car when she first married him, Leroy learned to drive quickly and masterfully albeit a standard transmission, as cars were back then. When asked for more information about the car, he explained nonchalantly, "It was just a Chevrolet – that was the days before all the other fancy names such as Impala, Biscayne, Bel-air, or Apache."

But it was not "just a Chevrolet." It was a distinctive chartreuse, ragtop convertible with a beautiful interior. Leroy ordered his dream car from Max Hobbs, owner of Hobbs Chrevolet in Portales. Like his mother, he paid cash for this beauty – $1,900. Leroy explained, "You really didn't have a choice in those days – no fancy, long drawn-out payment plans. You paid cash if you wanted a car – simple as that." Taking three weeks from the day Leroy ordered it, the car arrived in Portales on the train. Just as Mattie enjoyed the fun of sharing her car with other people, so did Leroy. And obviously, others – like Betty and Charlene – enjoyed riding in a stylish, eye-catching convertible car with a congenial driver.

Leroy demonstrating his "inherited" generosity with his two nieces, Betty and Charlene

Speaking of congenial people, let's get back to the "quaint old couple" in the picture that started Grandmother Mattie's reminiscing. She told me that Uncle Mitt and Aunt Alice were very kind and generous to her. They let Mattie and her children stay with them periodically after Harve died, and they continued to let two of her daughters stay with them after that. They never expected Mattie to contribute to the food budget or any other costs that additional residents created. This was about all Mattie ever told me about this quaint couple.

"If you cannot say anything nice about someone, do not say anything at all" was one of Mattie's favorite sayings, and she followed it faithfully. When I began interviewing family members to write this book, I found out just how Mattie truly "practiced what she preached." Aunt Lillie and Uncle Leroy both re-emphasized that Grandmother never revealed any information about this couple that could have possibly been perceived as negative or critical. For example, although Aunt Alice was a half-sister to Grandma Deatherage – Lewis' mother, Mattie never, ever referred to her as a "half" anything. In fact, she never referred to any relatives as "half" or "step" even though our family was replete with them because of deaths and remarriage of the survivors. Revealing very little about the quaint couple, Mattie left it at that – nothing but the "good stuff."

But other relatives heard information about this couple from various other sources as they grew up. As for the ability to buy their sleek, new Model T Ford, Aunt Alice had inherited some money before she moved from Texas to New Mexico with Uncle Mitt. That money helped them purchase their own New Mexico homestead. In addition, when people wanted to give up their homestead and return to their original home – as quite a few did, this enterprising couple "would buy them out cheap." Some people accused the couple of taking advantage of desperate people. In defense of the couple, this low purchase price was better than simply abandoning their homestead, as was often done. The income off Aunt Alice and Uncle Mitt's land holdings was probably added to the funds for buying the car.

Divorce was rare in the late 1890s and early 1900s. Aunt Alice was one of the rare divorced women. Only a few relatives knew that she had been married to a man in Texas. They adopted two children – both girls; they had no biological children. Rumor had it that Aunt Alice's husband was gay another choice or lifestyle rarely discussed in those days. At some point, the couple divorced, and one of the daughters who had married died – they had no children.

Next, Aunt Alice married her daughter's widower, none other than Uncle Mitt, and they moved to New Mexico to stake their claim on a homestead. If one looks closely at the picture of Uncle Mitt and Aunt Alice with their Model T Ford, their age difference might be discernible –

Aunt Alice was 25 years older than Uncle Mitt. Another interesting "tidbit" that Grandmother Mattie never mentioned.

The couple was known to be very frugal. Juanita could remember nearly freezing in their bathroom after bathing because in an effort to conserve fuel Aunt Alice would not "light the fire." Winnie recalled their humble meals. Once there was a bowl of sour cream on the table; someone had brought it along with some eggs from the Price Ranch. (Not to be confused with the Price Ranch that Granddad and then Johnny had served as foreman; Aunt Alice and Uncle Mitt had "built" this ranch by putting together land bought from homesteaders.) Winnie said she looked at that bowl of sour cream day after day until if finally turned to clabber. Aunt Alice seemed determined that it was going to be eaten. Winnie said, "I finally ate it just to get rid of it!"

House on Aunt Alice and Uncle Mitt's Price Ranch

As the couple acquired more land, Uncle Mitt also worked at a job in Portales. They put some of their money in the bank, but Winnie especially recalls stories of their stashing some of it in jars in holes dug in their back yard. Leroy said he heard that some was stored in a container in one of the barns. Uncle Mitt died before Aunt Alice. Before she died, as the rumor went, some of the hidden money quickly disappeared. Evidently someone else knew the hiding places; it was very coincidental that two different people – at least one of them a former co-worker with Uncle Mitt – suddenly had enough money to start businesses in Portales.

All the stories about Aunt Alice and Uncle Mitt would have been tongue-wagging fodder for gossips, but Grandmother never shared this titillating information. After learning all these details, I never looked at that picture of "this quaint-looking couple" and the shiny new Model T Ford quite the same as before.

Portales did indeed have some interesting individuals – not all of them relatives. Many of them were regular customers at Mattie's cafés, and she almost considered them as relatives. Someone asked Mattie if she was going to travel after she bought her first Hudson. Expressing sincere disbelief, she answered, "Why would I want to go somewhere else when Portales has so many interesting people?" If she had been asked to identify some of these interesting people, she most certainly would have included the renowned Jack Williamson. Jack ate at the café as did his wife, Blanch; Mattie considered both of them friends as well as customers. Even decades ago, Jack was making a name for himself with the publication of science fiction books. Any science fiction fan anywhere in the world knows the name Jack Williamson. Still writing, at the age of 95 or so, he has written 55 novels, about 136 short stories, and 88 appearances in collections of science fiction writing. He seemed to share Mattie's feeling that Portales was a good place to stay, but he also made sure he had a good car.

Although I shared Mattie and Jack Williamson's belief that Portales was a good place to live, I accepted a teaching offer several states away. Coincidentally, about that time the new 1965 Ford Mustangs were introduced. Popularity of this sporty little car spread like a wildfire on the dry, grassy plains of Eastern New Mexico. I shared Mattie's sentiment about a good car and my fervor for this beautiful car made it irresistible! Like Grandmother, I paid cash for it – $2,500!

New 1965 Ford Mustang and Barbara. Photo taken in August, 1965, by Mattie

Forty years have passed and I still have my grandmother's fervor – and my Mustang. Over the years it has lived up to Mattie's definition of a good car. It has taken me to work in a lot of interesting jobs, it has helped me to explore interesting places, and it has provided reliable – and fun – transportation for me to go see people I care about.

Old 1965 Mustang and Barbara. Photo taken in August, 2005, by Alan Hunt

Mattie truly did enjoy having a good car for work and for travel – but especially for travel with relatives and to go see relatives – wherever they happened to live. Martha and Brenda both recounted how they loved to go with our grandmother to Wink, Texas, to visit Paul and Barbara – and, of course, fun-loving cousins, Carolyn and Ronny. Trips to Fabens, Texas, to visit Leroy and Weesie were also fun. Martha and Brenda both said a highlight of that trip was the anticipation of "stopping at The Summit for a cup of coffee." That is the way Mattie always put it; the girls echoed the wording. They always felt so grownup and special traveling with Grandmother Mattie.

The Summit café was located in Mescalero, New Mexico, on the Mescalero Apache Indian Reservation on Highway 70 between Ruidoso and Tularosa. Well-named, the café was nestled atop a mountain with plenty of rich-green pine trees, a refreshing contrast to the flat, wind-swept plains of Eastern New Mexico with scatterings of elm trees – green only in the summer. Nothing like the lavish Inn of the Mountain Gods now in that area, this modest café still stands out in the memories of relatives Martha and Brenda and others accompanying Mattie on that trip in her good car.

Carolyn also holds some good memories of trips with Mattie, especially when she lived with her to attend college:

Grandmother and I made quite a few trips together to Roswell. At different times Mom and Dad lived there as did Ronny and his family. It never failed that on each and every trip Grandmother would tell me stories about when her mother and father and family homesteaded in the Elida area. She told about the sadness she suffered when her mother died – Grandmother had celebrated her eleventh birthday only one week before her mother's death. As a happy note, she told me how relieved she was after the first to year to learn that cotton didn't grow in the area. She would

tell me how hard it was on your hands to pick cotton. Don't get me wrong – she was NOT complaining.

She would get that faraway look in her eyes, thinking back into the past, with only the fondest of memories. She told me about going to a barn dance miles away from home. She worked in the fields during the day, put on her good dress (she had two!), and then got on the buckboard to go to the dance. She danced all night, got back into the buckboard, and returned home just in time to go back into the fields to work. She always concluded that they had a great time!

"Isn't this beautiful country?" Grandmother would also say at some point in the trip. The scenery was indeed beautiful.

Like Carolyn, I remember our grandmother commenting on the beauty of the countryside – it was always more of a statement than a question. Whatever, Mattie's words forced me to look around, to look long through the crisp, clean New Mexico air. Her words made me much more aware of the beauty. The images of Eastern New Mexico painted themselves on my mind and heart until I can still see the grand shapes even now when I close my eyes. Magnificent mesas erupt out of flatlands. Clouds, blazed by the bright sunshine, sometimes float effortlessly in majestic thunderheads, and at other times ripped by wind, streak across a boundless blue sky. The rising sun and the setting sun spotlight the desert's unyielding contours, lending rich texture and drama to every arroyo, every rise, every angle of sculpted landscape. Increasing awareness of the awe-inspiring scenery, Mattie's early pioneer experiences, and her love and interest in me as the car hummed along always made the trip fun and fulfilling.

On a practical note, we sometimes stopped alongside the road – there were no public restrooms between Portales and Roswell. We would get a new perspective on the landscape. Parked atop a high place (we never parked in "low places") so we could get a panoramic view let us grasp the largeness of the land. We could also see the small details – to see a cactus in bloom is to understand the allure of that part of the country. To hear the deafening silence and sense the mighty stillness gave the ability to think about life and all that was important.

One thing in life that was important to Mattie was her enjoyment of it – she loved life, and she laughed easily. This love and laughter were contagious. Just riding along in a car with her, you sensed a serenity, a peace of mind, and the ability to enjoy even the smallest of things. She could laugh – and help you laugh – at something without her keen perspective you would hardly notice. For example, if you had been driving along with her and seen what her great grandson Phillip Alan saw – and took this picture of – she would have laughed and laughed at the incongruity of it all. And you would've been laughing with her.

The trips across the plains were very enjoyable to Mattie and those fortunate enough to travel with her. Her first airplane ride was also a great joy! In 1966 Linda convinced her to fly with her to visit some relatives. Hesitant at first, Mattie thoroughly enjoyed flying to Arkansas to visit with Aunt Lillie and then onto Dallas where Del and I picked the travelers up for a few days visiting in Denton, where we lived at the time. Even as much as Mattie enjoyed flying, she quipped, "There's nothing like the thrill of being at the wheel of a good car."

In August, 1969, Charlene extended another invitation to Mattie that she could not resist. Here is Charlene's account of it:

> *…we were visiting Mother and Dad in Arkansas at the same time Grandmother was there. As we were preparing to leave, I said to her, "Grandmother, why don't you go home with us to Baltimore? Without hesitating, she said, "I think I will." We drove through Arkansas, Tennessee, and the Shenandoah Valley of Virginia before reaching Maryland. Grandmother enjoyed every minute of the long trip!*
>
> *I wanted her to see the sights of the city, so I took her downtown. This was before Baltimore cleaned up its inner harbor and made it into a wonderful tourist spot. At that time it was a mixture of warehouses and ghettos. The Civil War era battleship, The Constellation, was anchored at the wharf; that was our first stop. We climbed up and down ladders all over that ship and saw every inch of it. Then we started*

walking to the Betsy Ross Flag House; it was in an even worse section of the city. While we stood on the corner looking at the map, we heard sirens coming from all directions – police cars, ambulances, and fire trucks. I quickly decided I should get my 73-year-old grandmother and seven-year-old daughter to the car and get home!

As we approached the car, I realized it was directly across the apartment building where all the emergency equipment had gathered. The police were dragging a bleeding man from the building, and an angry mob was gathering. We obviously were out of our element! We hurriedly got into the car and locked the doors but had to wait until the police cars and ambulance left before we could pull out. I was shaking as we drove away from the volatile situation while Grandmother was amazingly calm.

Not fazed at all by the riot in Baltimore, Grandmother Mattie was ready the next day to get into the car and head for Washington, D.C. I will never forget her marveling at the things "she thought she would never see," how she always straightened up even more to pose for a picture, and her infectious laugh. As we drove around to see all the sights, we talked about the past and she said, "I don't feel any different inside than I did when I was 18." She was truly young at heart!

Mattie in Washington, D.C. standing near the fence around the White House. 1969

Another road trip Mattie enjoyed immensely was to Chama, New Mexico, where Coke and Juanita were working high on a ranch in the beautiful New Mexico mountains. Mattie was glad to grow up and be able to ride in a car rather than on horseback across a dusty pasture. But she loved riding a horse at Chama – it was her choice, and it was simply for pleasure. She reminisced about the days when horseback or horse-drawn buckboards were the only way to travel – trains were for riding long distances, like bringing homesteaders from faraway places to New Mexico.

But Mattie refused to let her memory surrender to the hardships of the past. She mentioned only the good, the pleasant, the fun times. Forever gallant, Mattie was a stoic woman who never yielded to self-pity. With her gentle manner, pioneer tenacity, and quiet humor, she clung to the solid values that had abetted her reconciliation to the extraordinary misfortunes she had endured. Her gentle, friendly smile, and dancing blue eyes belied a sharp intelligence, a deliberate determination, and a fiercely indomitable spirit.

In her late 60s, Mattie riding a horse at Chama, New Mexico

Strong as steel, Mattie had a contagious optimism. Her ability to see the good in all people and all places makes her one of the most memorable persons I have ever known. She was a woman at peace with her surroundings and herself. When I think about how she told me only "the good stuff" about Aunt Alice and Uncle Mitt, I admire her even more and am reminded frequently, "If you cannot say something good about someone, don't say anything at all."

When I think about Mattie's vow to someday own a good car, I consider how she achieved that dream and how it changed her life as it did the lives of many people. The automobile changed the American family more than one could imagine even a few generations ago.

Mattie's love of a good car revealed the richness of her personality and character and what she valued. She did not love a car just for the car's sake. She loved a good car because it helped her do the things that were important to her – it enabled her to get to work quickly and to help others hold down a job. A good car helped her to explore new places, to share her car and experiences with others – and to go see her kids!

To Mattie, life couldn't get any better than that.

Epilogue
A REMARKABLE LEGACY — LUCKY US!

A good person will be remembered as a blessing.
— Proverbs 10:7

When Mattie was 88, she collapsed in her front yard. The medics worked 40 frantic minutes to resuscitate her. From that day on, her mind skipped effortlessly back over her life. Working in the fields, washing clothes in an old-fashioned washtub, or managing cafes she had owned decades ago generally occupied her thoughts. Occasionally she cooked meals for her much-loved family members, still youngsters in her mind but grown gray with children and grandchildren of their own.

One particular day her body lay motionless on her nursing-home bed, but her mind was obviously traveling elsewhere. She might have been driving her new Hudson to visit one of her children. She might have been sightseeing in some of the places she had enjoyed decades ago. Her eyes reflected intense concentration but gave no hint of her destination.

My entering her room was obviously an unwelcome intrusion. "Who are you?" she demanded.

Quickly, I responded, "I am Barbara Jo."

"You couldn't be," she said with an all too familiar aura of authority and certainty I had heard throughout my growing up in her house. She studied my face, searching for someone she no longer remembered. I was a complete stranger to the person I had loved and called Grandmother for more than 40 years.

Mattie had always been a trim and not-so-tall person. But now, under the clinging white nursing home sheet, she appeared strikingly tiny. She reminded me of a doll with marble-hard, determined eyes. There had always been determination in her. It showed in that resolute thrust of her chin when she offered encouragement – frequently in the form of much-needed cash – to someone in dire distress and expressed faith that "things will work out." She always was a great one for helping people cope with whatever calamities befell them. She not only lived by the Golden Rule, she consistently went the second mile. She had an unrelenting work ethic, and she practiced unwavering honesty and fairness and principles of order and common sense. She treated all people with respect and dignity regardless of their station in life. She always saw the best in others – and she expected others to possess the wisdom to do likewise. If they didn't, she did not bombard them with harsh criticism or unsolicited advice. Rather, she inspired them by her own unassuming, impeccable behavior. Mattie was a role model beyond compare. Yet she did not want acclaim; she reserved that for others.

A formidable individual, Mattie was a true matriarch, a role thrust on her early in life. When she was barely 11, her mother died. When she was 22, her husband died in the Spanish Flu epidemic of 1918, leaving her with three young daughters to fend for. Her second husband died when she was still quite young, leaving her with two more young children to care for. One of her babies died one day before his first birthday. She suffered various misfortunes. An unscrupulous banker, for yet another example, left town with her children's meager inheritance, never to be apprehended.

Determined to survive and keep her children together as a family, Mattie hurled herself at life with awe inspiring resolve and a steady energy that made her seem always on the run. She ran after squawking chickens, committed to a beheading that would put dinner in the pot. She ran when she gathered clothes from the clothesline. (How she loved the fresh smell of clean sheets and towels dried in the New Mexico sunshine!) She ran when she made the beds, and she ran when she watered her roses, dahlias, and other flowers. She ran when she carried out the myriad responsibilities of her café – like dashing across town to give one of her employees a ride to work or checking on the preparation of the chicken fried steak, hot rolls, cherry cobbler and other delicious homemade food she was famous for.

Even when she was "relaxing," Mattie ran – like driving hours to spend a night or two with her children or grandchildren. She was genuinely "a people person" before that phrase existed. She ran the fastest when someone needed her help. She valued life, for she knew firsthand the pain suffered when the lives of loved ones are snuffed out. Life was an exhilarating challenge, and victory was not to the indifferent or lazy. So Mattie lived life fully – she ran!

But the time came when the inevitable was obvious and irrefutable: Mattie's running was over. On January 9, 1988, Mattie's revered, elderly body finally crossed over the finish line. Even though it is difficult, I try not to think about those last years of her life stricken by the infirmities of old age. Those days simply do not represent the Grandmother Mattie I knew; they distract from the significance and dignity of the many years of her tremendous life when she was a vibrant, triumphant person.

I like to let my mind move back across the years just as Mattie's mind did, and I think of myself as that young child Mattie saw in the nursing home. I envision myself sitting in the living room of her house enjoying the laughter and love of family members coming and going and gathering in her home. I feel the enthusiasm of her "I can do" determination. I swell with pride in how she embraced values that earned respect of everyone. I love it when she brings home yet another china dish someone gives to her as a tangible tribute to the admiration they hold for her. I sense the care and concern she gives to everyone. I appreciate how she is tender when the situation requires it and tough when that is needed. I enjoy the warmth of her engaging personality. These memories capture the true essence of the Mattie I most remember.

Even now when I think about this remarkable lady, I am overwhelmed. How lucky we are! The lessons of life she taught us and the immeasurable belief invested in each of us provide a precious legacy. The laughter and love of yesteryear give inexpressible confidence for the future. That is the way Mattie lived life and this is the way she would have it for each one of her descendants. I feel fully blessed for having experienced so much of my life with her. Others who knew her express these same heartfelt sentiments.

Mattie's running may be over, but her influence will live forever. Hopefully this book of family memories – woven into the fabric of my memories – will not only preserve but also carry on her legacy of grit, gumption, and grace.

Some of my most wonderful memories of Grandmother Mattie take me back to her kitchen where a favorite family pastime was sitting around the table with Mattie's friends and relatives enjoying the company of each other. As I see the Heritage china dishes displayed there, I gratefully voice the sentiments of each and every one of them:

My cup is running over, and I am drinking from the saucer.

Assorted Photos

Five generations! Taken in 1981 in Russellville, Arkansas, at Lillie's house, this picture shows Grandmother Mattie with her first great-great grandchild. From left to right is Grandmother Betty (Grandmother Mattie's first grandchild), Great-great-grandmother Mattie, proud father Steve Huett, baby Justin, and Great-grandmother Lillie Johnson.

Mattie and her five "kids": Back row, left to right is Lillie, Juanita, and Winnie. Front row, left to right is Paul, Leroy, and Mattie. (Photo by Albert Moss, Mr. Kinney's son-in-law, in about 1949).

Grandmother Mattie and Granddad Kinney are pictured with children and grandchildren in about 1949. Top row, left to right is Butch, Winnie, Charlene, Charlie, Betty, Coke, Barbara Lee, and Phillip. Front row, left to right is Leroy, Juanita, Linda, Ronny (on Paul's lap), Paul, Mattie, Barbara Jo, Mr. Kinney, Lea Norris, Lillie, and Lewis ("Bo"). (Photo by Albert Moss)

Janet Lenore Luttrell Duarte, Mattie's youngest grandchild, and Janet's son, Steve. Janet and her husband were killed in 1983 in an accident caused by a drunk driver. As of 2007, Janet is the only deceased grandchild.

Other grandchildren not pictured above, clockwise: Carolyn, Judy, Kathy, Martha and Brenda

Lewis and Martha

Emelia and John were married in a double ceremony with Mattie (called Martha then) and Lewis May 22, 1913.

Sarah Emelia Eminger Smith and daughter, Inez. Emelia was the wife of Mattie's brother John. John died in 1951, but Emelia lived 50 more years, reaching the age of 105. One of her greatest joys was the annual Smith Reunion, still held early each December. Photo courtesy of Louise Smith.

Jim and Ola Smith: Mattie kept in touch with all her brothers and one sister wherever they lived. But Jim and Ola lived in the Portales area – both were always willing and welcomed workers at Mattie's Café, disproving the old belief that relatives shouldn't work for relatives. Photo courtesy of Louise Smith.

Winnie
Nov. 6, 1917 – June 10, 2003

Celebrating Coke and Juanita's 50th anniversary – married Sept. 14, 1940, in Clovis, New Mexico. Among many other friends and relative attending the anniversary in Portales were Paul, Leroy, Lillie, Winnie, and Juanita.

At a celebration of Juanita's 86th birthday are Lillie, Paul, Leroy, and Juanita; March, 2002, in Huntsville, Texas

Mattie's five adult children in the early 1940s at the end of Mattie's house on what is now called South Dallas Avenue, in Portales, New Mexico. From left to right is Juanita, Paul, Winnie, Leroy, and Lillie.

Lewis Deatherage, 1913.

Harve Creek, 1920

Granddad Kinney, early 1940s

Smith family reunion – from left to right: Mattie, Mary, Emelia (John's wife), Ola (Jim's wife), Sally (Shelby's wife), Shelby, Alonzo Jackson, Charles Roy, and James William– or Uncle Jim, as he was affectionately called.

Juanita and Coke Chumbley with Lewis "Bo," Lea Norris "Lea," and Linda. About 1949 at Grandmother Mattie's house. Photo by Albert Moss.

Mattie loved to crochet and do other handwork. These two framed crochet pieces are typical examples of the beautiful things she made. She began early in life and mastered an amazing variety of sewing and handwork skills.

Making quilts was a necessity in Mattie's early days; they guarded against the cold winter nights before the days of electric blankets and central air. Later Mattie made them simply because she loved to make them. In addition, she enjoyed using scraps from clothes she had made for different people and herself – and she hated to throw any fabric away. The inset shows one of the decorative stitches she used.

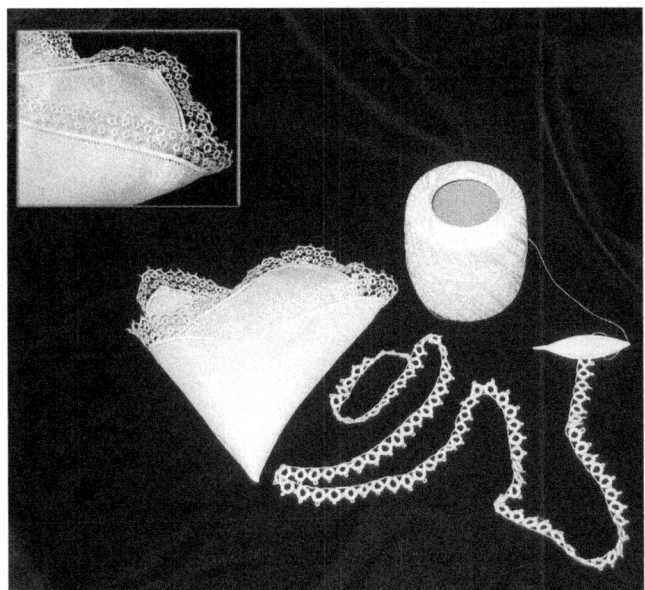

Tatting is almost a lost art now, but Mattie was a master of making fine lace by looping and knotting thread. She used tatting on handkerchiefs (as shown), pillow cases, and to decorate the edge of dress collars.

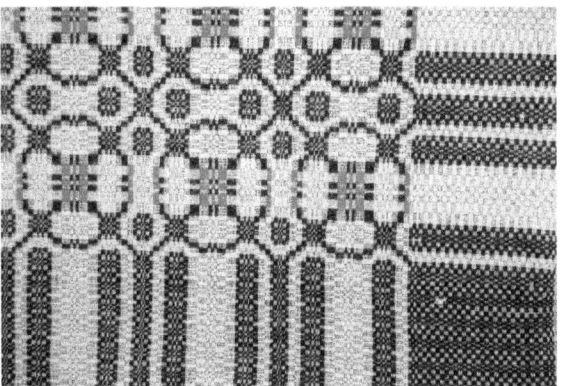

Mattie had this blue and white spread made from wool from sheep at the ranch where Mr. Kinney worked when the two got married.

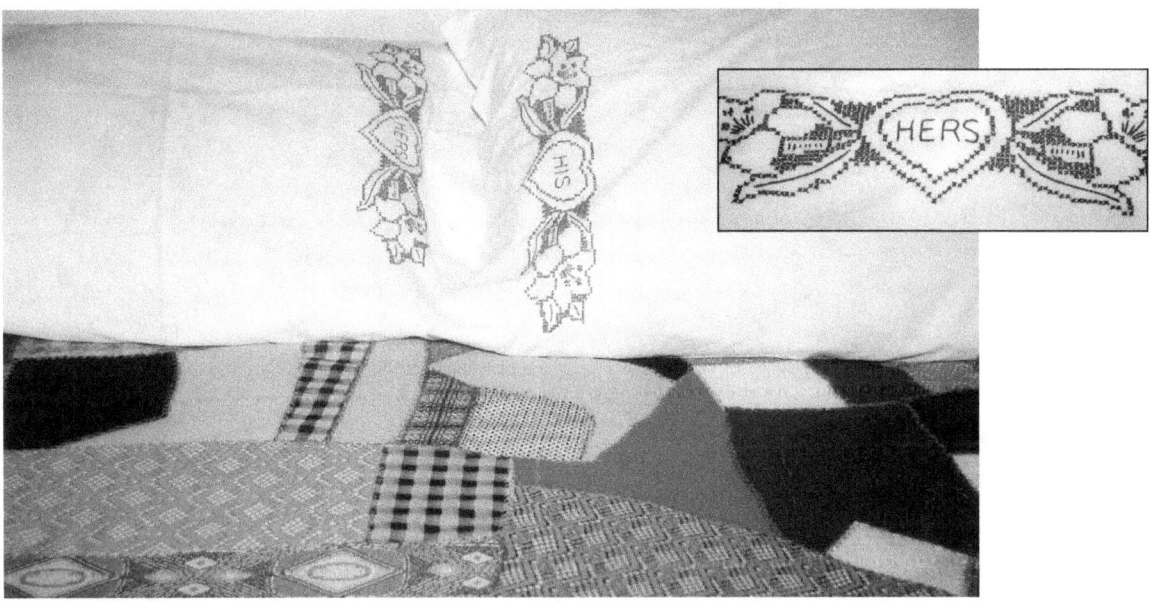

Using various ways – such as embroidery and cross stitch – to decorate pillow cases was another favorite pastime for Mattie as was making quilts from fabrics left over from her sewing projects.

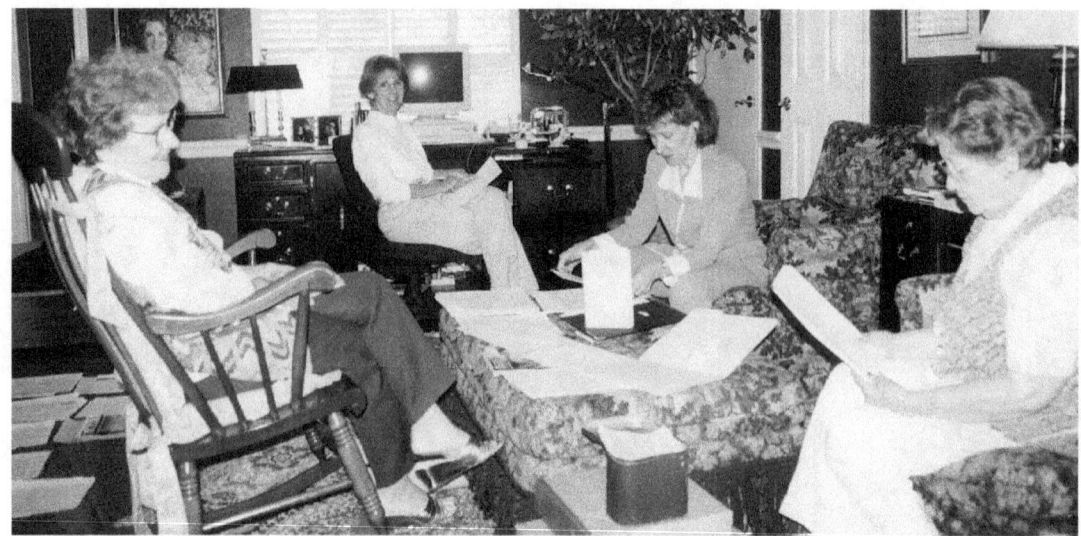

Getting started on this book about Mattie – Winnie, Charlene, Barbara Jo, and Lillie at Charlene's house in Dallas in 1998 going over stories sent in by various relatives of Mattie.

Phillip ("Russ") and Rita and Lewis ("Bo") and Marilyn Chumbley soon joined the mission to create a book to pay tribute to our remarkable grandmother.

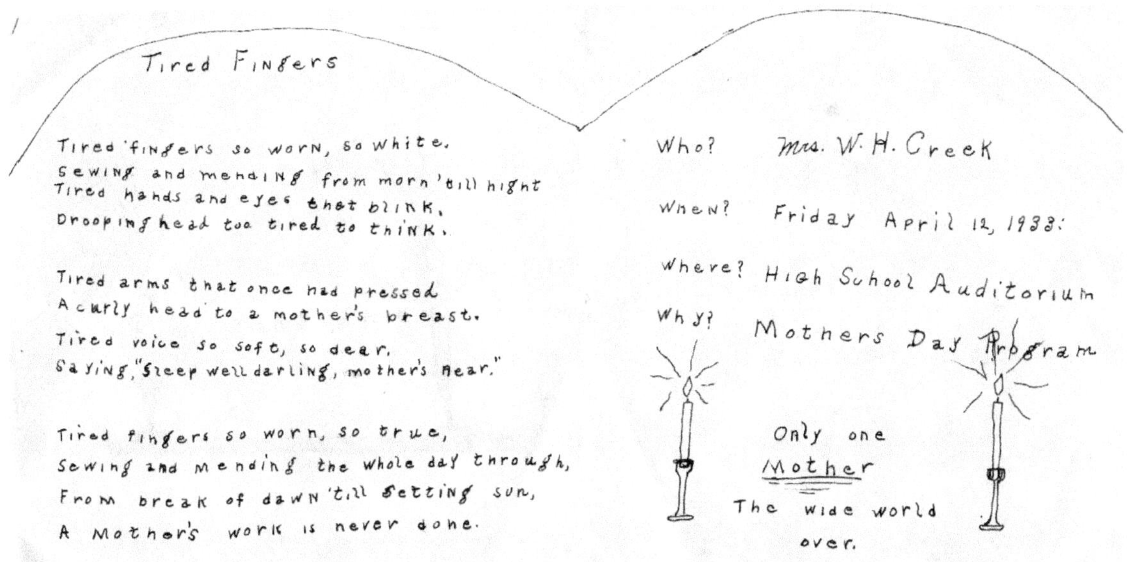

Tired Fingers

Tired fingers so worn, so white,
Sewing and mending from morn 'till night
Tired hands and eyes that blink,
Drooping head too tired to think.

Tired arms that once had pressed
A curly head to a mother's breast.
Tired voice so soft, so dear,
Saying, "Sleep well darling, mother's dear."

Tired fingers so worn, so true,
Sewing and mending the whole day through,
From break of dawn 'till setting sun,
A Mother's work is never done.

Who? Mrs. W. H. Creek
When? Friday April 12, 1933
Where? High School Auditorium
Why? Mothers Day Program

Only one Mother
The wide world over.

"Tired Fingers" given to Mattie by Paul as a nine-year-old April, 12, 1933, only a few weeks before his dad died May 1, 1933. The words of the poem described Mattie well.

All Mattie's children had special gifts and interests. Winnie loved to read and to write out passages or poems she particularly liked. This poem she wrote out reflects her love of the written word and her sense of humor. The poem also gives us all something to think about!

> Ancestors
>
> If you could see your ancestors
> All standing in a row
> Would you be proud of them or not
> Or don't you really know.
>
> Some strange discoveries are made
> In climbing family trees
> And some of these do, you know,
> Do not particularly please.
>
> If you could see your ancestors
> All standing in a row
> There might be some of them
> You wouldn't care to know.
>
> But heres another question
> Which requires a different view
> If you could meet your ancestors
> Would they be proud of you?
>
> Archernia - Raleigh

Every effort was made to determine the source of this poem. If the identity of the person who wrote it can be established, this information will be corrected in the next printing.

Family Histories

The McPeak Family

Martha Jane Smith's mother was a McPeak. Her mother's full name (after marrying Martha Jane's father) was Lillie Camilla McPeak Smith. Lillie's grandfather, Henry McPeak, was born in Pennsylvania in about 1777. But when his son, Isaac Shelby McPeak, was born in 1819, he and his wife, Mildred Arnold McPeak, were living in Carroll County Tennessee, which is in west-central Tennessee, west of Nashville. By the early 1840s, the McPeak family had relocated to Tunica County in northwest Mississippi.

Tunica County provided a rather interesting background for Martha Jane's family. In the late 1700s, Mississippi (which at the time included most of the land which is now Alabama) was wilderness populated by Native Americans, primarily Chickasaw and Choctaw Indians. In 1798, when Mississippi was organized as a U.S. territory, the white population was only about 4,000, with approximately the same number of black slaves.

Plantation bell used to alert residents of impending danger, meal times, or milestones such as the birth of a baby or the death of someone

Designation of Mississippi as a territory was accompanied by forcing the Indians to move further west – to Arkansas and the Oklahoma Territory. This opened the lands on the east side of the Mississippi river to settlement by whites. The Indian migration out and the influx of white settlers began in earnest early in the 1800s and continued for the next three decades.

Mississippi became a state in 1817, and Tunica County was organized in 1836 after the land in northwest Mississippi was ceded from the Chickasaw Indians. After 1836, this part of Mississippi experienced a large influx of settlers, many moving south from Tennessee. The driving forces were the availability of the lands recently obtained from the Indians and a huge demand for cotton, which grew very well in the flat, fertile valley of the Mississippi River.

House on the McPeak plantation at one time – probably not the original house. Photo provided by a McPeak descendant.

The McPeaks' close neighbors were Americus White and his wife, Amanda Bridges White, who had also moved to Tunica County from Tennessee. The McPeaks and Whites were among the few Anglo residents of Tunica County and were very prominent land owners. According to Mr. Ellis Koonce, a Tunica County historian, most of the population of the area was black slaves, with a few overseers. The white landowners primarily lived in the hillier regions to the north and east, where the climate was healthier. The McPeaks' house was the only plantation home in the area; it burned down in the late 1800s and was replaced by a red brick home.

Home currently on the land that was the McPeak plantation

The White and McPeak plantations included land along the banks of the Mississippi River. The land of the White and McPeak plantations was where the Tunica County casinos are now located.

In 1851, Isaac Shelby McPeak married Mary Jane White, the 14-year-old daughter of his neighbor, Americus White. Mary Jane was the second of six children born to Americus White and Amanda Bridges; Mary Jane was born in Tennessee in 1837. At the age of 32, Isaac was already a prominent land owner serving as the president of the Board of Police of Tunica County. Isaac and Mary Jane had 12 children over the next 20 years. Most (but not all), including the first and last, were born in Tunica County. Their fourth child, Mary Olivia McPeak, was born in 1858, and their sixth child was born in 1863 – Lillie Camilla McPeak, who would later become the mother of Martha Jane Smith, the subject of this book.

Isaac Shelby McPeak (Martha Jane Smith's grandfather) served as a scout in the Confederate Army during the Civil War, and after the war returned to Tunica County as something of a war hero. His name is listed on the "Wall of Honor" in the Tunica County Museum. This wall honors residents of Tunica County who have served in America's wars beginning with the Civil War. Also named on the wall is William McPeak, Isaac Shelby's nephew. William could not hear or talk and lived with Isaac and Mary while growing up. William also served as a scout for the Confederate Army during the Civil War.

Wall of Confederate Soldiers, Tunica County

Brothers James Lafayette Smith and Joseph Alonzo had moved to Tunica County in the 1870s from Fayette County in southwestern Tennessee after the death of their mother. Their father, Clark L. Smith, was born in about 1818 in Kentucky and died in the early 1850s in Tennessee. It is presumed that the two brothers were working as laborers on cotton plantations, probably plantations owned by the McPeaks and Whites.

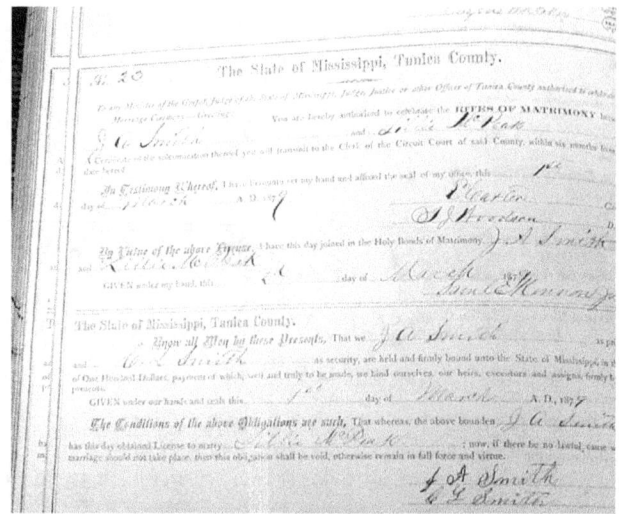
Record of marriage license, Lillie and Joseph

In 1877, James married Mary Olivia McPeak. Family tradition has it that the young couple was estranged from her family, as the McPeaks thought their daughter had married "beneath her status." Two years later, in 1879, Mary's younger sister, 16-year-old Lillie Camilla McPeak, married James' brother, Joseph Alonzo Smith.

Courthouse in Somerville where the two McPeak sisters married the two Smith brothers
1893 or 1894 Tunica Co Courthouse burned in 1920

It is not known whether the family rift was ever resolved or not. But soon after Joseph and Lillie married, the two young Smith families began moving from place to place. There is evidence that shortly after their marriage, James and Mary moved back to Tennessee for a time, then to Arkansas. Joseph and Lillie were in Mississippi until the early 1880s, and then they also moved to Arkansas. By the early 1890s, both families had settled in Wise County, Texas, northwest of Fort Worth.

Martha Jane Smith, the sixth of Joseph Alonzo and Lillie Camilla's eight children, was born in Alvord (Wise County), Texas, March 5 of 1896. The year before Martha Jane was born, her grandfather, Isaac Shelby McPeak, died in Gillet, Arkansas.

Mary Olivia McPeak, Lillie's sister and Martha Jane Smith's aunt, died in Wise County, Texas in 1899 soon after the birth of her last child. The child did not survive either, and both are buried together in the Ball Knob Cemetery in Wise County. James Lafayette, widower of Mary Olivia, remained in Texas, but several of his children and their families moved to New Mexico and homesteaded in the Blacktower community, west of what is now Clovis.

Joseph and Lillie Smith remained in Wise County, working the land, until 1906, when they moved to a homestead near Elida, in eastern New Mexico. Lillie died in 1907 at the age of 44. After her death, Joseph Alonzo spent time living with his grown children. When Martha Jane's first husband, Lewis Deatherage, died on his 27th birthday in the 1918 Spanish Flu epidemic, Joseph lived with her for a time and took care of her three young daughters while she worked. Joseph died in 1929; he and Lillie are both buried in the Elida, New Mexico, cemetery.

Although the children of the two sisters – Lillie Camilla and Mary Olivia – were double cousins and lived within 50 miles of each other, there is no evidence that they contacted each other after arriving in New Mexico.

— Photos taken by Marilyn Chumbley and Phill Russell

The Smith Family

Smith is the most common family name in the United States, the United Kingdom, Canada, Australia, and New Zealand. More than one out of every 100 persons in each of these countries is named Smith. So it is not surprising that tracing the lineage of Martha Jane Smith was difficult. Adding to the complexity of tracing the Smith lineage is the fact that since Smith is of English descent, it has often been taken by non-English individuals in order to blend into the majority culture more easily.

Because of these considerations, tracing the lineage of Martha Jane Smith was completed back only to her paternal grandparents, Clark L. and Mary G. Smith. Clark was born about 1818 in Kentucky, and Mary was born December 8, 1818, in Tennessee. As a couple, Clark and Mary lived in Tennessee, where they had seven children – six boys and a girl named Martha Jane. Their youngest child, Joseph Alonzo, would later become the father of Martha Jane Smith, the subject of this book.

Clark and Mary and their seven children lived in Fayette County, Tennessee, which is in the southwest corner near Memphis and only about 180 miles from Tunica, Mississippi. It was in Tunica that Joseph Alonzo met and married Lillie Camilla McPeak. Two years prior to Joseph and Lillie's marriage, Joseph's brother, James Lafeyette (nicknamed "Polk"), had married Lillie's sister, Mary Olivia. The two girls' father was a wealthy plantation owner, and "as the story goes" he disinherited both girls because of their marriages to day laborers on his plantation.

Clark and Mary's graves are located in the Liberty Hill Baptist Cemetery about 10 miles west of Somerville, Tennessee. Still active, the church was founded in 1824. The graves of Clark and Mary were the first ones in this cemetery. Clark's grave, dating back to the early 1850s, is the oldest surviving grave in the cemetery.

The Smith brothers and their families evidently cared for each other because there are indications that they moved to the same places and ultimately traveled west together to homestead on the developing frontier.

Home probably very similar to those the Smiths lived in. Photo by Phill Russell

Another brother, Francis Jackson ("Jack"), had two daughters, Lucy and Laura, born in Harrison, Arkansas. In 1894 Francis Jackson and his family moved to Alvord, Texas (Wise County), where more children were born. Joseph and Lillie and their children probably already lived there – Martha Jane was born in Alvord March 5, 1896.

James Lafeyette ("Polk") and Mary Olivia's daughter, Gertrude May, was born in Harrison in 1891. But at some time later, Polk and his family moved to Alvord; that is where the family was

The Jack Smith Family. Bottom row, left to right: Laura, Jack (father), Egbert, Lucy. Top row, left to right: Casey and Arthur.

living when Mary Olivia died January 20, 1899; she had given birth to a baby – Viola – nine months before her death. Only 14 months old, Baby Viola died April 25, 1899. Both mother and baby were buried in the Ball Knob Cemetery in Wise County, Texas.

In 1906 Joseph and Lillie and their children moved from Alvord to Elida, New Mexico, and staked out their homestead. One or two of their older boys traveled to New Mexico with the family but later returned to live in Texas. That same year – 1906 – Francis and his family moved to eastern New Mexico, west of Clovis. The next year, Lillie Camilla died March 16, 1907. Joseph lived until January 1, 1929.

The Smiths generally made their living farming and ranching; this tradition continued down through the generations. Terrell Smith, son of Jim Smith, grandson of Joseph Smith, and nephew of Martha Jane Smith Deatherage, started early learning to ride the donkeys used in the family farming operation.

Photo courtesy of Louise Smith

Little is known about the politics and community activities of the Smith family. However, records (Confederate pay vouchers) show that Joseph Alonzo's older brother, William ("Uncle Jap"), fought for the South in the Civil War. In addition, he was active in the Masonic Lodge, worked as a businessman, and served as sheriff of the county. In the 1890s, Uncle Jap owned a hotel in downtown Somerville. The building is still standing and houses an antique store (as of 2004).

Even in those days when communication and travel were difficult, Uncle Jap kept in touch with the family. In a letter to his niece, Gertrude Smith Castle (daughter of Mary Oliva and Polk), he wrote about a visit to New Mexico.

Naming their children after parents, grandparents, aunts, and uncles seemed customary among the Smiths. For example, the name "Jane" was used for at least six consecutive generations. Likewise, certain personality traits were characteristic of the Smiths, including kindness, good humor, and "strong wills" or determination.

Joseph Smith in his earlier days; shaggy things on each side of his head are "ear warmers" on his cap.

Joseph's grandchildren affectionately called him Grandpa Smith and remember him as a kind, gentle grandparent who helped watch after his grandchildren. For instance, he cared for the three young daughters of his daughter, Martha Jane Smith Deatherage, when she was working. Grandpa Smith enjoyed making toys for the young girls and playing with them. Grandpa Smith was also known never to lose his temper or "raise his voice" to them or others.

Joseph Smith in his later years; while he enjoyed comfortable clothes, he also liked being well-groomed – including his long beard.

Although Smith is a common name, as ancestors we can be proud of these "common folks." They left a rich heritage of uncommon values – especially in today's world. They reared their families, worked hard on their homesteads in a harsh land, were impeccably honest, and helped each other in times of hardships. Joseph Smith and Lewis Deatherage both played the fiddle at community dances that Martha and Lewis enjoyed so much. The Smiths left an invaluable legacy of laughing and dancing and celebrating life together – a rich legacy carried on by their numerous Smith descendants.

— Photos provided by Phill Russell and Marilyn Chumbley

The Deatherage Family

Never ask a Deatherage what they think, or to talk or to sing. Deatherages, as I know them, are truly extroverts and can entertain at the drop of a hat.
— Lucy Henry Deatherage in *The Deatherage Society Newsletter*

Lewis Campbell Deatherage was a handsome man with chiseled features, blue eyes, brown hair, and a deep cleft in his chin. Living up to the Deatherage family tradition, he was expressive, enjoyed being around people, and with his violin could "entertain at the drop of a hat."

Public records account for eight Deatherage children with Lewis being the youngest whereas his brother, Will, was 18 years older. These two brothers were the only Deatherage children to survive into adulthood. The oldest sister, Margaret, died at 16, while the other Deatherage children died as infants or youngsters.

Lewis, 1913

Lewis and mother, 1891

A much loved and pampered little boy, Lewis had long blond curls and fancy clothes as the many photographs of him show. He was about six or seven when his mother, Mattie, left him with his older brother, Will, while she went to town. Upon her return, she was devastated when she saw that Will had given Lewis a haircut. The doting mother kept one of the blond curls and only many years later gave it to Lewis' wife, Martha Jane, who kept it in her little tin box with her other "treasures."

Lewis with his parents

Lewis before his brother gave him his first haircut

"Home" to Lewis as a young boy was North Central Texas close to the Oklahoma border where his grandparents had settled. Around the turn of the century Lewis' family joined other settlers going to New Mexico to homestead. Surviving on the wind-swept High Plains was hard with little time for leisure and fun. Lewis' life, however, was enriched by a traveler with a fiddle who stopped by the Deatherage homestead. When he left, he asked to leave his fiddle for safe keeping until he returned. The traveler was never seen again, and Lewis did "guard" the fiddle, becoming a self-taught left-handed fiddle player well known in the area.

Pocahontas

Playing his fiddle at community dances may well have been the setting where he met Martha Jane Smith. The two met, fell in love, and were married in 1913. They lived mostly with his parents until they homesteaded their own place. Times were difficult for the young couple. But in love and happy, they had three daughters before he died in 1918 during the Spanish Flu epidemic. In his short life he probably knew nothing about his ancestors – immigrants from England, Ireland, Scotland, Holland, France, and Germany – nor about the probability that he was related to Native American Pocahontas.

Explanations of the origin of the Deatherage name are not consistent, and none of the pre-American origins are fully documented. *The First Four Generations of Deatherages in America*, by Richard Tobin II, is the most extensive research to be found. That publication and Tobin's web site, http://members.cox.net/rictobin/gen1.html, provided most of the following information.

A *Dictionary of British Surnames* lists Deatherage as a variation of Death. It also states that the rare occupational surname of DETHEWRIGHT, DEDEWRITHE, DEDEWRIGHT E means "fuel tender" and survives today as DEATHRIDGE and DETH(E)RIDGE. British genealogist J. S. Griffith explored the possibility that it was a variation of the English name Ditheridg. Lewis Campbell Deatherage's ancestor was possibly William, born in Worcestershire, England, to John and Mary DITHERIDG. William's baptism is documented, but no further record of him can be found.

Although family tradition contends that the Deatherages were English, at least one book says they were French Huguenot. Anderson Quisenberry wrote about the D'Etherage family in *Genealogical Memoranda of the Quisenberry Family and Other Families*, 1897, as one of the French

Huguenot families that spread to other parts of the United States from Monikin-Town (an old Indian town) in what was then Powhatan County but now Goochland County, Virginia.

Another story says that in the reign of Edward VI, William D'Aeth married Ann Vaugh of Erith. This couple had a son, Thomas D'Aeth, who married Joan Head. Their son was Thomas D'Aeth, who married Mary Barton. This couple had James Deatherage, who became the father of six children. The oldest son, Thomas, inherited the family estate and remained in England. The three younger brothers, William, John, and George, traveled to America and settled in Virginia.

While none of these foregoing speculations have been positively confirmed, most genealogists agree that there were three brothers – William, John, and George Deatherage – who came to Virginia.

The first documented record of a Deatherage in America is found in the Deedbook C (page 133) of Spotsylvania County, Virginia. A deed was executed in St. Mark's Parish, dated June 5, 1734, and witnessed by William Deatherage. In 1735 William Deatherage received a grant of 950 acres in what is now Culpepper County, Virginia, from George II of England. It is believed that this is the William Deatherage who married Susan Eastham; together they had six children. Although proof is not definitive, based on research down through the generations it has been an accepted conclusion that our lineage is from William. If this conclusion is valid, the descendants of Lewis Campbell Deatherage (husband of Martha Jane Smith) can claim these ancestors:

> Lewis Campbell Deatherage born 11 October 1891 in Nocona, Texas
> > to Lewis Jordan Deatherage born 18 February 1850 in Roane County, Tennessee
> > to John English Deatherage born 28 September 1819 in Green County, Tennessee
> > to Allen Deatherage born 20 July 1794 in Washington County, Tennessee
> > to Bird Deatherage born 1767 in Virginia
> > to George Deatherage born 1746 in Virginia
> > to William Deatherage born about 1685 in London, England

Most information included in this book about the Deatherages in America comes from John English Deatherage. Although he wrote primarily of his spiritual beliefs, sorrows, trials, and tribulations, he included a few details about his family including the following:

> *Grandfather Bird Deatherage's ancestors were from England, but whether English or French I do not know. Grandmother Sally English was of Irish descent and one of nature's noblest pieces of workmanship, both in beauty and virtue. She was of fair, ruddy skin, long flowing black hair and black eyes. Grandfather William Jolly on Mother's side was Irish and Grandmother Nancy Wheeler was of Dutch descent. Father was tall and…one of the most sweet singers ever heard. Mother was small and very active, of few words and seldom laughed or jested.*

John English Deatherage wrote of his early childhood – moving by water on flat bottomed boats, meeting friendly Indians, and seeing his Grandfather Bird (a Primitive Baptist Minister) baptize his mother and father. John English Deatherage also told that when he was about five, he started to school and his father died. The bulk of this diary was about his conviction that he was a hopeless sinner and how this conviction tortured him. His writings also detailed "his call from God to go preach" in Texas.

In March, 1833, John English Deatherage was baptized at the age of 15. He married Hannah Lackey Campbell in 1839. Hannah was of Scottish heritage and spoke with a thick Scottish brogue. She always pronounced Deatherage as D'Eatherage and said the Deatherage family had French origins. John English hardly mentioned her except for their disagreement on church doctrine. Hannah's Methodist beliefs were a source of pain to John English's Primitive Baptist doctrine. He also barely mentioned their children, but he did write about the sadness of losing two daughters to typhoid fever or pneumonia and a son killed in the Civil war fighting for the Confederates. John English wrote briefly about how he thought the election of Abe Lincoln to the presidency was a national disgrace and that he believed in the Confederacy because "It was ordained in the Bible."

Hannah wept bitterly when her husband insisted on going to Texas, but at last said, "I recon' you will have to go." John and Hannah and their children left Tennessee for Texas on the 7th of October, 1852. After a long hard wagon trip, they arrived in Grayson County, Texas, on November 26, 1852, and eventually settled a few miles west of Bonham. John was not a good provider because he traveled so much, preaching among the churches in Grayson, Fannin, Colin, and Dallas counties. The family was also plagued with poor crops, a bad land deal, and the typhoid epidemic that killed two daughters. Hannah almost died as well, and John was also very ill. All their misfortunes often forced them to have to accept the assistance of church members and friends.

Concluding the diary in 1865 on a despondent note, John English wrote about his fears for his country and his reflections on disobedient wives and disorderly children. He died in August, 1871, when his youngest son, William, was only eleven. Hannah Lackey Campbell Deatherage continued to live at their home place for the next 15 or more years and reared their children herself.

William, better known as Billy, went to medical school in Cincinnati and practiced in Dallas. Hannah lived with him in Dallas for the last 20 years of her life. Affectionally known as "Grandma Deatherage" to a great many people in Dallas, she died at the age of nearly 90 in 1908. Hannah was buried in the family cemetery next to her husband, John English.

Hannah Campbell Deatherage

Lewis Jordan Deatherage, father of Lewis Campbell Deatherage, was the sixth child of John English Deatherage and Hannah Campbell. Lewis Jordan was quite young when he made the trip from Tennessee to Texas and little is known about his youth. His father never mentioned any of his children by name in any of his writings. It is interesting to speculate that as a boy

Lewis Jordan may have known his future wife, Martha Edge, because when John English first began his church work in Grayson County, he met her uncle, Elder Hiram Savage. Hiram was the older brother of Susannah Savage Edge, who was Martha's mother.

Susannah and husband, Levi Edge, had come to Grayson County, Texas, with her brothers and their mother, Susan Williams Savage, the widow of Dr. William Savage of Dade County, Missouri. The Edges had five daughters – Margaret, Nancy, Sallie, Harriet, and Martha Levi (Named after her father, she was also called Mattie). Levi Edge died when Mattie was about a year old, so she understood many years later how her granddaughters felt when Lewis, their father, died and also when their mother remarried.

After Levi died, Susannah married Micajah Poindexter. Soon after their daughter, Mary Alice, was born, they divorced, leaving Susannah to rear her six daughters by herself.

After the daughters were grown, Susannah lived with Mary Alice and husband, William Whedby. The only other record found for Susannah was in Washburn Cemetery, Grayson County; her grave monument was engraved Susannah Edge, September 10, 1882.

Four of the Edge sisters; the one on the upper left is probably Martha Levi ("Mattie"), Lewis' mother.

Lewis Jordan Deatherage and Mattie Edge were married in 1871 and moved to Nocona, Texas, in north central Texas on the Oklahoma border. Lewis was most likely a tenant farmer growing cotton since it was the big cash crop in that area. Lewis Jordan and Mattie had eight children (maybe more); six died and were buried there. Around the turn of the century, the couple and their two surviving children traveled to New Mexico to homestead. Unlike the Smiths who traveled together, they left most of their extended family behind. Mattie's youngest sister, Mary Alice, was the exception. She probably traveled with them although some relatives thought she might have joined them later.

Both Mattie and Lewis Jordan signed up for a homestead and lived there for a time but sold them in the early 1920s and moved to Portales. They were loving, attentive parents and grandparents, helping daughter-in-law Martha Jane and children after Lewis Campbell's tragic death from the flu. Lillie, Juanita, and Winnie loved going to Grandma and Grandpa Deatherage's house. In 1929 Mattie died after a lengthy illness called dropsy at that time, but it was probably congestive heart failure. After Mattie's death Lewis Jordan lived with his remaining son, Will. He was known around town as "Doc" because he made a linament and sold it on the street. His granddaughter, Lillie, said that it smelled awful. By the time he was 88 he had become almost blind. One day in Portales he stepped from the curb into the street and was killed by a car. Lewis Jordan was buried with his wife, Mattie Levi, and their son, Lewis Campbell, in the Floyd (New Mexico) cemetery.

It is through Mattie Levi's ancestors that the ancestors of Lewis Deatherage and his wife, Mattie, may be related to well-known historical figures. This is how they have been traced back to the beginning of our country:

    Susannah Savage born in 1823 in Missouri
        to Susannah Bolling Williams 1786 in North Carolina
        to Elizabeth Bolling 1767 in North Carolina
        to Benjamin Bolling 1734 in Henry County, Virginia
        to John Bolling 1699/00
        to John Bolling 1675/76 in Kippax Virginia
        to Jane Rolfe 1653 in James Fort, Virginia
        toThomas Rolfe 1615 in Virginia
        to John Rolfe 1585 in Norfolk, England and Pocahontas about 1595
        to Powhatan, chief of the Powhatan Confederacy of Virginia, which included 30 different tribes totaling about 9,000 persons, in the Tidewater region of Virginia.

Thirteen years before the Mayflower brought the Pilgrims to Massachusetts, the Virginia colony of Jamestown was founded in 1607 as England's first permanent settlement in the area of the Powhatan Confederacy. The first few years were plagued by starvation, warring Indian tribes, and many deaths among the settlers. During a period of fighting between the white settlers and the Indians, Pocahontas, Powhatan's favorite daughter, was lured on board an English ship and held captive. There she and English settler John Rolfe met and fell in love. Pocahontas was converted to Christianity by Sir Thomas Dale and baptized with the English name Rebecca. John and Pocahontas were married in 1614 in the Jamestown church. In deference to his daughter, Powhatan declared peace with the settlers. Five years later, the first general assembly in the Western Hemisphere convened in the colony's church, laying the foundation for the form of representative government in the United States today.

Pocahontas in England

John Rolfe and Pocahontas, along with their son, Thomas, traveled to England. There Pocahontas was treated as an Indian Princess and presented to King James I and to the royal court.

Returning to America was their plan, but both Pocahontas and Thomas became seriously ill. So they stayed in England, where she died of smallpox, pneumonia, or possibly tuberculosis. With great honors, Pocahontas was buried at Gravesend, England. Thomas was left in England to be raised by relatives although at the age of twenty he moved back to Virginia to claim his parents' land.

Both John Rolfe and Pocahontas played an important role in the history of Jamestown. As a prosperous planter, Rolfe developed a successful export crop that was responsible for establishing a stable economy not only in Jamestown but in a much wider area. His efforts provided the colony with a cash crop for export to Europe.

Pocahontas' historic contribution was her father's signing the peace treaty with the colonists because of her persuasion. John Rolfe and Pocahontas' efforts caused Jamestown to begin to thrive, as did England's newer settlements along the James River.

Family history passed down from generation to generation and research indicate that descendants of Lewis Deatherage have a genetic link back to the 1500s to Pocahontas. Until additional documentation – or even DNA testing – indicates otherwise, Deatherage ancestors can entertain the longstanding belief that they are related to someone who helped establish the first permanent settlement iin the New World.

Furthermore they can take great pride in the indisputable family ties to the Deatherages who helped build America. They were a hardy clan, leaving familiar surroundings and frequently other family members to explore new frontiers. They left their homeland to ultimately sojourn to Texas and next to join the Westward Movement to stake their future on wind-scoured homesteads in Eastern New Mexico.

Each generation of Deatherage descendants can continue to carry on the pioneer spirit, exploring uncharted frontiers, conquering new challenges, making new friends, and treasuring each and every family member.

Deatherage family members can also celebrate the rich tradition of strong family values our forefathers – whoever they were – established. We can be proud of this historic kinship.

Lewis Deatherage and fellow musician, Steve Tatum
The Deatherages were congenial people who lived life fully.

— The photos of the Pocahontas statue and the two plaques provided by Phill Russell. The Deatherage family photos are from the album of Mattie Levi Edge Deatherage, now in the possession of Charlene Johnson Hutson.

The Creek Family

Mattie's second husband, William Harve Creek, brought a rich background of social gifts and religious principles to their marriage September 28, 1920. He also brought a family of fun-loving children left motherless by the Spanish Flu epidemic of 1918.

But let's go back a little further in Harve's background. On September 15, 1848, Harve's grandfather, Norris Creek, was born to William and Elizabeth Creek of Monroe County, Kentucky. Little is known about Norris' parents – Harve's grandparents. The census of 1850 indicates that William could neither read nor write; of course, this was true of many people at that time. The Creek farm was valued at $50, while nearby farms were valued much higher – from $75 to over $2,000. No explanation was given for this disparity. The census also says that Elizabeth was born in Tennessee in about 1817 and that William was born in Kentucky in about 1818. Two other sons, James and William, were living with them in 1850.

By the time of the 1870 census, William and Elizabeth, still living in Kentucky, had four other children, Mary, Rachel, John, and Willis. A neighboring farm was occupied in 1850 by John and Rebecca Creek, both born in Virginia in the late 18th century. They were related to William and could conceivably have been his parents.

The census of 1850 lists several other Creek families, all of them surely related to one another, in Monroe County, Kentucky. Among them were Radford and Elender Creek; Radford was born in Kentucky in 1825, and Elender, also in Kentucky, in 1820. Like William, Radford could not read or write although in 1850 three of his four children were enrolled in school. Soon after the

1850 census, Radford and Elender, along with their children, Josephine, John, Sarah, and Jane, migrated to Missouri, where another daughter, America, was born on May 27, 1854.

Two years later, on May 31, 1856, Radford was killed by a bolt of lightning while riding his horse. Family tradition tells us that he was buried where he was struck dead. His lone tombstone can still be seen near March, Missouri.

Like Radford and Elender in the 1850s, like several of their own sons a generation later, and like much of the nation throughout history, Norris Creek left his birthplace and headed west, probably around 1867. He migrated to Dallas County, Missouri, where he found his cousin, America Creek, and married her on April 29, 1869.

Over the next 22 years, Radford and America had 10 children – eight of them survived until adulthood. The first was William Harve, born in 1870, followed by James, Albert, Ben, Lula, Sherman, Everett, and Vivia.

Living in Berkely, California, at the time, a great, great grandson, Dennis Creek, interviewed these relatives of Radford and America in 1979, 1980, and 1981:

>Vivia Brundridge, Buffalo, MO (daughter, born in 1892)
>Paul Brundridge, Buffalo, MO (son of Vivia, birthdate not known)
>Georgie Agee, Visalia, CA (daughter of James, born in 1900)
>Lewis Norris "Buster" Creek, Merced, CA (son of Albert, born in 1909)
>Marvin Creek, Salida, CA (eldest son of Albert, born in 1899)
>Lola Hewitt, Salida, CA (daughter of Albert, born in 1914)
>Opal Evans, Salida, CA (daughter of Albert, born in 1916)

These interviews describe Radford and America from about 1900 to the time they died, in the 1920s. No one still alive at the time of these interviews knew them during their first 25 years together, and unfortunately, they did not pass on stories about their past. Some selected excerpts of the interviews capture the congenial personality and outstanding character of the Creek family. For example, Harve's sister, Opal, reveals Harve's generous nature in spite of widespread poverty:

> *Once Harve and his second wife, Mattie, came to Missouri to visit. I remember it real well because they went into town one day and brought each girl back a spool of thread. That was real special because we weren't used to getting gifts.*

Comments by other Creek relatives reveal how scarce money was; this helps understand just how remarkable Harve's generosity was:

> *At Christmas time Buster (one of Harve's nephews) remembers, "Grandma would put her arm around me and kiss me and say, 'That's all I got to give you for Christmas.' Besides that kiss I might get an apple or an orange in my stocking, but not toys."*

One of the interviews included this comment:

> *Everyone remembers Norris as one of the best respected men in the community. He ran his farm efficiently, he was a leader of his church, and he was a fair-minded man.*

Buster (Albert's son) recalls:

> *In the spring people would sometimes buy planting oats from Norris. He'd pile the oats high in the bushel measure instead of cutting it off flat at the top. "Give them good measure," he'd say to me.*

Religion was of great importance to the Creeks. Norris was a founder and deacon of two different Baptist churches in the Buffalo area, the Mount Pleasant Church in Flint Ridge and the Centerpoint Southern Baptist Church. Viva characterizes her parents simply:

> *My father was a good Christian man, and my mother was a good Christian woman. They went to church every single church day.*

Buster had this to say about his grandparents' religion:

> *Nothing would suit Grandpa and Grandma better in the evenings than to pop corn and get some apples from the fruit cellar and sit around the fireplace in their high backed rockers singing religious songs or reading from the family Bible.*

Another grandchild, Lola, pointed out that her grandparents took a stern view of "improprieties." She remembered once coming home from school and turning cartwheels on the way. Norris was riding in from town in his buggy when he saw her. Disturbed that her bloomers were visible, he warned her, "If I catch you doing that again, I'll make you put your legs in the air!" And America let everyone know that she did not approve of "rough jokes."

The Creeks were a self-sufficient family known for its generosity and love of good food and other people. They had 80 acres of "good bottom land" where they raised some livestock and grew wheat, corn, oats, sorghum, potatoes, apples, berries, grapes and other fruits, tobacco, and had a vegetable garden. Buster recalled:

> *Norris had two apple orchards covering about six acres with many varieties — Queen of the West, Jonathans, Grimes, Goldens, Arkansas Blacks, and Sheepnose. The ones that were still hard in the fall they'd put in the fruit cellar. Then they'd make a big vat of apple butter and can it. They had a big old copper bottom tub with wooden sides they'd make the apple butter in. They dried some apples for winter pies and also made 55 gallons of cider vinegar every other year. They used what they needed and gave the rest to whoever asked for it.*

The Creeks' congeniality and willingness to share their food goes way back, as pointed out by Buster:

> *Of a Sunday, there would be neighbors and relatives from all around and Grandma would make a big dinner for everyone. There would be molasses cakes for us kids to crumble in our milk and fried chicken or chicken and dumplings for dinner.*

Georgie, daughter of James, remembered best....

> *...the sweet potatoes and biscuits with homemade grape jelly or apple butter. Grandma's cooking was so good. She'd make rhubarb or huckleberry pies for dessert.*

Here is what Viva remembered:

> *...the big breakfasts every morning with fried meat and eggs and biscuits and gravy.*

"They were easy people to talk to," Buster said about his grandparents. He went on to explain:

> *For example, a passerby might stop for a drink of water, and he'd get to talking with Grandpa...before you knew it, Norris would make him stay for dinner...that's just the way he was.*

Harve Creek carried on the personality traits of his ancestors. He loved good food – he loved serving it to other people, and he loved the fun and festivities of being with family members and friends. Harve was a kind and generous man who loved mixing and mingling with other people and helping them in whatever way he could. He would literally "give the shirt off his back" to a person in need. The Creek family can be proud of the reputation William Harve Creek had for his congeniality, kindness, and concern for other people.

Mattie's Genealogy
The Smith Family – First Generation

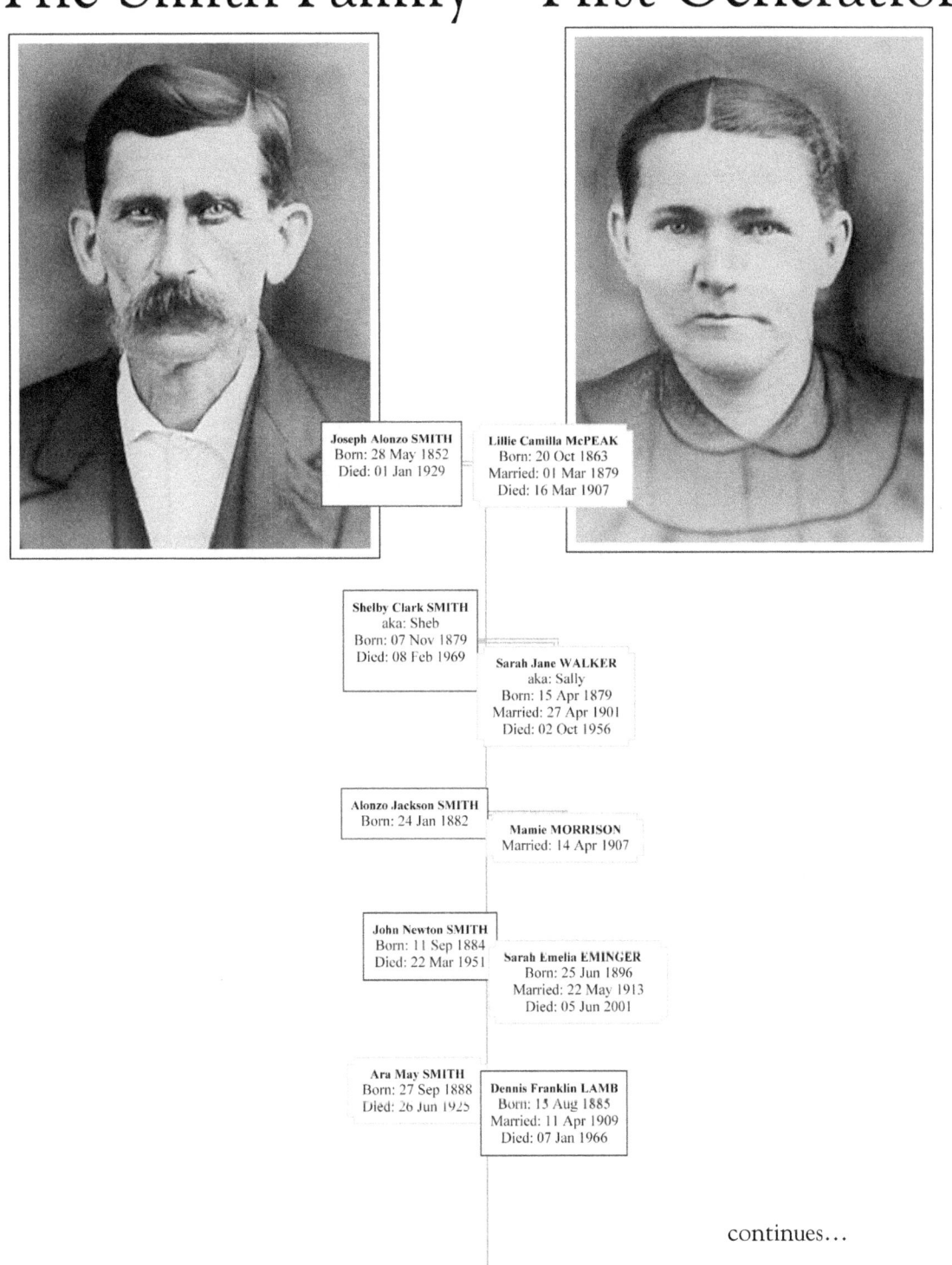

Joseph Alonzo SMITH
Born: 28 May 1852
Died: 01 Jan 1929

Lillie Camilla McPEAK
Born: 20 Oct 1863
Married: 01 Mar 1879
Died: 16 Mar 1907

Shelby Clark SMITH
aka: Sheb
Born: 07 Nov 1879
Died: 08 Feb 1969

Sarah Jane WALKER
aka: Sally
Born: 15 Apr 1879
Married: 27 Apr 1901
Died: 02 Oct 1956

Alonzo Jackson SMITH
Born: 24 Jan 1882

Mamie MORRISON
Married: 14 Apr 1907

John Newton SMITH
Born: 11 Sep 1884
Died: 22 Mar 1951

Sarah Emelia EMINGER
Born: 25 Jun 1896
Married: 22 May 1913
Died: 05 Jun 2001

Ara May SMITH
Born: 27 Sep 1888
Died: 26 Jun 1925

Dennis Franklin LAMB
Born: 13 Aug 1885
Married: 11 Apr 1909
Died: 07 Jan 1966

continues…

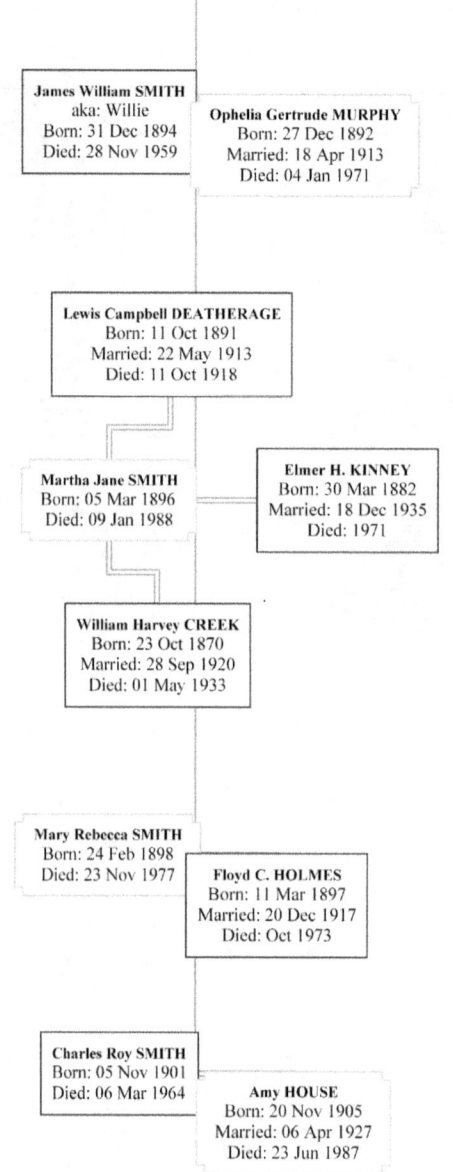

Mattie's Family – First Generation

- William Harvey CREEK 1870-1933
- Martha Jane SMITH 1896-1988
- Elmer H. KINNEY 1882-1971
- Lewis DEATHERAGE 1891-1918

- Harvey Joe CREEK 1921-1922
- Barbara Lee Durham 1929-1992
- Paul Norris CREEK 1924-
- Mary BIRD 1929-
- Leroy William CREEK 1928-
- Billie Louise BROWN 1929-

- Lillie L. DEATHERAGE 1914-
- Charlie R. JOHNSON 1910-1991
- Flora J. DEATHERAGE 1916-2008
- Coke E. CHUMBLEY 1911-1994
- JW ("Johnny") RUSSELL 1914-1941
- Winnie DEATHERAGE 1917-2003
- Kenneth Robert LUTTRELL 1913-1995

Martha/Mattie
TIMELINE

YEAR	MONTH	PLACE	EVENT
1896	5-Mar	Alvord, TX	Martha Jane Smith is born to Joseph Alonzo Smith and Lillie Camilla McPeak Smith.
1900			The turn of the Century: Martha Jane – and all other young people of that time – will face more social and technological changes in the 20th Century than others faced in all prior centuries since the beginning of time.
1904	Approx.	Alvord, TX	A rattlesnake bites Martha Jane, threatening her life and leaving her hobbling on a crutch for months.
1906		Elida, NM	The Smith family moves from Texas to the Territory of New Mexico and homesteads northwest of Elida.
1907	16-Mar	Elida, NM	Within days after Martha Jane's 11th birthday, her mother, Lillie Camilla McPeak Smith, dies suddenly – probably from a heart attack.
1912			The Territory of New Mexico becomes a state, making it the 47th state to join the U.S.A. The Titanic – a ship that was supposed to be unsinkable – sinks, taking the lives of 1523 people – more than the population of Elida, the largest town near the Smith homestead.
1913	22-May	Portales, NM	Martha Jane marries Lewis Campbell Deatherage in a double wedding ceremony. Martha Jane's brother, John, marries Sarah Emelia Eminger. Both couples staked homesteads near Elida.

YEAR	MONTH	PLACE	EVENT
1913			Henry Ford introduces the assembly line, making possible mass production of the automobile – a development that would create dramatic changes in the American way of life, including the life of Martha Jane.
1914	*	Clovis, NM	Martha Jane and Lewis' first baby, Lillie Levi, is born…and named after both grandmothers.
1914			World War I begins.
1916	*	Portales, NM	Martha Jane and Lewis' second baby, Flora Juanita, is born.
1917	6-Nov	Portales, NM	Martha Jane and Lewis' third baby, Winnie Mary, is born.
1918	11-Oct		Lewis Campbell Deatherage dies on his 27th birthday, a victim of the Spanish Flu epidemic that claimed the lives of 200,000 individuals in America.
1918			WWI ends.
1918-1920		Portales, NM	Martha grieves the loss of her husband and struggles to keep her girls together; she works in the fields by day and does laundry for other people in the evenings. Determined to create a more beautiful life for herself and her daughters, she creates and sews attractive dresses for herself and others.
1919-1920			Prohibition was ratified in 1919 and went into effect Jan. 16, 1920, but was repealed in 1933. Roosevelt Co. stayed "dry" for many years after the repeal and was last "dry" county in New Mexico – went "wet" in 1975.
1920	28-Sep	Clovis, NM	Martha marries William Harve Creek.

* To protect privacy and avoid identity theft, birthdates are not provided for living persons.

YEAR	MONTH	PLACE	EVENT
1920			Women are granted the right to vote in the U.S.A. Instead of Martha, many people are calling her Mattie.
1921	17-Oct	Portales, NM	Mattie and Harve's first baby, Harvey Joe Creek, is born.
1922	16-Oct	Mt. Zion (Dora), NM	Harvey Joe Creek dies and is buried on his first birthday. Cause of death is never determined.
1923			The "talking movie" is invented.
1924		Portales, NM	The "blended" Deatherage and Creek family moves to Mattie's "Little White House" in Portales.
1924	*	Portales, NM	Mattie and Harve's second son, Paul Norris Creek, is born.
1925		Buffalo, MO	Creek family goes to Buffalo, MO, where many of Harve's relatives live. Harve works as night watchman; entire family works in parks selling lemonade and hamburgers so they can return to NM.
1925		Portales, NM	The family returns to NM from MO and lives here briefly.
1925	Fall	Graham, TX	Creek family moves from Portales to Graham, TX.
1926	Spring	Portales, NM	Creek family returns to Portales and lives in Aunt Alice's rent house.
1926	Summer	Floyd, NM	Creek family moves to Slim Snell place near Floyd.
1927			Babe Ruth makes home-run record. Lindbergh flies solo across the Atlantic.
1928	Jan	Portales, NM	The Creek family moves to Poker Flats (near Portales).

YEAR	MONTH	PLACE	EVENT
1928	*	Portales, NM	Mattie and Harve's third child (and Mattie's sixth), Leroy Creek, is born. He is given no middle name. When he is in the first grade, "William" is legally made his middle name.
1928		Portales, NM	The Creek family moves to the white house across from the Portales Cemetery.
1928			Penicillin is discovered – a discovery that might have saved Little Harve's life; for sure, it will save many lives that would not have survived otherwise.
1929		Portales, NM	Mattie's father, Joseph Smith ("Grandpa Smith") dies.
1929		Portales, NM	Mattie and Harve open the Little Brick Front Café.
1929		Clovis, NM	Mattie and Harve operate a café called Our Place on Main Street.
1929	Summer	Portales, NM	Mattie's family moves back to Portales.
1929	Early Fall	Cloudcroft, NM	Mattie and Harve operate the "Café on Main Street," as it was called, and live in back of the café.
1929			The New York Stock Market crashes. The shock is felt around the world, including the remote plains of Eastern New Mexico.
1930	Fall	Portales, NM	Mattie's family moves to house on Lime Street and lives on a pension left by one of Harve's brothers.
1931	Fall	Witt Springs, AR	Harve trades 40 acres and two-room house on Poker Flat Road, (near Portales, NM), for some acreage and a four-room house near Witt Springs, Arkansas.
1931	Nov	Witt Springs, AR	The Creek family moves to Arkansas.
1932	30-Apr	Witt Springs, AR	Lillie marries Charlie Johnson.

* To protect privacy and avoid identity theft, birthdates are not provided for living persons.

YEAR	MONTH	PLACE	EVENT
1932		Oklahoma and Texas	The Creek family realizes the futility of trying to make a living in Arkansas and decides to move back to New Mexico. They pick cotton in Oklahoma and Texas to pay their expenses on the trip back to Portales.
1932			Air conditioning is invented, and scientists split the atom. Like many others, Mattie's family is concerned most with finding a place to live and putting food on the table.
1933	Jan	Portales, NM	After a long, hard trip, Mattie's family finally arrives in Portales.
1933	1-May	Portales, NM	Harve Creek dies suddenly after suffering briefly with chest pains. Martha is widowed for the second time.
1933	June	Portales, NM	Martha and her family move to the Price house.
1933	Sep	Portales, NM	Lillie and Charlie move to Portales from Arkansas and live for awhile with Mattie's family in the Price house.
1934		Portales, NM	Martha and her family move to the white square house on Third Street.
1934		Dora, NM	Lillie and Charlie move to Dora where they have rented a farm.
1935	*	Portales, NM	Mattie's first grandchild, Betty Jean, is born to Lillie and Charlie Johnson.
1935			Social Security is enacted in the United States. Although Mattie had survived widowhood twice and worked hard to keep her children without any government help, she is glad that help is available to others in dire circumstances.
1935	18-Dec	Clovis, NM	Mattie marries Elmer Kinney.

YEAR	MONTH	PLACE	EVENT
1936	Early summer	Floyd, NM	After school is out, Mattie and her family move to the Price Ranch, west of Floyd, to be with Elmer.
1937	25-Aug		Winnie marries JW ("Johnny") Russell and has an "instant family," two little boys – Bob and Bill – she adores.
1938	*	Portales, NM	Mattie's second grandchild, Charlene Jane, is born to Lillie and Charlie. Mattie is pleased to be the namesake of her second grandchild. She is also happy that Charlene Jane's birthday is in March – same month as hers.
1938	Fall	Portales, NM	Mattie and Elmer move from the ranch to a house on South Avenue B.
1938	*	Portales, NM	Mattie's third grandchild, Phillip Lewis, is born to Winnie and Johnny Russell.
1939			WWII begins in Europe.
1940	*	Portales, NM	Mattie's fourth grandchild, Leo Elmer ("Butch"), is born to Winnie and Johnny Russell.
1940	Spring	Hereford, TX	Mattie and Elmer move to a farm near Hereford where Elmer is the manager of the farm.
1940		Carlsbad, NM	Mattie and Elmer move to Carlsbad in hopes of Elmer's getting a job in the mines where his son, Russell, works.
1940	14-Sep	Clovis, NM	Mattie's daughter, Juanita, marries Coke Chumbley.
1941	Jan	Portales, NM	Mattie and Elmer move to a house on North Main. It has a commode – their first house with indoor plumbing!
1941	*	Portales, NM	Mattie's fifth grandchild, Barbara Jo, is born to Winnie and Johnny Russell.

* To protect privacy and avoid identity theft, birthdates are not provided for living persons.

YEAR	MONTH	PLACE	EVENT
1941		Portales, NM	Mattie leases the Chevrolet House Café in Portales.
1941	*	Snyder, TX	Mattie's sixth grandchild, Linda Janeice, is born to Coke and Juanita Chumbley.
1941	2-Nov	Floyd, NM	Johnny Russell is killed in an automobile accident.
1941	7-Dec		The Japanese attack Pearl Harbor and bring the United States actively into WWII. Only 17, Paul insists that Mattie sign for him to join the Navy. He is soon on his way to the Pacific Theater, where he serves until WWII is over.
1942	Spring	Portales, NM	Mattie and Elmer move to 821 Priddy Street. First named after an outstanding businessman, this street name was later changed to South Dallas Avenue when many of the streets are renamed after well-known cities, such as Abilene and Houston. Mattie and Elmer lived there the rest of their marriage. This is the place grandchildren gathered most of their memories of Grandmother Mattie.
1942	*	Clovis, NM	Mattie's seventh grandchild, Lewis Eugene, is born to Juanita and Coke.
1943	*	Clovis, NM	Mattie's eighth grandchild, Lea Norris, is born to Juanita and Coke.
1944		Portales, NM	Martha leases Miller's Coffee Shop on South Main.
1945			WWII ends when Germany and Japan surrender. Paul returns safely home.
1946		Russellville/Pottsville, AR	Lillie and Charlie move to their farm on Crow Mountain, near Russellville.

YEAR	MONTH	PLACE	EVENT
1946	15-Mar	Portales, NM	Leroy joins the Army.
1946	15-Sept		Leroy is discharged from Army.
1946	15- Sept	Hereford, TX	Paul marries Barbara Lee Durham, a co-ed he met when they both were students at E.N.M.U.
1948	*	Lubbock, TX	Mattie's ninth grandchild, Ronald Paul Creek, is born to Paul and Barbara.
1950	6-Apr	Clovis, NM	Leroy marries Louise ("Weesie") Brown, an art teacher at one of the elementary schools in Portales.
1950			The Korean War begins. Both of Mattie's sons are too old to serve, and none of the grandchildren are old enough to serve. But some of Mattie's café customers – who were like family – served.
1950	31-Dec	Portales NM	Winnie marries Kenneth Luttrell.
1951		Portales, NM	Mattie's lease on Miller's Coffee Shop is not renewed because the owner plans on opening his own café. Mattie opens the original Mattie's Café on Main Street. She has been called Mattie by most people for years; but after naming her café that, nearly everyone calls her Mattie.
1952	*	Portales, NM	Mattie welcomes her 10th grandchild, Carolyn Nan Creek – parents, Paul and Barbara.
1952	Feb	Russellville/Pottsville, AR	The Chumbley family moves from Clovis to a farm on Crow Mountain, close to Lillie and Charlie.
1952			Jonas Salk produces polio vaccine. While many will be spared of the death or crippling caused by polio, the vaccine is too late for several of Mattie's relatives.

* To protect privacy and avoid identity theft, birthdates are not provided for living persons.

YEAR	MONTH	PLACE	EVENT
1953		Portales, NM	Mattie's Café relocates to Second Street across from the Court House.
1953	*	Portales, NM	Mattie welcomes her 11th grandchild, Martha Leila Luttrell – parents, Kenneth and Winnie. Martha is named after her Grandmother Kinney. Now Mattie is the namesake of two of her grandchildren.
1954			Brown vs. Board of Education rules segregation illegal. This important ruling had little impact on Portales, for at this time there are no blacks living there.
1955	June	Portales, NM	The Chumbleys return to Portales and live in the apartments behind Mattie's house.
1955	Summer	Portales, NM	Charlene and Don Hutson move to Portales. Charlene has just graduated from high school while Don graduated the year before. Charlene enjoys working at Mattie's Café and Don works in construction before they return to Arkansas where Don goes to college.
1957	June	Artesia, NM	The Chumbleys move to Artesia where Coke has a new job.
1958	*	El Paso, TX	Mattie welcomes her 12th grandchild, Judy Creek – parents, Leroy and Weesie.
1960	*	Portales, NM	Mattie welcomes her 13th grandchild, Brenda Gay Luttrell – parents, Kenneth and Winnie.
1961	*	El Paso, TX	Mattie welcomes her 14th grandchild, Kathy Creek – parents, Leroy and Weesie.
1961			The Soviets launch the first man in space, generating more fear of the Russians. People everywhere, including Portales, build bomb shelters in their homes.
1962			John Glenn becomes the first American in space. Cusomers at Mattie's Café join the rest of the world in amazement at this accomplishment.

YEAR	MONTH	PLACE	EVENT
1963	July 2	Portales, NM	Mattie welcomes her 15th grandchild, Janet Lenore Luttrell – parents, Winnie and Kenneth.
1963	Aug	Portales, NM	With her new Pontiac, Mattie tows Barbara's small car, a Hillman Minx, to California. On the way to the San Francisco-Oakland area, Mattie enjoys a Las Vegas show and driving along the Strip. But she says she likes Los Angeles better, for they visit Russell (Elmer's son) and Eula. (Mattie was like that – she always liked people even more than places.)
1963			Times continue to change, and "things are happening": JFK is assassinated, and Martin Luther King delivers his "I Have a Dream" speech.
1965		Portales, NM	Since 1953, Mattie operates Mattie's Café except for fairly brief periods when it is leased to Bo King and sold to (then recovered from) Wayne Brannon. Lewis ("Bo") remembers going with Mattie and Elmer to Amarillo to "re-furbish" the apartments she received from Wayne in payment for the café.
1966			The U.S. commits a significantly larger buildup of troops to the Vietnam War. Two of Mattie's grandsons are serving in the military during this time – Phillip and Bob Russell made a life career of serving in the Navy.
1967	Summer		Mattie enjoys her first airplane ride when Linda flies with her from Lubbock, TX, to Little Rock, then to Dallas to visit Barbara Jo, and then back to Lubbock.
1968	Dec	Portales, NM	Mattie decides it is time to retire from the café business she has loved. She has the equipment from Mattie's Café auctioned off and closes the popular, longstanding "watering hole."

* To protect privacy and avoid identity theft, birthdates are not provided for living persons.

YEAR	MONTH	PLACE	EVENT
1969	Sep	Baltimore, MD Washington, D.C.	Mattie visits Charlene in Baltimore; they do a lot of sightseeing, including Washington, D.C. Mattie's frequent awe-filled comment is, "I never thought I would see this."
1970		Portales, NM	To the surprise of most, Mattie enjoys watching TV, including "As the World Turns." Of course, the whole time she is doing something – sewing, knitting, folding clothes, etc. She also enjoys TV for "keeping up with the world," as she put it – for example, watching as Neil Armstrong becomes the first man on the moon.
1970		Portales, NM	At the age of 74, Mattie enjoys working as a cook (with Mrs. Shrock) at the Portales Hotel. Her delicious homemade pies continue to be in great demand. She also works at Blanche's Children Shop. Both places give her an opportunity to visit people – very important to her.
1970	Feb	Portales, NM	Elmer almost dies. Family from far and near gather, including Lillie, Barbara Jo and husband, Del Chesser, who drive all night to New Mexico from Arkansas. Elmer miraculously survives.
1970	Oct	Fayetteville and Russellville, AR	Mattie, Elmer, and Juanita drive to Arkansas to see Del and Barbara Jo and their new baby, Christi, and to visit Lillie and Charlie. Mattie suffers back problems. Charlie drives her, Elmer, and Juanita back to New Mexico. Phill drives Charlie to Lubbock to catch the plane back to Arkansas.
1971	Feb	Portales, NM	Elmer dies after several weeks of critical illness. He is buried in Portales.
1973			Pocket calculators are introduced. Mattie says she still prefers to "work out things" in her head – she is surprisingly good at that.
1973		Portales, NM	Mattie begins having health problems.

YEAR	MONTH	PLACE	EVENT
1979	4-Mar	Portales, NM	Mattie enjoys her most memorable birthday when a party is given in her honor. All five adult "kids" and nearly all the grandkids are present with their families. Relatives from Illinois and many friends are there to celebrate with Mattie.
1979		Portales, NM	At age 83, Mattie needs some help with the lawn, orchard, etc. Juanita and Coke move into her house to help out.
1982	Apr	Russellville, AR	Mattie attends Lillie and Charlie's 50th wedding anniversary.
1983	2-Sep	Portales, NM	Mattie's youngest grandchild, Janet Luttrell Duarte, is killed in a tragic auto accident caused by a drunk driver. Janet's husband, Robert, also dies in this accident.
1984	Aug	Portales, NM	Mattie's health deteriorates significantly after a 40-minute episode of unconsciousness.
1985		Portales, NM	Mattie spends some time in the hospital and then is transferred to the nursing home. When Lillie visits Mattie, she decides to take her back to Arkansas so she and Charlie can provide better care for her.
1985		Russellville, AR	Because of increasing health problems, Mattie goes to live with Lillie and Charlie.
1986		Carlsbad, NM	When Charlie is diagnosed with cancer, Leroy and Weesie go to Arkansas and drive Mattie to a nursing home in Carlsbad.
1988	9-Jan	Carlsbad, NM	Martha Jane ("Mattie") Smith Deatherage Creek Kinney dies peacefully after a long and remarkable life.
1988	14-Jan	Portales, NM	Mattie is buried in the Portales Cemetery.

* To protect privacy and avoid identity theft, birthdates are not provided for living persons.

Mattie's golden influence and indomitable spirit

…Her grit, gumption, and grace…

can live on forever

And never die

As long as each one of us lives in such a way that we pass on

The legacy she left to each one of us.

www.ingramcontent.com/pod-product-compliance
Lightning Source LLC
Chambersburg PA
CBHW080542230426
43663CB00015B/2684